UNITED STATES SPORTS A
One Academy Drive
Daphne, AL 36526

W9-BWQ-119

Applied Sociology of Sport

Andrew Yiannakis, PhD
The University of Connecticut

Susan L. Greendorfer, PhD
University of Illinois at Urbana-Champaign

Editors

Human Kinetics Books
Champaign, Illinois

Library of Congress Cataloging-in-Publication Data

Applied sociology of sport / editors, Andrew Yiannakis, Susan L.
  Greendorfer.
      p.   cm.
  Includes bibliographical references (p.) and index.
  ISBN 0-87322-320-9
  1. Sports--Sociological aspects. I. Yiannakis, Andrew.
II. Greendorfer, Susan L.
GV706.5.A66 1992   90-29002
306.4'83--dc20   CIP

ISBN: 0-87322-320-9

Development Editors: Christine M. Drews and Jan Progen, EdD
Assistant Editors: Elizabeth Bridgett, Timothy Ryan, Laura Bofinger,
                and Julia Anderson
Copyeditor: Meg Reynolds
Proofreader: Laurie McGee
Indexer: Barbara Cohen
Production Director: Ernie Noa
Typesetters: Brad Colson, Kathy Fuoss, Julie Overholt, and Marsha Wildhagen
Text Design: Keith Blomberg
Text Layout: Denise Lowry and Tara Welsch
Cover Design: Jack Davis
Illustrations: Gretchen Walters
Printer: Edwards Brothers

Printed in the United States of America

10 9 8 7 6 5 4 3 2 1

Human Kinetics Books
A Division of Human Kinetics Publishers, Inc.
Box 5076, Champaign, IL 61825-5076
1-800-747-4457

Canada Office:
Human Kinetics Publishers, Inc.
P.O. Box 2503, Windsor, ON N8Y 4S2
1-800-465-7301 (in Canada only)

UK Office:
Human Kinetics Publishers (UK) Ltd.
P.O. Box 18
Rawdon, Leeds LS19 6TG
England
(0532) 504211

Contents

Preface

The issue of application in the sociology of sport is not a new one. Debates first surfaced about 20 years ago, initially in early position papers, then in papers that considered the pedagogical significance of the new subdiscipline. The adamant sentiments expressed in these position statements set the stage for considerable resistance to application, and efforts to make research usable for practitioners have been infrequent. By 1985, however, attitudes seemed to have mellowed somewhat, and applied sociology of sport was officially launched as an independent thematic area at the Fifth Annual Conference of the North American Society for the Sociology of Sport (NASSS). The papers presented awakened a dormant concern, and applied sport sociology sessions were included on programs at subsequent meetings of NASSS and the American Alliance of Physical Education, Recreation and Dance (AAHPERD). With the legitimacy of application no longer in question, sport sociologists began trying to translate research into practical knowledge.

Quite recently journal articles have extended the application debate. As we move into the 1990s the call for a more self-reflexive system of social knowledge—one concerned with the consequences of social scientific conceptions—presents additional challenges.

It is in the context of this challenge to be concerned with application that we have edited this collection of readings. This anthology contains papers presented at the NASSS and AAHPERD national conferences as well as previously published articles that have some bearing on issues of application in both sociology and the subdiscipline of sport sociology. The book is perhaps the first systematic attempt to illustrate the various ways in which existing work touches the concepts of relevance, application, implementation, social policy, and practical sport sociology. Although the articles selected do not represent every domain of research or all facets of application, they include a range of themes that illustrate either conceptual or methodological issues of the application process. Our aim in producing this anthology is to bridge the present gap between researchers and practitioners by extending the existing knowledge base in sociology of sport into the domain of application.

We believe the strength of this anthology lies in its uniqueness. The text does more than present a collection of articles on organizing and developing social knowledge so that it can be disseminated for policy analysis, problem solving, and consumer application. It also represents an attempt to articulate a theoretical framework for the conceptual development of an applied sociology of sport, and only articles that either provide a context for or appropriately demonstrate specific aspects of the proposed framework have been selected. We feel this approach not only tests the validity of the proposed framework, or model, but it also provides a set of conceptual principles that can be critically examined and subjected to further debate. Therefore, the reader should understand that we see application and relevance as more than issues, position papers, and specific techniques or methods. We consider applied sociology of sport a legitimate body of substantive and theoretical knowledge, a position that has been supported in more recent discussions of knowledge utilization and action-oriented sport sociology that is practical, political, and supportive of social change.

To illustrate the value of a conceptual framework, we have divided the anthology into five sections. Although Section 1 contains only one chapter, we consider the issues discussed there pivotal to understanding. It provides the conceptual model that explains levels of abstraction in sociology of sport—ranging from basic research and theory building and testing to implementation—as well as the framework for the rest of the anthology. Although not directly linked to components of the framework outlined in Section 1, the three articles in Section 2 should help you understand underlying issues that ultimately led to the formation of an applied sociology of sport. Sections 3 and 4 shift from this broad conceptual background to more specific aspects of application. Each article in these sections specifically illustrates and contributes in some way to the framework outlined in Section 1. With an eye toward expansion and continued debate, Section 5 focuses on future directions of an applied or practical sociology of sport.

This anthology was organized with both students and practitioners in mind. We intend it for students in sociology of sport who want to understand the applied as well as the theoretical nature of the field; sociologists of sport who wish to extend their work into the realm of practice, policy, and advocacy; and professionals in sport-related jobs who want to incorporate knowledge and insight from existing research into their work. We hope that students as well as professionals in teaching, coaching, sport and leisure management, sport administration, and counseling will appreciate the intent and purpose of this text. With the goal of translating theory into application, we share this book with friends, colleagues, and others ready to enter the challenging new era of application and relevance.

SECTION 1
A Theoretical Framework

The purpose of this anthology is to extend existing knowledge in the sport sociology literature by developing new understandings related to application. To do this, however, we must begin with an original perspective that presents a general framework or basis from which knowledge can be applied. Although the framework we have selected has already been subjected to criticism (see Ingham & Donnelly article in Section 5), we feel that the conceptualization advocated by Yiannakis is an appropriate vehicle for introducing the topic of applied sociology of sport. Although it is important for you to have some understanding of issues and barriers that have retarded the growth of an applied sociology of sport, we feel the strength of the Yiannakis paper lies in his discussion of the relationship between theory and application. This section of the paper is significant for at least two reasons. First, it makes conceptual distinctions between the levels of theory and application or implementation. But more critically, it emphasizes the importance of *good* research regardless of type (basic or applied). Embedded in his discussion is Yiannakis's underlying assumption that knowledge stems from conceptually grounded research that has broad-base implications for application. From this assumption it follows that application and implementation stem from a sound, substantive knowledge base.

After describing the distinctions between levels of abstraction in sport sociology research, Yiannakis outlines four phases of application: explanatory research, operational research, knowledge transfer, and implementation. These phases become the foundation of his conceptual model, which considers various work roles within specific contexts of application. These contexts—physical education and athletics (e.g., teaching, coaching, sport management), policy analysis (e.g., athletic or program director, facility planning and use), management and marketing (e.g., sporting goods manufacturing, facility development), and counseling (e.g., education or drug)—become the means through which different types of applied knowledge may be delivered to practitioners.

Whether you agree with the model or not, Yiannakis has provided a theoretical rationale and basis from which applied sociology of sport can be developed. In keeping with his rationale, the phases of application present the big picture for considerations related to applied sociology of sport. They also provide the organizing structure for this anthology.

Chapter 1

Toward an Applied Sociology of Sport: The Next Generation

Andrew Yiannakis
The University of Connecticut

The issue of application in sociology of sport surfaced in the literature almost 20 years ago. Since those early works by Schafer (1971), Lenk (1973), and Voight (1974), the need for an applied sociology of sport has been the subject of considerable debate in published works and presentations (Greendorfer, 1977, 1985; Heinemann, 1983; Hellison, 1986; Kjeldsen, 1988; Krawczyk, 1977; Lueschen, 1985; Massengale, 1985; McPherson, 1986; Melnick, 1975, 1980; Rees, 1984; Sack, 1986; Sage; 1977, 1985; Santomier, 1988; Ulrich, 1979; Widmer, 1977; Yiannakis, 1986, 1988) and has been the focus of deliberation at three major national conferences (NASSS, Boston, 1985; AAHPERD, Cincinnati, 1986; NASSS, Cincinnati, 1988). Yet despite an increasing interest in the field today, little has been done to further either conceptually or methodologically the work of first-generation pioneers such as Schafer, Voight, and Melnick, among others.

Among sociologists, the issue of relevance and application has been the subject of discussion for a number of years, as evidenced by a variety of published works (Berk, 1981; Boros & Adamek, 1981; Bulmer, 1985; Coller, 1955; DeMartini, 1979; Foote, 1985; Gelfand, 1975; Jalowiecki, 1967; Kalmuss, 1981; Klein, 1984; Lyson & Squires, 1984; Murphy, 1981; Rossi, 1980; Sherohman, 1984; Street & Weinstein, 1975; Veidemanis, 1964; Watts, Short, & Schultz, 1983; Yonebayashi, 1960), conferences on the topic, job advertisements, and new course and program developments. Several journals are devoted exclusively to works in applied sociology (e.g., *Applied Sociology, Sociological Practice, Journal of Applied Sociology, Journal of Sociology and Social Welfare*, and *The Journal of Applied Behavioral Science*, among others).

Note. From *Sociology of Sport Journal, 1989,* **6**, pp. 1–16. Reprinted by permission.

In developing an applied sociology of sport, therefore, what might we learn from sociology? What issues and problems did sociologists encounter? What efforts were made to address them? Were these successful? How is applied sociology conceptualized today? How does it differ from basic work? And how were ethical issues addressed and resolved by the parent discipline?

The discussion that follows presents those key issues that preoccupied many sociologists in the 1960s and 1970s in their efforts to develop applied sociology. The various perspectives that such an approach yields are essential in the present debate, for what appears to be hindering the growth of applied sport sociology today is the absence of a broad theoretical context in which the current thinking may be grounded. The lessons from sociology are therefore instructive since they provide essential insights. A careful scrutiny of the pitfalls, challenges, and lessons learned by earlier sociologists is therefore a necessary exercise.

Lessons From Sociology

Street and Weinstein (1975) provide a broad historical perspective of the issues and problems that confronted applied sociology up to 1975. What is especially noteworthy about their analysis of the sociocultural changes of the 1960s and early 1970s is their upbeat perspective and optimism regarding the growth of the field and the demand for applied work. It will be remembered that during this period the United States was experiencing major social upheavals that included opposition to the Vietnam War, student demonstrations, race riots, and a general questioning of the basic values of society. No institution was immune from scrutiny or challenge, including sport. It was a period that spawned much of the early critical sport literature, and works such as Jack Scott's *The Athletic Revolution* (1971), Dave Meggyesy's *Out of Their League* (1970), and Paul Hoch's *Rip Off the Big Game* (1972) became cause for much heated debate.

For sociologists interested in the study of conflict and social change, this period must be considered one of the most challenging in recent history. Where else could one find a field setting as rich and as stimulating, a sociological laboratory on one's front doorstep? It was not surprising, therefore, that opinion leaders and others looked to sociology for solutions during these troubled times. And it was not surprising that interest in sociology grew dramatically in the 1960s. Street and Weinstein point out that the demand for sociology during this period took many forms: in universities, sociology faculties and enrollments grew rapidly; there was talk of introducing sociology at the high school level; federal spending on applied social research increased; sociological analyses and columns were introduced in various popular magazines; and the inclusion of sociological terms such as "power structure," "social class," "role," and "norm" in everyday parlance became commonplace (Street & Weinstein, 1975, p. 66). Clearly society was in need of answers—answers whose practical significance could provide effective solutions to the problems which, to some degree at least, touched almost everyone.

Society's call, which went mostly unheeded, was one for relevance and application; the plea was for an applied form of sociology. Unfortunately, we believe that sociologists failed to fully meet this challenge. They failed to provide society with the short-term remedies it wanted and the long-term solutions it needed. Instead, sociologists mostly grappled with theoretical and ethical issues inherent in applied work and failed to provide adequate solutions to societal problems. Street and Weinstein identify and discuss in detail many of these, including the problems of product and user, value neutrality, and ideological bias, among others.

And yet, Rossi (1980) points out, even today applied work is still approached with mixed feelings by sociologists who on the one hand see it as an important reason for sociology's existence, while at the same time believing that applied work is not really worthy of their best efforts. Thus, because applied social research does not rate high on "the academic totem pole of prestige," universities and social science departments have not participated to any great degree in "the burgeoning market for applied social research" (Rossi, 1980, p. 902). This, Rossi laments, has caused sociologists to miss out on some important opportunities with the result that the intellectual health of the discipline may have suffered. For applied work "provides important opportunities to learn more about how society works for building theory and for strengthening our base of empirical knowledge" (Rossi, 1980, p. 902).

But there are some other important organizational reasons for such participation. Academic employment opportunities for sociologists are limited, undergraduate curricula that fail to provide students with some viable occupational skills are shrinking, and junior level research opportunities in the private sector are simply missed due to lack of training in applied research skills. Therefore, Rossi suggests, closer links need to be established between academic sociology and applied social research; and graduate students should be trained in applied research methods so as to compete successfully for available funds. Finally, Rossi recommends that universities themselves should consider building their own research centers where applied research may be carried out.

Sociology's failure to adequately meet the challenge for solutions and answers in the 1960s and 1970s was, I suspect, one of the major setbacks of the field; in the eyes of society, sociology had failed the litmus test. The repercussions, and there were many, were felt in the late 1970s and early 1980s and are discussed in detail by Rossi (1980) in his presidential address to the American Sociological Association.

It would be inaccurate, however, to suggest that sociologists were totally unresponsive during this rather volatile period of American history; nor was the field totally to blame. On the contrary, much good work emerged during this period (Cloward & Ohlin, 1960; Coleman et al., 1966; Moynihan, 1965; Schur, 1965; Sewell, Hauser, & Featherman, 1976; Wright, Rossi, Wright, & Weber-Burdin, 1979), reports were published, and efforts were made to communicate "the message." A combination of factors conspired to undermine the impact of sociologists' efforts, however, and a brief discussion at this point would be instructive for the emerging field of applied sociology of sport. These may be summarized as follows:

1. Much applied research by sociologists failed to incorporate a practitioner's definition of what application really entails. In fact, to many sociologists even today, the application of sociological theory and methods to the study of any issue automatically defines the end product as applied research. This is of course not the case (Lyson & Squires, 1984), a point that is further addressed elsewhere in this paper.

2. Published works in applied sociology often failed to reach consumers, government agencies, and the private sector since most such works appear in scholarly journals. Additionally, scant efforts were made to communicate the findings in language that the consumer can understand or in media that are accessible to the public.

3. Most sociologists generally shied away not only from applied research, since it was not considered worthy of their best effort (Rossi, 1980), but also from actual implementation, that is, the process of actually installing, carrying out, and evaluating the effectiveness of particular courses of action.

4. There was little organized and coordinated activity by sociological organizations and societies to penetrate societal institutions, organizations, and communities to promote the potential contributions of applied sociology.

5. Discussions, and at times heated debates, over the ethical issues arising out of a commitment to applied work mired the field in pitched intellectual battles—battles that in the long run diverted much attention from the social issues and the more immediate social problems of society. Though such debates and occasional conflict are needed to keep the field alive and vibrant, they were conducted at the expense of searching for solutions to societal problems. And while the debates went on, the "patient" either sought help elsewhere or simply perished.

6. And finally, we cannot ignore the fact that the lowly status of applied work in universities contributed in some measure to the general lack of interest and expertise in applied sociology.

However, despite the stigma associated with applied work, Rossi points out that many of the most prominent sociologists in the world such as Durkheim, Stouffer, Park, Lazarsfeld, Duncan, and Coleman, among others, conducted some significant applied research. Yet many are not remembered for their applied work because, over time, many of their significant contributions have been redefined as basic work (Rossi, 1980).

Today the demand for applied researchers, particularly in the private sector, appears to be quite high. According to estimates (Abt, 1980), federal spending on applied social research in the last few years has varied from about $1 billion to possibly $2 billion, thus making applied social research a significant growth sector of the economy, although a substantial amount of this figure does not go to universities but to private research organizations employing mostly social science PhDs.

Clearly a demand for applied social research exists, and because universities have been slow to respond, especially among sociology departments, private organizations and others loosely connected with universities have expanded to meet this demand. This should be an important lesson for sport sociologists who continue to ignore the potential for applied research in the huge sport and leisure industry and the public sector.

What Are the Issues?

Progress in applied sociology of sport appears to have been hindered by a failure to adequately address, and resolve, many of the very same issues that confronted sociologists in the 1960s and 1970s. For sport sociology, these include (a) the relationship of theory to application and, more specifically, that between basic and applied forms of research; (b) the need to evaluate models from sociology and determine what might logically be incorporated within the emerging field of applied sport sociology; (c) problems of precise definition with the term "application," which appears to have a variety of meanings; some include such interpretations as the application of theory to the study of a phenomenon or phenomena, others refer explicitly to usage in practical settings, while to others the term refers to efforts to provide solutions or to change things; (d) the need to clarify how different levels of theoretical abstraction relate to, and give rise to, different forms of applied activity, and to map out the boundaries that these levels of abstraction are associated with; and (e) a clarification of the role of the applied sport sociologist and the ethical issues that applied activities often raise.

To achieve meaningful social change, concerned sport sociologists take on a variety of roles. What are these roles and what are the nature and boundaries of their spheres of action? And more important, what are the ethical issues that a commitment to an applied sociology of sport raises? A satisfactory resolution of the above issues is clearly essential, therefore, if we are to develop a conceptual model that can serve as a basis for guiding future developments in applied sociology of sport. The ensuing discussion seeks to attain this end.

The Relationship of Theory to Application

The distinction often made between theory and application, or more specifically between basic and applied forms of research, suggests an inadequate understanding between two essentially interdependent processes, that is, the process of formulating and implementing, designing and executing. For it is through experience that we observe, learn, and develop generalizations (formulations) about the world around us (inductive process); and it is through the testing of experiential maps (theories) that we verify or refute the validity of our generalizations in different contexts (deductive process).

We recognize of course that when a social scientist engages in inductive-deductive operations, the primary goal is the development and testing of theory and its contributions to the larger body of knowledge. Thus, providing solutions to practical problems, contributing to change, and ameliorating the human condition are not often of primary concern in basic research, although spinoffs from basic discoveries often do have implications for practice. However, even in basic research the ultimate test of a theory is the extent to which it explains and predicts social reality. Thus if sport sociologists are truly interested in the worth of their research, logic dictates that their findings be put to the test in the world of sport. Engaging in good applied sport sociology (applied research, knowledge transfer activity, and implementation) should not be seen as something less than true social science and therefore not worthy of their best efforts, but rather as a necessary process in both the inductive and deductive phases of the research enterprise.

Of course there is good and bad applied research. Research that is not theoretically informed, not grounded in the existing body of knowledge, or of the "shotgun" variety that fails to raise and investigate conceptually grounded questions, is likely to generate findings of a narrow and ungeneralizable value. This is often the case when researchers attack a problem as though it were a unique phenomenon rather than a specific manifestation of a broader pattern of events. Figure 1.1 underscores both the importance of the relationship between basic and applied research and the need to ground applied activity in basic knowledge and theory.

While the distinction between basic and applied forms of research is not always clear, as Rossi (1980) points out, broad generalizations are still possible. Such generalizations are useful at this early stage in the development of the field since they provide us with the only available markers in this mostly conceptually uncharted terrain.

In contrast to applied research, basic research focuses on the analysis, description, and explanation of particular phenomena for the purpose of discovering stable broader patterns and trends; such discoveries enable social scientists to make generalizations about human behavior whose applicability transcends the phenomenon under scrutiny. For the ultimate goal of all social science is the development of micro and macro theories of human social behavior. Thus the particular phenomenon under study is often relatively unimportant in and of itself, except for what it can contribute to our understanding of a broader set of explanations about such phenomena. That is, the phenomenon under study serves as a *means* to some other end.

For applied research, however, the phenomenon under investigation is important in and of itself (Berk, 1981). The applied researcher wishes to know, for example, why certain countries win more Olympic medals than others (Levine, 1974), why certain individuals persist in fitness programs and others drop out (Snyder & Spreitzer, 1984), and whether winning in collegiate sports increases alumni giving (Sigelman & Bookheimer, 1984). Such information, which reflects research in the explanatory phase, is essential since it provides the knowledge base upon which

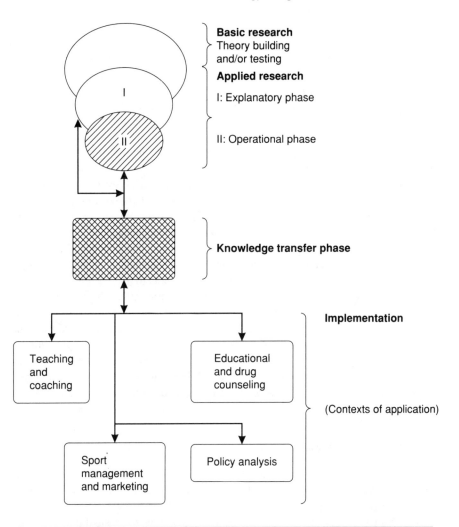

Figure 1.1 Relationships among levels of abstraction in sociology of sport research, knowledge transfer, and implementation. Arrows indicate direction and exchange of information.

works seeking more narrow technical solutions (research in the operational phase) may be based.

Given the logical interdependence of different levels of research activity, as portrayed in Figure 1.1, that is, the interdependence of basic, explanatory, and operational research, it also follows that a good applied social scientist must be sensitive to the fact that even narrow technical problems are grounded in the larger social structure. For example, achieving success in international competition is a process that is intimately tied to many other micro and macro social processes, as Levine (1974) points out. Thus, in order to appreciate the true ramifications of a problem requiring a solution, one must be able to see the larger picture, for it affords a wider set of solutions to select from than the narrow focus of an untheoretically guided practitioner. Thus, effective application must be grounded in good social science; and good social science, by definition, demands that all research, applied or otherwise, be linked to a larger body of knowledge, or theory.

In summary therefore, good applied research is a major dimension of the inductive-deductive phase of the research enterprise, and the primary goal of applied research is not the development of theory—although good theory can come of it—or "to advance the current level of discourse within the discipline" (Berk, 1981, p. 205), but the amelioration of the human condition and the solution of human problems. Therefore we view the role of sport sociology as one of discovery, description, explanation, and prediction, and that of applied sociology of sport as one of service to society. Thus the insights, methods, and theoretical perspectives from sport sociology are treated as means to an end, that end being the solution of problems and concerns of practical importance and significance to society.

Street and Weinstein (1975), in discussing the problems that mainstream sociology encountered in grappling with issues of relevance and application, suggest that application can take four forms: the Enlightenment Model, the Social Engineering Model, the Radical Model, and Mixed Models. Since these conceptualizations are instructive in developing an applied sociology of sport, a brief review of each will shed light on the discussion that follows.

The Enlightenment Model

This position suggests that the sociologist's task should be to communicate to the client "the broad range of problematics of theory and data, enlightening the user to the sociological perspective" (Street & Weinstein, 1975, p. 70). In other words, the sociologist should use explanatory knowledge to create the intellectual conditions for problem solving and decision making. In a strict sense, this is not applied sociology as the practitioner would wish it. Instead, the Enlightenment Model serves to provide the explanatory knowledge that may serve as a foundation for more narrowly focused research (operational research) and subsequent planning and decision making. We call this the explanatory research phase.

The Social Engineering Model

This model comes closest to a practitioner's definition of true application, for it seeks to provide narrow and specific technical solutions for specific social or professional problems. This model suggests that the role of applied research should be to translate practical problems into researchable form, seek solutions by applying sociological theory and methodology, and make specific recommendations that the practitioner may readily employ. We call this model the operational research phase.

Radical Sociology Model

According to Street and Weinstein, this is a conflict model of society that emphasizes the amelioration of social conditions resulting from inequality, exploitation, and the like. Applied sociology (and sport sociology) from this perspective stresses the search for, and commitment to, discovering the causes and consequences of social inequality for the purpose of bringing about meaningful social change. Advocates of this orientation may begin, for example, by conducting applied research and then continue by engaging in the implementation phase as change agents (praxis). Therefore adherents to the radical model are often both producers and practitioners (change agents) of sociological knowledge.

Although Street and Weinstein fail to address this same issue from a reactionary perspective, assuming that the political continuum has at its polar extremes a radical and a reactionary dimension, it is possible to extend the model further to include all forms of implementation. Thus, when a sport sociologist chooses to become a change agent, he or she is naturally free to engage in any form of activity, be it radical, reactionary, or otherwise.

Mixed Models

Finally, Street and Weinstein discuss a fourth category which they refer to as Mixed Models. Since different models tend to be more effective for different levels of decision making, the authors point out, "An applied sociology cannot be exclusively any one because the range and variety of questions to which it is legitimately directed cannot all be handled within a single model" (p. 70).

What Is Meant by Application?

The term application in the context of this paper is employed in relation to the business of life activity, that is, the business of providing *solutions* to questions of practical importance, assisting in *changing* behavior, and contributing to the *amelioration* of the human condition. Thus applied work concerns itself with what ought to be rather than with discovery, explanation, and prediction of what is, the latter clearly being the business of all science. Applied sociology of sport is therefore the process of generating knowledge of practical value and importance, and translating and delivering it to professionals for use in diverse contexts of application. Typically these contexts include physical education, coaching, policy, management, marketing, and counseling settings, among others. In either case, whether a sport sociologist serves as a consultant to the various professions or becomes the actual change agent, the objective is clearly to solve, change, and ameliorate.

If these criteria are indeed the yardstick by which societies judge the practical value of a profession, it behooves sport sociologists during these early formative stages to consider carefully what applied sociology of sport ought to become. For alternative viewpoints argue that the sociology of sport is already an applied area in the same way that criminology, family, and race are (for sociology), by virtue of having general sociology theory applied to them. This of course is a totally inadequate conceptualization of the meaning of application because it fails to address those key life activity concerns of solving, changing, and ameliorating. Such a viewpoint clearly reflects an academic's definition of application without considering the practitioner's perspective. In fact, in a survey of nonacademic employers, Lyson and Squires (1984) found that individuals with PhD degrees in sociology found it difficult to relate to the needs and realities of agencies in nonacademic settings.

Therefore, while such scholarly activity produces knowledge that explains "what is" about such social phenomena, it often fails to address the needs of practitioners concerned with the business of attempting to rehabilitate delinquents, solving the problems of single-parent families, facilitating the process of racial desegregation, or counseling academically marginal athletes. Therefore we cannot accept the position that the application of sociological theory to the study of a phenomenon automatically defines the enterprise as applied work.

The Phases of Application

Applied sociology of sport is characterized by several levels of abstraction which in this paper are called Phases of Application (see Figure 1.2): the Applied Research Phase, the Knowledge Transfer Phase, and the Implementation Phase.

The Applied Research Phase

The Applied Research Phase consists of two levels of abstraction. The higher level, which we call the Explanatory Phase, provides the foundation upon which more narrowly focused research may be based. Explanatory research therefore (a) addresses questions of practical importance or significance, (b) helps explain those underlying causes or influential factors contributing to the existence of the problem, (c) and provides explanations of relatively narrower theoretical scope than basic forms of research. Thus, explanatory research serves to illuminate issues and creates the intellectual conditions for problem solving, decision making, and more focused applied research. Street and Weinstein (1975) refer to this as the Enlightenment Model.

The next (lower) level of abstraction in applied research, called the Operational Research Phase, provides narrow technical solutions to problems of practical

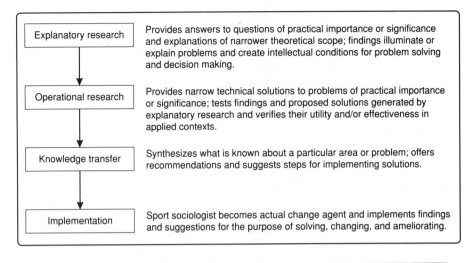

Figure 1.2   Phases of application in applied sociology of sport.

importance. Researchers at this level will often take the findings and proposed solutions advanced by explanatory research and test them in applied contexts in order to verify their utility. Various forms of evaluation research also fall into this category. Street and Weinstein refer to this as the Social Engineering Model. It is the aim of operational research to deliver the kind of knowledge that is most readily transferable to an array of application contexts (see Figure 1.1 for types of application contexts).

The Knowledge Transfer Phase

Good operational research takes the findings and proposed solutions generated in the explanatory research phase and investigates their utility in specific contexts of application (e.g., classroom, playing field, international arena). Of particular importance to the practitioner, however, are the recommendations in such works suggesting ways of solving, changing, and ameliorating. However, effective contextual application requires one final step. As one professional said about the knowledge transfer phase, "It explains the means by which your supplies are delivered to the fort." That is, it bridges the gap between knowledge and practical action. There is a need, therefore, for systematic efforts to translate the solutions provided by applied research into applied knowledge pertinent to specific contexts of application—knowledge that speaks to objectives, deficits, and recommendations for action by practitioners, and knowledge that is free of jargon and technical information which the practitioner can use.

This step, which we call the Knowledge Transfer Phase, requires a synthesis of what is known about a specific issue (e.g., sport and juvenile delinquency) together with a specification of the strategies for solving, changing, and perhaps ameliorating the situation. The Knowledge Transfer Phase consists of the following operations: (a) The applied sport sociologist identifies and defines the problem, and reviews and summarizes what is known about it by examining the findings of pertinent works from explanatory and operational research. (b) He or she reviews and assesses solutions for given contexts of application and recommends courses of action, and also provides a rationale for suggested courses of action. (c) He or she specifies steps or makes recommendations for implementing solutions in specific professional settings (e.g., physical education, sport management).

The Implementation Phase

Implementation is herein defined as the process by which program or policy recommendations are converted into programs of action, installed in specific contexts, and actually carried out. Implementation is the final stage in the chain of activities that characterize applied sociology of sport. It may occur, of course, in various contexts of application including the ones depicted in Figure 1.1, that is, teaching and coaching, educational counseling, sport management and market-ing contexts, and the like.

In this phase of application the sport sociologist becomes totally immersed in the process by becoming the change agent. This process involves the application of a model or method to the solution of a problem, for the purpose of changing behavior or achieving other objectives. Becoming a change agent sometimes poses problems for the sport sociologist. While some sport sociologists believe that direct involvement in social change enhances their effectiveness and chances of success, there is inevitably some loss of scientific objectivity. The problem is further compounded if such activity is client-financed (see Rossi, 1980, for an extended discussion).

Given this apparent conflict in roles, does the applied sport sociologist have any reasonable courses of action? At one extreme we can retain our pristine scientific purity by remaining "huddled behind self barricaded intellectual ghettos" as Gouldner (1963, p. 43) aptly stated over a quarter of a century ago, or we may opt to participate in the business of life and take both the criticism when deserved and the rewards when earned. It is clear that good judgment must be employed if the interests of science and the problems of society are to be effec-tively addressed. However, it is important to distinguish among the different roles available to the sport sociologist that differentiate academic from professional activity. As a change agent, for example, it is clear that one may no longer behave as an academic in the dispassionate pursuit of truth, but rather as someone whose efforts seek to solve, change, and ameliorate (hopefully) the human condition.

Thus a sport sociologist in the role of change agent must of necessity be concerned with what ought to be rather than with what is. This inevitably requires that value judgments be made about what is good and worthwhile. Therefore, so long as a sport sociologist/change agent recognizes that such an unabashed and committed declaration of what "ought to be" is incompatible with the more dispassionate stance expected of a social scientist, many potential role conflicts may be avoided. However, when the role of scientist is confused with the role of change agent, the dispassionate and objective search for truth, to the degree that this is in fact possible (Friedricks, 1970; Gouldner, 1963), can be easily contaminated or compromised.

There is clearly a need for applied sport sociology and for the diverse roles in which sport sociologists may legitimately engage. However, as Lyson and Squires (1984) prudently point out regarding applied sociology, "the potential contributions of sociology as an intellectual enterprise, not the declining academic job market, is the principal justification for an expansion of nonacademic work" (p. 13), for "graduate programs that tailor their training to meet the perceived needs of nonacademic employers reduce sociology to the status of a mere service station" (p. 11) whose aims can be dictated by narrow political, social, or economic demands.

The conflict of interest inherent in client/employer-defined forms of applied sociology (and sport sociology) are sufficiently important to merit separate treatment in another paper. Suffice it to say that we agree with Lyson and Squires and do not wish to see an applied form of sport sociology develop in which aims, training, and academic focus are dictated by the marketplace. However, sport sociologists have ignored societal concerns for too long, with the result that the field is now perceived as being mostly a theoretical/research area of study for students wishing to earn a doctorate and teach at the college level. Surely, as Bulmer (1985) noted in a book review on applied sociology, there are more strings to our bow than this!

Who Is an Applied Sport Sociologist?

In our discussion so far, we have identified at least four clusters of activities that can be subsumed under the general rubric of applied sociology of sport. We can state that a sport sociologist is said to be engaging in applied sport sociology if he or she (a) engages in explanatory or operational research and disseminates findings to various client groups, that is, he/she becomes an applied researcher; (b) serves as a consultant by assisting sport professionals (e.g., teachers, managers, policymakers) to improve their effectiveness through expert advice, referrals, and problem-solving activity; (c) becomes a knowledge broker, translating and delivering explanatory and operational knowledge to sport professionals through workshops, books, newsletters, and the like (engages in the process of knowledge transfer); (d) becomes a change agent and implements findings from applied research for the purpose of solving, changing, and ameliorating; designs, implements, and evaluates programs in specific contexts of application.

Specific Recommendations for Developing Applied Sociology of Sport

It is clear that a sharp distinction exists between the abstract and theoretical concerns of sport sociology and the practical, professional, and policy-oriented concerns of managers, teachers, sporting goods manufacturers, and coaches. If applied sociology of sport is to speak to the needs of society and the concerns of the various constituencies that stand to benefit from such research and involvement, sport sociologists must be encouraged to pursue with vigor and commitment the roles of applied researcher, consultant, knowledge broker, and change agent. Since these work roles form a structural link between the phases of application and the contexts of application (see Figure 1.3), they provide the only means through which the different types of applied knowledge may be delivered to practitioners.

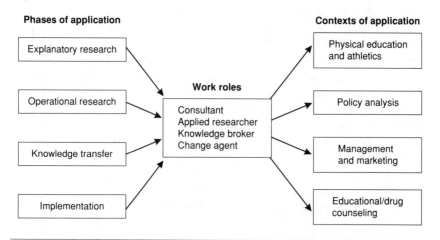

Figure 1.3 Relationship of applied sociology of sport with work roles and contexts of application.

The profession must also develop delivery systems such that the information generated by applied sport sociologists reaches professionals in physical education, coaching, policy formulation, counseling, management, and marketing, among others. There is a clear need for newsletters, a journal of applied sociology of sport, workshops, conferences, and other forums whereby the mutual interests of applied sport sociologists and practitioners may be fruitfully addressed. And there is clearly a need to develop graduate and undergraduate programs for the training of applied researchers (Berk, 1981; Rossi, 1980; Watts et al., 1983). Then perhaps the gulf that presently separates academics and practitioners will not seem so vast.

There is also a dire need to further develop the Knowledge Transfer Phase both on a conceptual level and as a vehicle for "getting our supplies to the fort." Since this phase of application clarifies the process of extracting, synthesizing, and packaging technical findings for delivery to practitioners in diverse contexts of application, it is clearly a significant point of linkage between academia and the professions. Ultimately it would be in the best interest of society and sport sociology if this were developed and strengthened.

Individual efforts by applied sport sociologists to venture into the public and private sectors should be coupled with initiatives at the organizational level. The North American Society for the Sociology of Sport, the Sport Sociology Academy, and ICSS [International Committee for Sociology of Sport], among others, should be mobilized to address societal problems and concerns, and also educate the public and private sectors about the potential contributions of applied sociology of sport. Of necessity, some of this activity will include efforts to promote the field (Santomier, 1988; Yiannakis, 1986), for there is a definite need to create a more positive image than the one that sport professionals presently have of both sociology and sport sociology.

References

Abt, C.C. (1980). What's wrong with social policy research? In C.C. Abt (Ed.), *Problems in American social policy research*. Cambridge, MA: Abt Books.

Berk, R.A. (1981). On the compatibility of applied and basic sociological research: An effort in marriage counseling. *The American Sociologist, 16*, 204-211.

Boros, A., & Adamek, R. (1981). Developing applied sociology programs: Some results. *Teaching Sociology, 8*, 387-399.

Bulmer, M. (1985). Applied sociology: There are more strings to your bow than this. *Contemporary Sociology, 4*, 304-306.

Cloward, R.A., & Ohlin, L.E. (1960). *Delinquency and opportunity: A theory of gangs*. New York: Free Press.

Coleman, J.S., Campbell, E.Q., Hobson, C., McPartland, J., Mood, A., Weinfeld, F., & York, R.L. (1966). *Equality of educational opportunity*. Washington, DC: U.S. Government Printing Office.

Coller, R. (1955). Notes on applied sociology. *Philippine Sociological Review, 3*(2), 11-14.

DeMartini, J. (1979). Applied sociology: An attempt at clarification and assessment. *Teaching Sociology, 6*, 331-354.

Foote, N. (1985). Challenge to apply sociology in business. *Sociological Practice, 5*, 165-174.

Friedricks, R. (1970). *A sociology of sociology*. New York: Free Press.

Gelfand, D. (1975). The challenge of applied sociology. *The American Sociologist, 10*, 13-18.

Gouldner, A. (1963). Anti-minotaur. The myth of a value-free sociology. In M. Stein & A. Vidich (Eds.), *Sociology on trial* (pp. 35-52). Englewood Cliffs, NJ: Prentice-Hall.

Greendorfer, S. (1977). Sociology of sport: Knowledge of what? *Quest, 28*, 58-65.

Greendorfer, S. (1985, November). *Sociology of sport and the issue of relevance.* Paper presented at Sixth Annual Conference of the North American Society for the Sociology of Sport, Boston.

Heinemann, K. (1983). Practical orientation and function of sport sociology. *International Review of Sport Sociology, 18*(1), 21-34.

Hellison, D. (1986, April). *The relevance of sport sociology for teachers and coaches.* Paper presented at the Annual Convention of the American Alliance for Health, Physical Education, Recreation and Dance, Cincinnati.

Hoch, P. (1972) *Rip off the big game.* Garden City, NY: Doubleday & Co.

Jalowiecki, B. (1967). Applied sociology as an instrument of area planning. *The Polish Sociological Bulletin, 15*, 69-77.

Kalmuss, D. (1981). Scholars in the classroom: Two models of applied social science. *The American Sociologist, 16*, 212-223.

Kjeldsen, E. (1988, November). *The utility of the sport sociological perspective in the preparation of sport practitioners.* Paper presented at Annual Conference of the North American Society for the Sociology of Sport, Cincinnati.

Klein, G. (1984). Applied sociology and social policy: Are we reformers, oppressors, social engineers, or marginal men? A review of the literature. *Sociological Practice, 5*(1), 85-160.

Krawczyk, Z. (1977). Theory and empiricism in the social sciences regarding physical culture. *International Review of Sport Sociology, 12*, 71-92.

Lenk, H. (1973). The pedagogical significance of sport sociology. *International Journal of Physical Education, 10*, 16-20.

Levine, N. (1974). Why do countries win Olympic medals? Some structural correlates of Olympic Games success: 1972. *Sociology and Social Research, 58*, 353-360.

Lueschen, G. (1985). The practical uses of sociology of sport: Some methodological issues. In R. Rees & A. Miracle (Eds.), *Sport and social theory* (pp. 245-254). Champaign, IL: Human Kinetics.

Lyson, T., & Squires G. (1984). The promise and perils of applied sociology: A survey of nonacademic employers. *Sociological Enquiry, 54*(1), 1-15.

Massengale, J. (1985, November). *Applications of sport sociology to the teaching profession.* Paper presented at the Sixth Annual Conference of the North American Society for the Sociology of Sport, Boston.

McPherson, B. (1986). Policy-oriented research in youth sport: An analysis of the process and product. In R. Rees & A. Miracle (Eds.), *Sport and social theory* (pp. 255-287). Champaign, IL: Human Kinetics.

Meggyesy, D. (1970). *Out of their league.* Berkeley, CA: Ramparts.

Melnick, M. (1975). A critical look at sociology of sport. *Quest, 24*, 34-47.

Melnick, M. (1980). Toward an applied sociology of sport. *Journal of Sport and Social Issues, 4*(2), 1-12.

Moynihan, D.P. (1965). *The negro family: The case for national action*. Washington, DC: U.S. Government Printing Office.

Murphy, J. (1981). Applied sociology, social engineering, and human rationality. *Journal of Sociology and Social Welfare*, **8**(1), 10-18.

Rees, R. (1984). Applying sociology to physical education. Who needs it? In N. Struna (Ed.), *Proceedings of the National Association for Physical Education in Higher Education*, **5**, 54-59.

Rossi, P.H. (1980). The presidential address: The challenge and opportunities of applied research. *American Sociological Review*, **45**, 889-904.

Sack, A. (1986, April). *Applications of sport sociology to sport management*. Paper presented at the Annual Convention of the American Alliance for Health, Physical Education, Recreation and Dance, Cincinnati.

Sage, G. (1977). Sport sociology: The state of the art and implications for physical education. *NAPECW/NCPEAM Proceedings*, pp. 310-318.

Sage, G. (1985). *The role of sport studies in sport pedagogy*. Paper presented at AIESEP World Conference, New York.

Santomier, J. (1988, November). *Marketing and promoting the sport sociologist*. Paper presented at Annual Conference of the North American Society for the Sociology of Sport, Cincinnati.

Schafer, W. (1971). *Sport, socialization and the school: Toward maturity or enculturation?* Paper presented at Third International Symposium on the Sociology of Sport, Waterloo, Canada.

Schur, E.M. (1965). *Crimes without victims*. Englewood Cliffs, NJ: Prentice-Hall.

Scott, J. (1971). *The athletic revolution*. New York: The Free Press.

Sewell, W.H., Hauser, R.M., & Featherman, D. (1976). *Schooling and achievement in American society*. New York: Academic Press.

Sherohman, J. (1984). Applied sociology and social work. *The Wisconsin Sociologist*, **21**(1), 37-44.

Sigelman, L., & Bookheimer, S. (1984). Is it whether you win or lose? Monetary contributions to big-time college athletic programs. *Social Science Quarterly*, **64**, 347-359.

Snyder, E., & Spreitzer, E. (1984). Patterns of adherence to a physical conditioning program. *Sociology of Sport Journal*, **1**, 103-116.

Street, D., & Weinstein, E. (1975). Problems and prospects of applied sociology. *The American Sociologist*, **10**, 65-72.

Ulrich, C. (1979). The significance of sport sociology to the profession. In M. Krotee (Ed.), *The dimensions of sport sociology* (pp. 11-19). West Point, NY: Leisure Press.

Veidemanis, J. (1964). Applied sociology and the refugee problem. *Indian Journal of Social Research*, **5**(1), 74-82.

Voight, D. (1974). Sociology in the training of the sport teacher and of the teacher in general. *International Journal of Physical Education*, **10**, 26-40.

Watts, D., Short, A., & Schultz, C. (1983). Applied sociology and the current crisis. *Teaching Sociology*, **11**, 47-61.

Widmer, K. (1977). Social sciences of sport and sport pedagogy as part aspect of sport science. *International Journal of Physical Education,* **14**, 21-35.

Wright, J.D., Rossi, P.H., Wright, S.R., & Weber-Burdin, E. (1979). *After the clean-up: Long range effects of natural disasters.* Beverly Hills, CA: Sage.

Yiannakis, A. (1986, April). *Applications of sport sociology to sport and leisure marketing.* Paper presented at the Annual Convention of the American Alliance for Health, Physical Education, Recreation and Dance, Cincinnati.

Yiannakis, A. (1988, November). *A conceptual framework for applied sociology of sport.* Paper presented at Annual Conference of the North American Society for the Sociology of Sport, Cincinnati.

Yonebayashi, T. (1960). Application of sociology and applied sociology. *Japanese Sociological Review,* **10**(3-4), 33-50.

SECTION 2

Issues and Problems in Developing an Applied Sociology of Sport

The three articles in this section offer a general orientation to issues, problems, and controversies that have surrounded the topic of application in both the parent discipline of sociology and the subdiscipline of sport sociology. Despite the fact that they are not directly linked to components of the framework outlined in chapter 1, the articles identify specific themes that set the tone and provide the basis of support for the development of an applied sport sociology.

Assuming that lessons can be learned from sociology in general, we have included one paper that outlines the difficulties faced when the parent discipline was confronted with the issue of application. Although the two subsequent articles address exclusively sport sociology, they tend to support the general contention underlying the more general article—that the line between applied and basic research is a thin one and that both terms are in need of redefinition. Each author recognizes and is receptive to the impact of assimilating knowledge into practice while at the same time maintaining some ambivalence toward applied research. Given the strong sentiments toward outright rejection of application at the point in history that these papers were written, their overall message represents a receptivity that was essential for continued consideration of application. After reading the articles in Section 2 you should have sufficient background to understand the underlying issues and debates that ultimately contributed to the formation of the theoretical framework in chapter 1.

Chapter 2

The Presidential Address: The Challenge and Opportunities of Applied Social Research

Peter H. Rossi
University of Massachusetts, Amherst

This chapter focuses on the inability of sociology to respond (and on the repercussions of such failure) to the challenges and demands for *relevance* of education to everyday life and the perceived need to solve such social problems as poverty, racism, and social upheaval. In his presidential address to the American Sociological Association, Rossi describes the mixed feelings sociologists have when they deal with the challenges, pitfalls, and opportunities of applied research. On one hand they view applied research as an important reason for sociology's existence; yet they also believe that applied work is not really worthy of their best efforts. Despite the stigma associated with applied work, Rossi quite appropriately mentions that some of the most prominent social theorists have conducted significant applied research.

The stance of our profession toward applied work of all sorts in sociology has been one of considerable ambivalence. On the one hand, applied work is decidedly below basic or theoretical work in the hierarchy of preference, prestige, and esteem. Correspondingly, academic employment is very strongly preferred over nonacademic positions, even though salary levels for the latter are often considerably higher. When we scan the credentials of job applicants or bibliographies appended to grant applications, articles published in journals that feature applied work are assumed to be of lesser quality than ones published in mainstream

Paper presented at the meeting of the American Sociological Association, New York, NY, 1980. Grateful acknowledgments are due to James F. Short, Alice S. Rossi, Stanley Lieberson, Clark C. Abt, James D. Wright, Howard Freeman, and Richard Berk whose comments on an early draft helped to improve this paper. *Note.* From *American Sociological Review*, 1980, **45**, pp. 889–904. Copyright 1980 by the American Sociological Association. Reprinted by permission.

professional journals. Most sociologists are embarrassed when we are confused with social work or with family therapists. Indeed, some of our colleagues gloss over their applied work as if it were a vice best kept from public view.

On the other hand, our roots in applied concerns are old and very much alive. Our ranks always have been full of ministers and ex-ministers, radicals and ex-radicals, even a few conservatives and ex-conservatives, all of whom were attracted to sociology because our discipline appeared to have some relevance to social reform or its prevention. And when it comes to facing outward toward the public—and especially toward our benefactors—we are very quick to point to the many complicated social problems that justify our existence and need for support. Our public stance is often enough that a properly supported sociology will point the way to a better society with a lowered level of social troubles.

Thus, our ambivalence consists in believing—at one and the same time—that applied work is not worthy of our best efforts and our best minds and that an important reason for our existence is that sociology will lead to important practical applications.

Some of our critics apparently understand this ambivalence sufficiently to be able to exploit it and, occasionally, will criticize us on both counts. For example, earlier this year, Congressman Ashbrook (Ohio) spoke out in support of his proposal to slash the NSF [National Science Foundation] appropriation for the basic research program in the social and behavioral sciences—a sterile title that hides sociology, political science, and economics in a plain brown envelope. He accused us (on the one hand) of being off in the cloudy heights of theory and speculation and, hence, not attending to the very real needs of our society, yet (on the other hand) of seriously endangering the moral order of our society by implicitly endorsing, through research on such matters, the dreadful patterns of deviance that afflict our society.

It should be pointed out that sociology is not the only discipline that holds an ambivalent view of applied work: This is a viewpoint we share with the other social sciences and with the natural physical sciences as well.

There must be some important reasons why this ambivalence persists, over time, in sociology and other disciplines. I will leave it to the sociologists of science to provide an understanding of why we have such mixed feelings toward applied work. My task here is to examine more closely the relationships between applied and basic work in our field, through taking up four themes:

First, I will explore what the differences are between basic and applied work, showing that the lines between the two are difficult, if not impossible, to draw.

Second, I will attempt to show that there has been considerable commerce between the two parts of our discipline, to the considerable enrichment of both. For polemical reasons, I will emphasize the contributions that applied research has made to basic sociology, an argument that may not give appropriate attention to the fact that the commerce between basic and applied work is certainly a two-way exchange. No one knows whether, in the long- or short-run, the balance of trade favors the one or the other side of the exchange—although there are many opinions on this issue.

Third, I will belabor the obvious a bit, pointing out what many of us already know quite well—namely, that applied social research has enjoyed a boom period over the last two decades, a prosperity in which sociology as a discipline has not participated strongly.

As my final theme, I will point out some of the implications of the current boom in applied social science for our field, indicating why we should become more involved and how we can do so.

There are several varieties of applied work in sociology, including clinical practice, policy analysis, consultation to businesses and government agencies on substantive issues, and applied social research. My main concern will be with applied social research, although many of the points made are, most likely, relevant to other kinds of applied work in sociology. I confine myself to applied social research mainly because I know more about that subfield of applied sociology.

The general argument running through this article is that applied social research has been a firm and fruitful part of the tradition of our discipline. Practitioners and their applied social research have not been given sufficient credit for their contributions to the development of our discipline. I argue for greater recognition to be given to applied social research—in the form of more attention to that activity within our curricula, in our professional journals, and in the rewards our profession gives for scholarly accomplishments.

A Modest Contribution
Toward Conceptual Clarity

It is easy to distinguish between applied and basic work in sociology if you consider only extreme cases. Using examples from my own work, it appears to be quite obvious that *After the Clean-Up* . . . (Wright et al., 1979) is applied social research, being an attempt to estimate the long-term effects of natural disasters (tornadoes, floods, and hurricanes) on the population and housing stocks of small areas. It is, clearly, applied research because its main purpose was to assess whether there was any need for changes in federal policy to provide aid to communities and neighborhoods ameliorating the impacts of long-term negative effects of such natural-hazard happenings. In contrast, an apparently clear example of basic research is my recent article (Alves & Rossi, 1978) on uncovering the normative bases for distributive justice judgments concerning household earnings. What is it that appears to differentiate between the two examples? First of all, the research on the long-term effects of natural disasters was designed to serve an existing need for information for social policy decision making while the distributive justice study is far from current policy concerns. In contrast, income redistribution issues involving wage rates are not explicit issues on current political agendas of legislatures. Nor is there any consideration given to regulating earnings in the interest of increasing popular feelings about how just income discrepancies are among households. The fact that we found no discernible long-term community effects, stemming out of a decade's experience with natural disasters, meant that no relief measures designed to meet the needs of small areas were necessary. In contrast, there likely are no policy makers who are currently concerned with altering wages in order to increase the average sense of justice.

Note, however, that implied in the foregoing is the argument that for a given research to be clearly applied requires the existence of policy makers who would be interested in the outcome as well as in the possibility or existence of some policy to which the research was immediately addressed. So far, this does not appear to be a very satisfactory definition as its main provisions are not linked to the research activities per se but, rather, to the purposes to which the research might be put by some segment of our society. Indeed, this consideration points to the historical specificity of just what is often called applied social research. Because the interests and concerns of policy makers and other political partisans change, over time, research that is applied in one historical period may be basic research in another period—and vice versa. Legislatures might not be concerned *currently* with establishing new (and presumably more equitable) principles for setting wages and salaries, but it is certainly conceivable that they *might* do so. In that event, Alves and Rossi's 1979 study would become applied social research! (We will return again to this issue of historical specificity.)

A second point of difference between the two research examples lies, in the first instance, in the existence of a "client" who underwrote the costs of the research and who also had a direct interest in the outcomes of the research. The NSF-RANN program financed the research that went into the *After the Clean-up* study because it showed promise (indeed, we actually *did* promise) to be relevant to policy issues. But the social science panel of NIMH that approved the distributive justice study apparently "couldn't have cared less" whether the research was needed for social policy or not. Nor did that grant application promise policy-relevant findings.

Having a client who is concerned about the outcome of a research project that he or she has sponsored often means a continuing connection between the researcher and client throughout the conduct of the research project. While the connection may take a variety of forms, all the way from "oppressive" supervision at the one extreme and benign neglect at the other extreme, applied research always means that somewhere there is less autonomy for the applied (as compared with the basic) researcher.

In applied work, there is more time-consciousness, deadlines to be met, interim and final reports to clients to be written; and, often, there is some specific person or group that is intensely enough interested in your work to attempt constantly to find out what you are up to, and doing, in quite specific terms. In contrast, even though basic researchers have to report to someone and be responsible in a general way for doing a job, the detail and constancy of supervision is simply not as great. I am sure that this is one of the reasons that applied research is valued less than basic research in which the autonomy of the researcher is always greater. Although the NSF-RANN program was far from the most intrusive clients I have had dealings with, my colleagues and I did have to suffer, albeit mildly, through a succession of advisory committee meetings, conferences with RANN [Research Applied to National Needs] staff members, and consultations with federal agencies that were concerned with disaster relief.

Basic research presents quite a contrast. I never again heard from NIMH [National Institute of Mental Health] once the distributive justice grant was awarded. As requested, I sent copies of articles published as a result of work done under the support grant. If anyone on the NIMH staff actually read any of them, he/she certainly did not feel impelled to communicate either pleasure or displeasure or, for that matter, any other reaction. From almost any researcher's point of view, it is better to operate either without a client or with a very un-intrusive client. Certainly, in that sense, basic research is to be preferred over applied research.

The major implication that flows from this discussion, so far, is that whether or not a given research or scholarly work is regarded as basic or applied is, at least partially, historically bound. Thus, subsequent history may treat very differently research conducted in an earlier period. For example, the now-classic 1947 NORC [National Opinion Research Center] (Reiss, 1961) study of occupational prestige was originally applied social research conducted for a federal agency concerned at the time with the recruitment of natural scientists to federal employment. The agency was convinced that the prestige of federal employment had suffered a severe blow in the years immediately following World War II and had sponsored the research simply to get a better reading on how government scientists were viewed by the general public—as compared with their views of scientists who worked for private industry or for universities. What was, originally, a piece of applied work done for a particular client has become, with time, primarily basic research—at least in the way it has been viewed in the sociological literature.

Indeed, the NORC-North-Hatt occupational prestige research is rather instructive as an illustration of the interpenetration of applied and basic interests. It certainly would have been possible for NORC to have undertaken a study of occupational prestige that was focused exclusively on the occupations of interest to the client. However, the researchers in charge of the project convinced the client that the agency's interests would be better served by a research design that placed the occupations of policy interest into the context of the entire occupational structure. This enlargement of the original narrowly focused interest of the client into a much larger framework was guided largely by North and Hatt's interests in social stratification. The resulting study, of course, was considerably enhanced in value for basic sociology as a consequence.

Another example of applied research becoming basic is W. Lloyd Warner's study of Newburyport (Warner & Lunt, 1941). The immediate motivation for the Yankee City studies was to add a community context to the study of industrial work forces, an interest that had grown out of the Mayo and Roethlisberger Western Electric Hawthorne studies (Roethlisberger & Dickson, 1939). One can dispute whether or not the Yankee City studies were even at all relevant to the applied concerns they were designed to serve, but the fact remains that, initially, Warner was working for a client with quite specific interests and the Yankee City studies were initially conceived of as applied research.

The course of history may also turn a basic study into an applied one. Thus, Benjamin Bloom's work (Bloom, 1964) on the stability of IQ during early childhood became one of the intellectual pillars of President Johnson's Head Start program, as policy makers and their staffs searched through existing literature to find data on where best in the lives of children to intervene with compensatory educational programs. Bloom's work noted the apparent stability of IQ from the first grade on, suggesting that preschool intervention would be most effective. In the same way, E. Franklin Frazier's monograph (Frazier, 1939) on the Negro family had almost slipped into scholarly oblivion when revived by Moynihan (Moynihan, 1965) to provide an apparent explanation of why there was so much "pathology" among contemporary black families.

I started out this discussion of the differences between basic and applied social research with examples in which the distinction is easy to make. For many researches, particularly large-scale studies, the distinctions are much more difficult to draw and, at the margins, the lines between applied and basic research are almost impossible to discern. For example, the Income Dynamics Study (Morgan et al., 1974) was sponsored initially by the Office of Economic Opportunity to provide information on how often, and why, families apparently drifted back and forth across the poverty line. Currently, this longitudinal study is being supported as basic research by the Social Science Division of the National Science Foundation. There can be little doubt that this study has simultaneously contributed to applied concerns and basic social science, aided considerably by the wide diffusion of public use data sets. Essentially nothing about the design changed as sponsorship shifted from OEO to NSF, nor was there much shift in subject matter. The question of whether this is basic or applied social research is somewhat irrelevant—as it seems to have been both. Of course, it should be emphasized that the principal investigators played an important role in designing the study (and its continuation) so that findings would be relevant both to current social welfare policy and to a host of basic concerns in several social sciences.

Another interesting example is the Equality of Educational Opportunity report (Coleman et al., 1966) and the data sets lying behind that report. In its inception, Coleman and associates' study was certainly applied, mandated as it was in the 1964 equal rights legislation. While there were some policy concerns expressed specifically in the federal legislation, it was relatively general in character, calling as it did for a survey to ascertain whether or not educational opportunities were equal across ethnic groups. The design created—and the analysis followed—by Coleman and his associates went considerably beyond the mandate of the Congress to provide, among other things, estimates of the effects of schools on the achievement of pupils. Is this an example of basic or applied research? The answer is that it is both: It is applied research—by virtue of having a client and a set of policy concerns to which the research was at least partially directed; but it is also basic research—in that the researchers went beyond a narrow research mandate to consider some general issues in the sociology of education.

Special note should be taken of the important role played by the researchers in the design of applied social research. A particular applied-research study may be so narrowly designed that basic sociological (or other social science) concerns would find very little of interest in the study or in its findings, or it can be designed to accommodate basic concerns as well. Indeed, given the fact that policy concerns are often vaguely stated and, furthermore, often shift over short periods of time, broad-focused applied studies are likely to be more useful to policy interests, as well as being of greater disciplinary interest.

I hope that I have given sufficient examples to illustrate that the line between basic and applied research is a fuzzy one, subject to redefinition by the researchers, by clients, and by the drift of historical change. The implication of such fuzzy boundaries is that it is difficult to decide what is applied work and what is not. Good applied work tends to be transformed into basic contributions, a process that does not disturb the conventional view of applied social research being, somehow, lower in value and quality than is basic research. A proper recognition of the origins of much of the work that we value in our history would support a more positive view of the contribution of applied work to the growth of our discipline.

Of course, the counter-arguments can be made that (1) I have selectively skimmed the best of applied social research in order to bolster unfairly the argument I have presented, and (2) the bulk of applied social research is of poor quality and hardly likely to contribute even to the discipline, let alone to the solution of social problems. There is some truth in this argument: Much of applied social research is best left in the fugitive Xerox reports in which they were issued. But low quality and irrelevance are characteristic of most of the work in our discipline, whether applied or basic. For example, more than three-fourths of all articles submitted to *ASR* [*American Sociological Review*] are turned down. Whether or not applied work has more low-quality output than does basic work is problematic.

Some General Contributions of Applied Social Research to Basic Concerns

Because the line between basic and applied work in sociology is fuzzy and indeterminate, it is correspondingly difficult to make a definitive assessment of the interchange between basic and applied work. Today's applied work may be tomorrow's basic science—and vice versa. Furthermore, what I may classify as "basic" may be defined by another sociologist as "applied." Indeed, about the best one can do is to provide examples of notable transactions in which applied work has made obviously significant contributions to basic social science concerns, in the optimistic hope that these outstanding examples are fair indicators of what is true generally.

To begin with, it is important to recognize that many of the most prominent sociologists have devoted some significant portions of their careers to applied social research: Even an incomplete listing of such persons is quite impressive, including Durkheim, Giddings, Ogburn, Stouffer, Park, Hughes, Lazarsfeld, K. Davis, Phillip Hauser, Sewell, O.D. Duncan, and Coleman. Indeed, a rough and informal count I made of the last thirty presidents of the American Sociological Association yielded an estimate that eighteen had been involved significantly in applied social research. Clearly, this is an underestimate, relying as it does on the fallibility of one observer's memory. Among the remaining twelve, there are a few who did some applied work—as, for example, Pitirim Sorokin, though his general work was certainly not of that vein. Indeed, there are likely more than a few among the twelve others who may have been "closet" applied social researchers.

Most interesting and revealing, in light of the earlier discussion about the lower esteem accorded applied work, is that so many of the eighteen presidents are not generally remembered as applied social researchers because, over time, some of their most important applied research has been redefined as basic work. For example, how many of us recall (or ever knew) that Lazarsfeld's seminal work on personal influence (Katz & Lazarsfeld, 1955) stemmed from very applied work financed by MacFadden Publications in an effort to obtain evidence that would convince would-be advertisers that placing ads in *True Story* magazine would reach opinion leaders? Or that the very influential series of researches by Sewell and his associates (Sewell et al., 1976) on status attainment had its beginnings in a state-sponsored survey of Wisconsin high school seniors, the major purpose of which was to forecast the demand for higher education in that state?

One of the more visible characteristics of prominent sociologists who have participated in applied work is the predominance of quantitative empirical researchers in that group. This is a feature of some importance, as I will develop more fully later in this discussion. For the present, this characterization is noteworthy as evidence that one of the more important contributions of applied research has been to technical developments in research methods.

Most of us are familiar with the fact that much of the basic work in statistical methods has come out of applied concerns in other fields, experimental work in agriculture, psychological test construction, quality control in industry, and so on. The outstanding examples are quite numerous, as the following list demonstrates: Student's t, analysis of variance, factor analysis, regression, and on and on. By and large, sociologists have been net borrowers of research methods vis-à-vis other fields, especially with respect to statistical models.

Sociologists have played a more important role in the development of data collection methods. Along with other social scientists, we have made important contributions to the science and art of sample surveys. Much of the early work that went into the development of sampling methods, interview construction, and the like was undertaken within applied contexts, by sociologists in collaboration with other social scientists. Area probability sampling was developed at the Bureau of the

Census out of a need to conduct valid periodic estimates of the labor force. Psychologists and sociologists—working for the most part with the advertising industry, newspapers, and political candidates—developed the attitude survey. Scaling methods, at least in part, developed out of the work in Stouffer's (Stouffer et al., 1950) Research Branch in the Information and Education Division of the War Department. Indeed, the Research Branch, a decidedly applied activity, did a great deal to train a fairly large set of young sociologists who became the postwar specialists in sample surveys and, more generally, helped to establish the use of sample surveys of all sorts as a prime research tool for our field. The most recent development in sample surveys, random digit dialing, was developed initially by persons working on commercial sample surveys; it is now gradually finding its way into use by sociological researchers.

In addition, one must recall that Hollerith was a Census employee when he came up with the idea of the punch card and mechanical tabulating equipment. And the first commercial version of the electronic computer, UNIVAC I, was at least partially speeded toward development by the demand for its use in the 1950 Census of Population and Housing.

Other frequently used techniques in social research were also either developed in pursuit of applied interests or heavily influenced by being used in applied research. For example, the intense postwar public policy interest in the issue of overpopulation gave a large impetus to the further development of demographic methods. Sociometric techniques had their start as Moreno (1934) developed a device for optimizing the residential arrangements of young women in a training school. Social field experiments had an early start with Dodd's (1934) randomized experiment in Syria on techniques for instilling appropriate drinking water treatment procedures in rural areas.

Qualitative research methods also have roots in applied work. The earliest American community study (Williams, 1906), conducted by a rural sociologist housed in an experimental station, was concerned with the impact of changing agricultural technology on a rural town. As mentioned earlier, Warner's study of Newburyport grew out of the Mayo and Roethlisberger work on worker productivity. The Lynds' first Middletown study (Lynd & Lynd, 1938) was financed by a foundation with a concern for studying the impact of social change on the moral life of Americans.

The technological and methodological contributions of applied to basic sociology loom large because new methods are easier to transfer across substantive fields. In contrast, theory and empirical knowledge are most closely tied to substantive fields and, hence, do not travel as easily. Perhaps most of the transfer from applied to basic work in substantive theory and empirical findings has occurred because much applied work has dealt with subject matters that are at the very heart of sociological concerns—stratification and inequality, organizations, collective behavior, deviance and social control, race relations and discrimination, life chances and health care, family, work and occupations, and so on. Indeed, there are few substantive areas that have not been studied with an applied focus.

Yet, it is difficult to point out clear one-way contributions of applied work to basic work—mainly because the interchange has been an interactive one. Some contributions of applied work (such as the concept of personal influence and opinion leadership) are directly and easily traceable to the applied work from which they originated. Others (such as the concept of relative deprivation) are indirect contributions arising out of commentaries upon or secondary analyses of applied work. In still other cases, concepts arising in theoretical work have been refined in applied work—and vice versa. Examples of the joint development of concepts include status attainment, occupational prestige, and anomie. Other examples, I am sure, will occur to the reader. Of course, one of the more important contributions of applied social research has been to the refinement of—and sometimes negations of—concepts derived from general sociology. The empirical testing of concepts that are incorporated into applied research has led often enough to their being disconfirmed. For examples: There is little empirical evidence for labelling theory, virtually no evidence for a "culture of poverty," meager support for differential association, and so on. Although it would certainly be an exaggeration to state that sociology would not have advanced at all over the past three decades without the help of applied work, it would be equally foolish to claim that applied work has not made a strong contribution to the progress that sociology has made in that period. Basic and applied work in our discipline are complementary.

Some Challenges and Pitfalls of Applied Social Research

The products of applied social research have made, as I have attempted to show, strong contributions to the development of our discipline. Although the hope of making such contributions might be sufficient to motivate one to engage in applied social research, there are also some intrinsic satisfactions to be derived from the inherent nature of applied work. There are also some pitfalls of which the would-be applied social researcher must at least be aware. Both the attractions and the dangers of applied social research have their roots in the politicized nature of such research, as I will now attempt to show.

Applied social research often demands greater technical skills than does basic research. Because the results of applied social research may be used in the political process, it is clearly important that it be done well. After all, an article in a major professional journal, or a monograph, has little consequence except upon the career of the writer and, perhaps, except for attracting the attention of the handful of other social scientists who have been doing work on the same topic. In contrast, the product of applied social research might be used in the formation and change of public policy; and an error in applied work might have consequences not only for the social scientists involved but also for institutions, agencies, policy makers, and the intended beneficiaries of the policies in question.

Although the discipline may be concerned with whether research reported upon in an *ASR* or *AJS* [*American Journal of Sociology*] article is based on good samples, used good measurement instruments, used a research design of appropriate power and methods of analyses that are robust, such concerns are not as salient as in applied work. This is one of the main reasons why much applied social research is on a so-much-larger scale than discipline-oriented research. Of course, editors and readers do deduct points for defects in any of these respects, but the fact of the matter is that there are so few good ideas and data in sociology that Type I errors are clearly less important than Type II errors in the judging of articles. In contrast, for example, estimating the work disincentive effects of transfer payments calls for good samples, precision and validity in measurement, and virtuosity in analysis—because an error in any of these might be translated into social policy affecting the well-being of poor households across the nation.

Of course, the fact that applied social research may be used in policy formation is also one of the pitfalls into which it is easy to stumble. It is very easy to become the center of rancorous controversy; contending parties in some policy dispute may use and abuse your work. There are few major applied researches that have not sparked controversy, as, for example, in the cases of the Coleman Report, the evaluation of Head Start, or the Income Maintenance experiments. Indeed, the controversial character of applied social research has spawned part-time employment of researchers as methodological critics hired by partisans to provide devastating criticisms of some applied social research.

Conflict over the results of applied social research is not without its positive side, however. The competition among divergent points of view has led to a considerable acceleration of progress toward higher and higher quality in applied social research. For example, the heavy criticism directed at quasi-experimental estimates of program effectiveness has sparked considerable progress toward understanding the role of a priori theory in devising research designs (Heckman, 1980).

New methodologies have been invented, old ones adapted to new problems; and interdisciplinary transfer of ideas has been accelerated through the critical evaluation of applied research. Of course, so-called basic and theoretical work is also subject to criticism, but the critical process for applied work is more timely and more intense, characteristics which may be somewhat more painful to the applied social researcher but which are more productive of relatively rapid progress in technical and conceptual quality.

The political character of applied social research is the source of another of its attractions, at least to those of us who are still concerned with improving our society. There is the possibility that the results of applied social research will do some good. Thus, one might be tempted to undertake research on the child-care arrangements used by working mothers in the hope that the resulting findings might pave the way for better and more effective child-care policies. There are, however, some restrictions on what one can do as an applied social researcher. First of all, problems are not set by the researcher alone but, often, are worked out on the initiative of some policy-oriented agency and, sometimes, by negotiation between the researcher and the agency in question. In practice, this means that, as an applied social scientist, one is not entirely free to frame research problems in the form that appears most fruitful to the researcher. One is ordinarily restricted to what is called "policy space"—that is, the range of alternative remedies for a social policy that appears to be politically acceptable. Thus, for example, the income maintenance experiments defined a set of payment plans that were thought to span what would be acceptable to Congress, a space that did not include what you and I might consider to be very generous payment plans. In short, there are politically imposed limits on subject matter and policy issues that can be considered in applied social research.

Applied social research tends to be conservative, devoted mainly to the examination of policy alternatives that are not radically different from existing social policies. Fine tuning, rather than revolution, is on the political agenda. At best, applied social research is politically congenial, both to those who are liberals and to the right of liberals.

While applied social research will not bring about revolutionary changes, it is in practice neither reactionary nor completely supportive of the status quo. At least in the present historical period, applied social research has had the characteristics of being a demystifying instrument, exposing the faults and inadequacies of existing institutions. Criminologists in their research have had profound impacts on American prisons. Applied research on schools has raised fundamental questions about what schools do. Applied research on alcoholism has certainly changed our understanding of that disorder. Such examples can be easily multiplied. The fact of the matter is that the social policy of the past few decades was conceived by persons with—at best—amateur social scientist status and, hence, most of it (as well as most long-standing institutions) cannot stand up very well under the scrutiny of a thoroughgoing empirical testing.

It should be kept in mind, however, that applied social research is no occupation for would-be philosopher kings. The applied researcher ordinarily does not get very close to the seats of decision making and policy formation. Often enough, policy appears impermeable to both the results of research and the advice of the researcher. Even at its best, applied social research does not substitute for the political process. It merely provides another input into the policy-making process. Indeed, who would have it otherwise? One of the virtues of our political system is that decisions are made often enough as the outcome of the pulling and hauling among a variety of interest groups, a process that may value the input of social science work but does not place the work on a pedestal of absolute authority.

It is not at all clear to me how one may measure whether the attractions of applied social research are outweighed by the negative aspects of politicized work, or vice versa. If you are attracted both to technically challenging work involving the fine tuning of our existing society and to the opportunities presented by relatively high levels of resources, and are not put off by the possibility that your work will be seemingly ignored by decision makers and possibly come under attack from fellow social scientists, then applied social research is an attractive activity. If you cannot stand verbal and written abuse, or want to work on fundamental changes in our society, then applied social research is clearly not for you.

These foregoing remarks are addressed to the question of whether one would or would not find the politicized aspects of applied social research a deterrent to participation. The negative consequences account, in part, for the reasons that applied social research is undervalued in our discipline. But such arguments do not address themselves to the scholarly contributions such work may make to the growth of our discipline. Applied social research is harder on the participant, but that is at least partially balanced by the greater intellectual challenges such work may provide and by the positive contributions it may make to our society and to the discipline.

Opportunities in Applied Social Research Today

Applied social research may or may not be as attractive as I have described it, but if there are no opportunities for participation in such activities, then that message may be enlightening—but irrelevant—to our discipline. Such is decidedly not the case, however: Applied social research must be described as having been, during the last two decades, one of the growth sectors in our economy. Estimates (Abt, 1980) of the amounts spent in the federal budgets of the last few years on applied social research, in one form or another, vary from a high of $2 billion to a low of about $1 billion. The amount spent on the evaluation of educational programs alone was estimated to be more than $100 million in 1976. Whatever estimate one accepts, the numbers indicate that applied social research is big, strong, and flourishing—especially when compared to the support of basic social research program funds, which amount to only several hundred million dollars for all the social sciences combined. In addition, private foundations also provide support, although on a smaller scale.

Note that these funds count only the federal budget allocations. State and local governments also support applied social research, perhaps not to the same extent but adding at least several hundred million dollars more.

With all these funds going for applied social research, one might predict that sociology and sociologists would be wallowing in prosperity. Such appears to be far from the current state of our discipline. While we are not on the threshold of destitution and widespread unemployment, it does not appear that sociologists generally have participated fully in the last two decades of growth in applied social research. There are a variety of reasons for our failure to participate.

First of all, applied social research is certainly not the monopoly of sociology. Economics, psychology, political science, education, geography, anthropology, and such hybrid fields as business, communication, social work, and operations research are all fields that can and do participate in applied social research. Indeed, my best estimate is that economists, psychologists, and educational researchers are more deeply involved in applied social research than any other field. Of course, the three leaders in applied social research are bigger fields than sociology and, hence, such leadership reflects in part the fact that there are simply many more psychologists, educators, and economists than sociologists. But it also reflects the fact that, within those fields, applied work is accorded higher regard than in sociology. Sociology has been primarily an academic field, with far fewer sociologists employed outside the groves of academe, compared to the profile of economists and psychologists.

Second, many of the funds available for applied social research do not go to universities but to nonacademic organizations. Within the last decade, new organizations have appeared on the scene to provide the applied social research that was demanded by the existence of research funds. Older, nonacademic research organizations have also responded by increasing their staffs. Research organizations loosely connected with universities, such as NORC and Michigan's ISR, have expanded as well. Some of the larger research firms now dwarf university social science divisions. For example, Abt Associates, Inc., located in Cambridge, employs more social science Ph.D.'s on its staff than any of the universities in the Boston area. The Rand Corporation in Santa Monica has enough social scientists on its staff to offer a Ph.D. program in the social sciences.

The rapid increase in effective demand for applied social research has not been without accompanying problems. First of all, it appears that legislators often imposed impossible research demands—yet, at the same time, offered funds to do those impossible tasks, a situation that is a structured strain toward hypocrisy, and fraud on the part of suppliers. Literally scores of "beltway bandit" firms were started to bid on the offered contracts, often to accomplish tasks that could be done or completed within the allotted time or budget or with existing research technology. Second, the demand for applied social researchers exceeded the available supply, with the result that there were many persons who became social researchers by fiat. A serious negative consequence of the rapid growth in applied social research was that the quality of much of such research was exceedingly poor—especially in the earliest part of the growth period and especially on the state and local level. Fortunately, there is an apparent secular trend toward increased quality accompanied by a high failure rate among the "beltway bandits." The low quality of some of this research, however, has not helped to raise the status of applied social research among the academic disciplines.

Not all of the quality problems of applied social research have been solved. There are still many applied research projects that are ill-conceived, sloppily executed, and presented in a misleading fashion. Yet the best of applied social research is as good as the best social science going. Furthermore, the average quality is rising as quality standards diffuse more widely and as the critical process described earlier takes hold.

It is especially striking that the research-oriented universities and social science departments have not participated very much in the burgeoning market for applied social research. One of the major reasons has just been alluded to: Often, the research tasks were impossible to accomplish and inadequately funded. But there are also additional reasons. First, applied social research is not very high on the academic totem pole of prestige. Second, even when the research tasks are attractive and of intrinsic interest, academicians find it difficult to respond quickly to the research procurement process and to mount the often-extensive, large-scale research projects that are called for. Whatever the reasons, the concentration of applied social research activities outside the university walls has meant that sociology as primarily an academic discipline has not been reached by this new prosperity.

Third, applied social research demands skills that not all sociologists have received through training or through practice. By and large, applied social research is quantitative research and I would venture that the level of relevant skills achieved on the average by sociologists is considerably below that of the social science fields that have been more successful in applied work. In addition, applied work requires an attentiveness to policy-related structural features of our society.

Whatever the reasons for our discipline's lack of participation in applied social research, it is clear that we are missing out on some important opportunities. Primary among these missed opportunities are those that relate to the intellectual health of our discipline. Applied social research, as I have tried to argue earlier here, provides important opportunities to learn more about how society works for building theory and for strengthening our base of empirical knowledge.

There are also organizational reasons for building a stronger level of participation in applied social research. Academic employment for sociologists at present—and even more so in the future—is drying up. We can no longer afford to run undergraduate curricula that lead to no specific vocational opportunities for graduates. Few departments in the country are experiencing any increases in undergraduate enrollment and in majors. We appear to be losing out to fields in which there are clear employment opportunities beyond graduation. I suggest that junior-level applied research opportunity is one such vocational goal that we could emphasize in our teaching and training programs.

Applied social research is even more important for graduate-level training in our discipline. There are jobs out there in the applied social research "industry" that properly trained new sociology Ph.D.'s could enter.

In order to take greater advantage of these occupational opportunities for our undergraduate majors and those who earn graduate degrees, it is necessary for the discipline to build linkages to applied social research as an institutionalized activity. This means that academic sociologists will have to participate more in applied work. We have to learn how to compete successfully for the funds that are available, learn how to undertake the more complicated and extensive research tasks that are involved. This last point may mean that we have to build research organizations within universities or loosely connected with them that can efficiently and skillfully carry out the research tasks involved. Building such organizations will mean that academicians will have the experience to understand properly the research tasks involved and will be able to provide the apprenticeship-like hands-on experiences for undergraduate majors and graduate students that can make academicians attractive as researchers. We will also have to revamp our undergraduate and graduate curricula to reflect a greater emphasis on quantitative research and on policy-oriented research. Note that I am not suggesting that sociology become a monolithic discipline as far as research methods are concerned. All I am advocating is greater emphasis, especially at the undergraduate level.

Of course, all the changes suggested above imply a greater recognition to be given to applied work as crucial to the health of our discipline. That means that we should not lift our eyebrows when our better graduate students take non-academic research positions, conveying the notion that by so doing they have left the company of the elect. It means that we evaluate applied social research as research and not automatically deduct points because it is applied. It also means that those of us who do both basic and applied work should be as proud of the latter as of the former. Applied social researchers should come out of the closet!

There are other institutional changes that would also be helpful. Our professional association currently has an academic bias that manifests itself in a variety of ways: Our employment bulletin lists few nonacademic positions, and the editors of our professional journals are reluctant to consider articles that are clearly applied research. The American Sociological Association should be taking the lead in helping to bridge the distance between our discipline and the intellectual and employment opportunities in applied social research.

Sociology has deep roots in humanity's desire to understand and control the turmoil of social change and in its striving for ways to lessen the toll of humankind. It would be to deny our heritage to become more and more turned inward to an increasingly precious academic discipline. For the sake of our intellectual growth and our disciplinary strength, we need to provide a more respectable place for applied work, a move that will surely redound to our benefit in excitement, theoretical progress, and a renewed sense of the relevance of our work to the world around us.

References

Abt, C.C.
   1980   "What's wrong with social policy research?" In C.C. Abt (ed.), Problems in American Social Policy Research, Cambridge: Abt Books.
Alves, W., and P.H. Rossi
   1978   "Who should get what? Fairness judgments in the distribution of earnings." American Journal of Sociology, 34:541–64.
Berk, R.A., K. Lenihan, and P.H. Rossi
   1980   "Crime and poverty: some experimental evidence from ex-offenders." American Sociological Review, 45:766–86.
Bloom, B.
   1964   Stability and Change in Human Characteristics. New York: Wiley.

Coleman, J.S., E.Q. Campbell, C. Hobson, J. McPartland, A. Mood, F. Weinfeld, and R.L. York
1966   Equality of Educational Opportunity. Washington, D.C.: U.S. Government Printing Office.

Dodd, S.C.
1934   A Controlled Experiment on Rural Hygiene in Syria. Beirut: Publications of the American University of Beirut Social Science Series, No. 7.

Frazer, E.F.
1939   The Negro Family in America. Chicago: University of Chicago Press.

Heckman, J.
1980   "Sample selection bias as a specification error." In E.W. Stormsdorfer and G. Farkas (eds.) Evaluation Studies Annual Review. Beverly Hills: Sage.

Katz, E. and P.F. Lazarsfeld
1955   Personal Influence. Glencoe, Illinois: Free Press.

Lenihan, K.
1978   Opening the Second Gate. Washington, D.C.: U.S. Government Printing Office.

Lynd, R.S., and H.M. Lynd
1928   Middletown. New York: Harcourt Brace.

Moreno, J.L.
1934   Who Shall Survive? Washington: Nervous and Mental Disease Publishing Co.

Morgan, J.N., K. Dickinson, J. Dickinson, J. Bemus, and G. Duncan
1974   Five Thousand American Families: Patterns of Economic Progress, (Vol. 1.) Ann Arbor: Institute for Social Research.

Moynihan, D.P.
1965   The Negro Family: The Case for National Action. Washington, D.C.: U.S. Government Printing Office.

Reiss, A.E.
1961   Occupations and Social Status. Glencoe: Free Press.

Roethlisberger, F., and W.J. Dickson
1939   Management and the Worker. Cambridge: Harvard University Press.

Rossi, P.H., R.A. Berk, and K. Lenihan
1980   Money, Work and Crime. New York: Academic Press.

Sewell, W.H., R.M. Hauser, and D. Featherman
1976   Schooling and Achievement in American Society. New York: Academic Press.

Stouffer, S.A., L. Guttman, E. Suchman, P. Lazarsfeld, S. Star, and J. Clausen
1950   Measurement and Prediction: Studies in Social Psychology in World War II, Vol. 4. Princeton: Princeton University Press.

Warner, W.L., and P.S. Lunt
1941   The Social Life of a Modern Community. New Haven: Yale University Press.

Williams, J.M.
   1906   An American Town. New York: Lippincott.
Wright, J.D., P.H. Rossi, S.R. Wright, and E. Weber-Burdin
   1979   After the Clean-Up: Long Range Effects of Natural Disasters. Beverly Hills: Sage.

Chapter 3
Toward an Applied Sociology of Sport

Merrill J. Melnick
State University of New York, College at Brockport

Melnick provides a general overview and identifies key issues (e.g., value freeness, disinterest in applied perspectives, academic respectability, and emphasis on the natural science model) in the development of sport sociology that mitigated against its becoming more applied. He discusses the future development of an applied sociology of sport in relationship to the adoption of a more humanistic commitment, redefinition of alternative work roles, and expanded forms of professional preparation to enhance understanding of policy making in sporting practice. Ironically, Melnick's words seem to carry a greater impact today than they did when the article was first published.

Somewhere amidst all the excitement and fervor that came with discovering its identity and pronouncing its existence to the academic world, sociology of sport chose an investigative paradigm which, in recent years, has become the subject of considerable scrutiny and debate (Gruneau, 1976; Melnick, 1975). Flushed with early successes and motivated by a frenetic desire for academic respectability, sociology of sport adopted a scientific frame of reference which, upon closer inspection, demonstrated, at least to some of its critics, a narrow form of positivism rather than an accurate depiction of science itself. Furthermore, the quest for social scientific laws similar to the laws of the natural sciences to explain the social phenomenon of sport has not imposed the anticipated scientific rigor on the field nor generated the hoped-for law-like generalizations (Gruneau, 1976).

While the early stance taken in support of "value-neutrality" proved valuable insofar as it called for the control of *a priori* assumptions when doing sociological research, its insistence on "value-freeness" served the latent function of

Note. From *Journal of Sport and Social Issues*, 1980, **4**(2), pp. 1–12. Copyright 1980 by *Journal of Sport and Social Issues*. Reprinted by permission.

encouraging a detached, almost aloof attitude toward the need for a more critical, contextual and evaluative type of sociological research. Lastly, the strong suggestion that the roles of sport sociologist and private citizen needed to be differentiated and kept separate helped define the former in exceedingly narrow terms. Cautions against the sport sociologist influencing public opinion, shaping attitudes and values and/or participating in community action programs operated in the main to encourage the adoption of a dispassionate academic work role, one seemingly lacking concern for the sport actor. Thus, what evolved was a sociology of sport committed to a rather mechanistic application of the natural scientific model of inquiry to sport rather than a sociology of sport that was at once critical, evaluative and action-oriented (Gruneau, 1978).

Greendorfer (1978) has cautioned against being overly harsh on this relatively new sub-field for perspectives adopted 15 years ago, and I certainly concur. Despite inherent weaknesses in the natural scientific model, its proponents must be credited with being largely responsible for the sub-field's very existence. The record shows that approximately 200 institutions of higher education in the United States and Canada now offer courses in sociology of sport, with several offering graduate programs through the Ph.D. degree; an information retrieval system for the sociology and social psychology of leisure and sport, located at the University of Waterloo, contains well over 5,000 bibliographical entries; regional and national sociological meetings usually include at least one section devoted entirely to sociology of sport; entire issues of scholarly journals *outside of* physical education and sport have featured the theoretical and empirical writings of sport sociologists[1]; the plethora of anthologies, textbooks, monographs, annual reviews and journals attests vividly to the "publication boom" of the past five years; and from an organizational standpoint, the Sport Sociology Academy, the North American Society for the Sociology of Sport, the Canadian Association of Sports Sciences and the International Committee for Sociology of Sport provide frequent opportunities for regular, on-going professional interaction (Loy, McPherson & Kenyon, 1979). All of this, I submit, is due in no small measure to the first- and second-generation sport sociologists who had the intellectual acumen and courage to envision such a field.

The growing interest among an increasing number of American sport sociologists in social problems, applied concerns and sport-related issues also needs to be recognized. Special attention should be made of the work of the Sports Institute for Research, a voluntary, mutual-benefit service organization consisting of University of Windsor physical and health faculty, community scientists, educators and technicians. Its commitment to applied, change-agent research has resulted in dramatic improvements in several Windsor community sport organizations (Guilmette & Moriarty, 1978; Moriarty & Guilmette, 1976). McPherson's (1975) mid-1970s prediction that the late 1970s and early 1980s will bear witness to an increased interest by North American sport sociologists in the study of applied sport problems is worth considering; however, on balance, I do not share his optimism for reasons to be discussed later.

Even recognizing the number of applied investigations that have been initiated since the late 1960s, it is my judgment that a truly applied perspective is sorely lacking in American sociology of sport today. Whitson (1978) poses some provocative questions on this point when he asks: (1) What has the development of the sub-field meant for the sports participant, the community planner, the general public? (2) What role has sociology of sport come to play in the development of public policies toward competitive sport and mass leisure? (3) Has sociology of sport shown any interest in those issues which *ordinary* participants experience as problems in their encounters with sport and leisure institutions? And (4) ". . . is the sociology of sport one group of people (sociologists) making observations about others (participants), according to their own determinations of what is important to find out? Or is it sociologists working together with those who are part of sport . . . to enhance their *collective* understanding of those problems which are most real and urgent to them . . . ?" (p. 74). Schafer (1971) offers the more strident opinion that

> . . . sport sociologists need to leap forth from the academic tower of irrelevance with its entangling and blinding vines of useless theorizing and pedestrian descriptive studies into the open and fertile fields of practical, applicable research of a policy-related, experimental or evaluative kind . . .

The voice of moderation hopefully would argue that the proponents of both applied and basic research perspectives are guilty of constructing a false dichotomy in the sense that they couch the issue in "either/or" terms. I believe, as Luschen (1979) does, that sociology of sport should assume some responsibility for delivering ". . . information and insight useful for the practical problems of sport in regard to teaching, coaching and organizational decision making" (pp. 19-20). On the other hand, Kenyon (1969) observes quite correctly that if the sport sociologist ". . . is limited to problems reflecting current social problems or some practical need, the development of the very knowledge upon which social action depends could be greatly delayed" (p. 172). What seems appropriate, therefore, is an eclectic approach to the study of sport as a social phenomenon, one which encourages the sport sociologist to choose from a variety of work roles, e.g., basic researcher, applied researcher, muckraker, policy-oriented reformer, etc., and investigative paradigms, e.g., structural-functionalist, positivist, radical, reflexive-critical, etc.

What does seem true today, however, is the failure of sociology of sport to clearly identify and articulate an applied or action-oriented perspective ". . . devoted to acquiring knowledge for the more effective administration of athletes and/or the more humanistic understanding of sport" (Loy & Segrave, 1974, p. 292). Parenthetically, it is somewhat comforting to note that the basic versus applied issue is not unique to sociology of sport. As Loy and Segrave point out, "the problem of the utility of knowledge, for what purposes and for whose use, has long plagued sociologists" (p. 291). However, Deutsch (1970) has observed that a combination of traditional liberalism coupled with a renewed interest in Marxist traditions has promoted, to some degree, an advocacy framework in sociology today which manifests itself in a literature that is replete with applied and action research.

Closer to home, I recently read with considerable interest an article by sport psychologist Rainer Martens (1979) entitled, "About Smocks and Jocks." Reading more like the "confessions of a born-again sport psychologist," Martens brings the following charges against his own field: (1) sport psychology has had little or no influence in the world of sport; (2) sport psychology has failed to address the critical sport issues of the day; and (3) sport psychology has failed to do applied research. Since the same charges have been leveled against sociology of sport in recent years, Martens's belief in the need for a socially relevant, applied field-based research tradition for the sport sciences is as appropriate for sociology of sport as it is for sport psychology.

Sociology of Sport and Physical Education

Nowhere is the gap between basic research and its application more evident than in the schism which presently exists between sociology of sport and physical education. The author recently did a content analysis of the *Research Quarterly* for the years 1965-1979 and found only *one* study which investigated a sociological parameter within the context of a school physical education class.[2] Typically, sport sociologists have shown a decided preference for studying varsity and elite athletes in highly visible sport milieus rather than physical education students learning and interacting within school physical education programs (Ulrich, 1979). And Sage (1977) cautions that it may not be until the mid-1980s before sociology of sport will have produced any work useful to the physical educator.

The fact that so little applied research has actually been undertaken in sociology of sport is partly understandable, given the fact that the initial priorities of any fledgling sub-field must clearly favor the development of a sound knowledge base derived from uninhibited basic research (Henry, 1978). The applied research can then follow and provide the rational basis for related professions or technologies. However, the introduction of an applied perspective at this juncture in the history of American sociology of sport would seem especially opportune since a very impressive body of knowledge is presently available in several substantive areas directly related to the work of the physical educator (Greendorfer, 1977). Rather than create another sub-field, e.g., "sociology of physical education," as some have suggested (Saunders, 1976), a closer, functional relationship between the sub-field and the profession can be achieved by improving communication and encouraging collaboration between sport sociologists and physical educators (Greendorfer, 1975). Commitment to an applied perspective would reinforce this liaison by encouraging expanded research pursuits and the seeking of answers to those sociological questions which have particular relevance for sports practitioners. Parenthetically, it is of interest to note that European sport sociologists believe very strongly that sociology of sport holds knowledge directly useful for physical education teachers and has much to contribute to sport pedagogics (Lenk, 1973; Voigt, 1964; Widmer, 1977).

Counter-Forces to the Development of an Applied Sociology of Sport

Although in recent years we have witnessed some sporadic and isolated examples of applied research in sociology of sport, one would be hard-pressed to conclude that the application of sociological principles and insights to the analysis and understanding of concrete sport systems and the solving of particular sport problems have taken place in any systematic fashion. The following speculations are offered as tentative explanations for the current state of affairs.

1. *"Courtship" of sociology.* Motivated perhaps by the multi-need to gain greater academic respectability, to have more direct access to institutional reward systems, to be better able to procure research funding and/or to once and for all shed the mantle of "second-class citizenship," a growing number of sport sociologists trained in departments of physical education are seeking professional ties with the parent discipline, sociology, while putting as much distance between themselves and their academic roots as possible.

This "courtship" of sociology manifests itself in a variety of ways including: (1) seeking joint faculty appointments; (2) choosing research problems largely informed by theories which enjoy particular favor and popularity within sociology, (3) publishing in sociological rather than physical education and sport journals; and (4) preferring sociological forums rather than physical education meetings and conferences for the presentation of papers. There is nothing inherently good or bad about these actions and no criticism is intended. However, if a truly applied tradition is to take shape within sociology of sport, sufficient numbers of sport sociologists will need to maintain their professional and scholarly ties with the academic discipline of physical education in general and the profession in particular. From the standpoint of developing such a tradition, membership in AAHPERD and The National Association for Physical Education in Higher Education is just as important for a sport sociologist as membership in the American Sociological Association. Henry (1978) recently observed that the pattern of professional mobility described above is symptomatic of a general over-emphasis in physical education today on unitary disciplines or sub-fields and a corresponding disinterest in the academic discipline of physical education.

2. *Professional training of sport sociologists.* When we look at the professional training of third-generation sport sociologists, that is, those who are presently in the process of completing advanced degrees, we find that many do not hold undergraduate degrees in physical education but in one of the social sciences and that they are taking the bulk of their graduate course work in sociology. McPherson

(1975) has further observed that this generation will pursue an emphasis on quantitative techniques and theory construction in sociology and be as well-trained in these areas as any sociologist. Certainly, a professional regimen which emphasizes theory construction, causal modeling and multi-variate statistical approaches is laudable. Such training should go a long way in helping to improve upon the atheoretical, single-system, descriptive studies which characterized the early years of sociology of sport. However, one has to seriously question whether such a professional training, disembodied from the academic and professional concerns of physical education, can nurture the interest and concern needed for addressing the specific and immediate practical needs of the sports practitioner. Surely, applied sociology of sport is not for everyone—there will always be a need for the basic researcher uninhibited by the requirement that his or her research serve any need of practical application. In fact, as Henry (1978) points out, "the fundamental knowledge derived from uninhibited basic research is the very life blood of any respectable profession" (p. 25). However, if we are truly interested in seeing the development of an applied sociology of sport, then serious attention will need to be given to the ways in which sport sociologists are presently being trained and appropriate modifications and adjustments will have to be made where necessary.

3. *Value system of sport sociologists*. Extant within the sub-culture of sport sociologists today is a value system which offers a formidable barrier to the development of any type of applied perspective. Prominent in this system is the value which suggests, either explicitly or implicitly, that applied research is simply not as scientific or scholarly as basic research. Space does not permit a full and complete rebuttal; however, it should be pointed out that there is nothing inherent in applied research that renders it atheoretical or intellectually sterile. The applied researcher requires no less competency in research methods and theory construction than does his counterpart in basic research. The distinction between the two rests more with the particular research problems each chooses to investigate than with any fundamental difference in their commitment to the canons of scientific inquiry. Belief in the dual values of scientific rigor and the majesty of established science also operate in concert to steer the sport sociologist away from applied problems, either because the latter are deemed too complicated (and thus labeled "nonscientific") or they do not readily lend themselves to available conceptual and analytical tools. This worship of what is available thus "leads to what is known best, rather than what is know least" (Hammond, 1976, p. 37).

Another value which tends to deflect attention from the conduct of research investigations on contemporary problems is the mystical belief in serendipity, that is, the defense of "any and all scientific work on the grounds that no one can really predict the ultimate consequences" (Hammond, p. 38). It may well be time for sport sociologists to consider rank-ordering their research interests according to some definition of potential social value. On this point, sociologist David Gray (1975) has argued that we must begin to "discriminate among things worth doing versus those less so or not at all . . . only a combination of 'objective' pretense and timidity . . . can encourage one to take the position that 'all of the traditional content areas are, in principle, equal . . .' " (p. 278). A strong commitment to an applied perspective can help bring into bold relief those socially significant problems which presently prevent the sport institution from best serving its clientele.

4. *Sociology of sport as a "game."* There is a popular style of scholarship within the subculture of sport sociologists which I believe runs counter to the development of a serious and committed applied tradition. This *style* to which I refer is a remnant of a couple of hundred years ago when science was practiced as a *hobby* by a few people who had independent wealth (Hammond, 1976). What lingers on today is a style of scholarship which regards the pursuit of scientific questions as a *game*, somewhat in the comfortable, classical tradition of the past. Pursuit of science for the sake of the game and the seeking of elegant and sometimes-amusing solutions to esoteric problems for personal gain, be it monetary, status or identity-related, is a luxury which this sub-field may not be able to afford as it struggles for its professional existence during especially difficult economic times. If science is indeed a tool to be used in the service of humankind, then those newly developed academic sub-disciplines best able to serve the social order in some demonstrable way will in all likelihood have the greatest chance of survival. The future of those sub-disciplines which merely "play at science" while eschewing any serious commitment to applied research would seem much more problematical.

Humanism and an Applied Sociology of Sport

The future development of an applied sociology of sport must involve more than the selection and investigation of a "different set of research problems." What is initially called for is the adoption of a *humanistic* perspective, one which welcomes speculation, prediction and theorizing about the future. Such a perspective would contribute to a greatly enlarged view of science by taking the researcher beyond the narrow goals of scientific control and prediction (Glass, 1971). The humanistic sport sociologist's highest commitment would not be to a worship of the majesty of science but rather, to a concern for human beings and the self-actualizing potential of the institutional structures they create. What is being suggested is not an ideology or a perspective for radical change, but rather, a perspective which does not treat the institutional arrangements which characterize contemporary sport as unchangeable givens, which is prepared to devise alternatives to those structures which are stultifying and overly restrictive or punitive, which can foresee a future for sport that is essentially better than the present and which is prepared to struggle against those conditions which deny human beings their dignity and respect (Gouldner, 1970). An applied perspective would thus have a central and rightful place in a humanistically oriented sub-field so conceived.

At the same time, I am well aware of the criticisms that have been proffered against those sport sociologists who have, through their words and/or deeds, earned such appelations as "missionaries," "do-gooders" and "ameliorators of society." Their critics argue that given the fact that ignorance presently outdistances knowledge in sociology of sport, the best that our "savers of mankind" can hope to be are "one-eyed missionaries," if that (Ingham, 1974). I would counter by saying that normative zeal is not necessarily incompatible with scientific objectivity. I see no reason why a properly trained, humanistically oriented applied sport sociologist should be any less "scientific" than a basic researcher. While it is true that the sub-field is short on axiomatic theories and lawlike propositions, I do not believe that these shortcomings allow critics to plead that a state of ignorance exists. Some very important research studies in several substantive areas have been undertaken in recent years which clearly suggest informed, applied directions. The time may indeed be right, as Krawczyk (1977) suggests, to stop the procrastinating and get on with the business of constructing normative sport models based on historical and contemporary experience and the research at hand.

Re-Defining the Role of Sport Sociologist

The work role of the American sport sociologist, as defined in the contemporary literature, tends to be carefully circumscribed in terms of a recommended investigative paradigm, a set of appropriate theoretical and empirical work tools and an overall research objective, to wit, to study "the underlying regularity of human social behavior within situations involving sport" (Kenyon, 1969, p. 165). If an applied perspective is to emerge from sociology of sport, new role definitions will need to be written since those presently promulgated fail to suggest that a sport sociologist is also a man or woman of *action, applied action*, that is.

Gruneau (1978) has contributed to this task by observing that "the idea of the sociology of sport as a free-floating, knowledge-for-its-own-sake conception betrays the classical sociological concern for issues of social structure and crises in human values, [and] also disguises the ideological character of science itself" (p. 87). For Gruneau, the most desirable state of affairs "is to merge disciplined scholarly analysis with evaluation, and ultimately, with personal action" (p. 90). If planning, implementation and evaluation are to become part of a new job description for sport sociologists so inclined, then the training of researchers for career opportunities *outside* academia will need to go forward.

Training Applied Sport Sociologists

A growing interest among sport sociologists in applied research, coupled with an anticipated increase in job opportunities outside the university, will require sociology of sport to define its relationship to application more clearly as well as provide professional training appropriate for working in applied sports settings. For example, in the same way that applied sociologists have contributed in recent years to better understanding and policy implementation in such areas as school busing, mental health, drug addiction, education, housing and welfare, the applied sport sociologist should find increasing professional opportunities in such areas as: (1) developing recreational sport facilities; (2) providing consultant services to community sport organizations; (3) formulating and implementing policy as members of local, regional, national and international sports commissions and agencies; (4) planning and developing recreational sports programs for retirement communities; (5) advising state and national governmental agencies on politically related sport issues; and (6) serving as consultants to amateur and professional sport groups and organizations.[3]

Given these possibilities, how then should applied sport sociologists be prepared? Firstly, the more specialized training required by the applied researcher should not be interpreted to mean the abandonment of a mainstream sociological education. Courses in sociological theory, research methods, statistical analysis and substantive fields of sociological knowledge are important for all sport sociologists—basic, applied or otherwise. However, the standard research methods course typically required in the preparation of the basic researcher will need to be revised because it does not adequately prepare the student for work in the applied sports setting. Matters of cost, efficiency of operation and time will probably reduce the usefulness of some traditional research methodologies, e.g., survey research, participant observation, etc. (Gelfand, 1975). New methods will develop mainly out of the researcher's experience, although it is anticipated that expertise in such areas as interviewing, systems analysis, organizational development, organizational auditing, natural observation, sociometry and interaction process analysis will prove useful.

The ubiquitous nature of an applied sociology of sport will also require the researcher to pursue an *inter-disciplinary* program of studies. Because of their work in applied sports settings, applied researchers, in all likelihood, will find themselves serving on inter-disciplinary investigative teams. This will require at least a cursory background in such diverse disciplines as psychology, economics, business management, political science, recreation and perhaps, law. The requirement of an extended field internship will also distinguish the applied sport researcher's professional training from that of the basic researcher. This internship could be served with any one of a number of groups, organizations or institutions, e.g., professional sports team, voluntary sports organization, governmental agency, etc. Because applied sport sociologists will need to interact with colleagues from other disciplines, the staffs of public and private agencies and organizations and the public-at-large, it is extremely important that they be able to speak and write both effectively and clearly. For example, a communications core course structured around the learning of effective speaking skills, extemporaneous speech-making, the giving of formal group presentations and the writing of grant proposals and news releases would be of considerable value.

To summarize, the professional preparation of applied sport sociologists would include the following necessary components: (1) foundational knowledge, understandings and skills drawn for sociology; (2) a thorough comprehension of the basic and applied literature of sociology of sport; (3) research skills appropriate for solving the problems of the clients served; (4) an interdisciplinary background composed of selected courses from a variety of disciplines; (5) specialized course work and experience in policy planning and implementation; (6) a field internship experience with an appropriate sport system; and (7) a strong background in the communication arts.

Conclusion

The arguments presented in support of the development of an applied sociology of sport should in no way be interpreted as an indictment of the basic research paradigm which has ruled American sociology of sport for the past 15 years (Sage, 1979). Sociology of sport needs to make no apologies for the body of knowledge it has accumulated to date, the methods of inquiry it has used to generate that body of knowledge or the degree to which it has contributed to the general understanding of the social phenomenon of sport. What has been suggested, however, is the need for an alternative direction for the field, one which promises to generate the kinds of professional and technological knowledge needed by the sports practitioner.

The gap between researchers and practitioners in physical education is growing wider all the time and this is no less true for sport sociologists and the clients whom they could be presently serving. A humanistically oriented, applied sociology of sport can help close this gap while, at the same time, furthering the theoretical and substantive development of the field. If sociology of sport is indeed at a cross-roads stage in its evolutionary development and in need of renewed vigor and purpose, an applied perspective can help revitalize the field, create new models for solving sport problems and substantially augment existing sport theory. In my judgment, the promise is too great not to seize the moment.

References

Deutsch, Steven E.
  1970 "The radical perspective in sociology." *Sociological Inquiry* 40:85-93.
Gelfand, Donald E.
  1975 "The challenge of applied sociology." *American Sociologist* 10:13-18.
Glass, John F.
  1971 "The humanistic challenge to sociology." *Journal of Humanistic Psychology* 11:170-183.
Gouldner, Alvin W.
  1970 *The Coming Crisis of Western Sociology*. New York: Avon Books.

Gray, David J.
1975 "State of the field: Commentary." *The Sociological Quarterly* 16:277-280.
Greendorfer, Susan L.
1978 "On false dichotomies." *NAPECW/NCPEAM Proceedings* 164-168.
Greendorfer, Susan L.
1977 "Sociology of sport: Knowledge of what?" *Quest* 28:58-65.
Greendorfer, Susan L.
1975 "The social science of sport: A need for further knowledge." *NCPEAM Proceedings* 25-33.
Gruneau, Richard S.
1978 "Conflicting standards and problems of personal action in the sociology of sport." *Quest* 30:80-90.
Gruneau, Richard S.
1976 "Sport as an area of sociological study; An introduction to major themes and perspectives." In Richard S. Gruneau and John G. Albinson (Eds.), *Canadian Sport: Sociological Perspectives*. Don Mills: Addison-Wesley, Canada.
Guilmette, Anne Marie, and Dick Moriarty
1978 "Crisis in amateur sports organizations viewed by change agent research (CAR)." In F. Landry and W. A. Orban (Eds.), *Sociology of Sport*. Miami: Symposia Specialists.
Hammond, George S.
1976 "The value system in the scientific subculture." *The Bulletin of the Atomic Scientists* 32:36-40.
Henry, Franklin M.
1978 "The academic discipline of physical education." *Quest* 29:13-29.
Ingham, Alan G.
1975 *In the Land of the Blind, the One-Eyed Missionary Can Become King*. Paper presented at the Western College Men's Physical Education Society Annual Conference, Reno, Nevada.
Kenyon, Gerald S.
1969 "A sociology of sport: On becoming a sub-discipline." In Bryant J. Cratty and Roscoe Brown (Eds.), *New Perspectives of Man in Action*. Englewood Cliffs: Prentice-Hall.
Krawczyk, Zbigniew
1977 "Theory and empiricism in the social sciences regarding physical culture." *International Review of Sport Sociology* 12:71-92.
Lenk, Hans
1973 "The pedagogical significance of sport sociology." *International Journal of Physical Education* 10:16-20.
Loy, John W., Barry D. McPherson and Gerald S. Kenyon
1978 *The Sociology of Sport as an Academic Specialty: An Episodic Essay on the Development of an Hybrid Sub-Field in North America*. Ottawa: CAHPER.

Loy, John W., and Jeffrey O. Segrave
 1974   "Research methodology in the sociology of sport." In Jack H. Wilmore
        (Ed.), *Exercise and Sport Sciences Reviews*. New York: Academic Press.
Luschen, Gunther
 1979   "Sociology of sport in the context of a sport science—three issues of
        methodology." In March L. Krotee (Ed.), *The Dimensions of Sport
        Sociology*. West Point: Leisure Press.
McPherson, Barry D.
 1975   "Past, present and future perspectives for research in sport sociology."
        International Review of Sport Sociology 10:55-72.
Martens, Rainer.
 1979   "About smocks and jocks." *Journal of Sport Psychology* 1:94-99.
Melnick, Merrill J.
 1975   "A critical look at sociology of sport." *Quest* 25:34-47.
Moriarty, Dick, and Anne Marie Guilmette
 1976   "Sport institute for research/change agent research (SIR/CAR)."
        NCPEAM Proceedings 81-99.
Nelson, Jack K., and Barry L. Johnson
 1968   "Effects of varied techniques in organizing class competition upon
        changes in sociometric status." *Research Quarterly* 39:634-639.
Sage, George H.
 1979   "The current status and trends of sport sociology." In March L. Krotee
        (Ed.), *The Dimensions of Sport Sociology*. West Point: Leisure Press.
Sage, George H.
 1977   "Sport sociology: The state of the art and implications for physical educa-
        tion." *NAPECW/NCPEAM Proceedings* 310:318.
Saunders, E.D.
 1976   "Sociology, sport and physical education." *Review of Sport & Leisure*
        1:122-138.
Schafer, Walter E.
 1971   *Sport, Socialization and the School: Toward Maturity or Enculturation?*
        Paper presented at the Third International Symposium on the Sociology
        of Sport, Waterloo, Ontario, Canada.
Ulrich, Celeste
 1979   "The significance of sport sociology to the profession." In March L.
        Krotee (Ed.), *The Dimensions of Sport Sociology*. West Point: Leisure
        Press.
Voigt, Dieter
 1974   "Sociology in the training of the sport teacher and of the teacher in
        general." *International Journal of Physical Education* 10:26-40.
Whitson, David J.
 1978   "Sociology, psychology and Canadian sport." *Canadian Journal of
        Applied Sport Sciences* 3:71-78.

Widmer, Konrad
    1977   "Social sciences of sport and sport pedagogy as part aspect of sport science." *International Journal of Physical Education* 14:21-35.

Notes

[1]See the November 1979 issue of *The Annals* of the prestigious American Academy of Political and Social Science.

[2]Nelson and Johnson (1968) earned this distinction when they studied different methods of organizing class competition on the sociometric status of students enrolled in a college badminton activity class.

[3]The author would like to acknowledge an important point raised by one of the reviewers of this paper concerning whether or not the work of applied sport sociologists might prove profitable enough to warrant their full-time employment in either the public or private sector. The question of whether an applied sport sociologist could be of sufficient economic value to pay for himself or herself probably cannot be answered until the "waters are tested." One would like to think, however, that an applied sport sociologist capable of rendering valuable consultant services and/or conducting sophisticated market research would indeed be deserving of a permanent position and satisfactory compensation from some progressive-thinking sport organization.

Chapter 4

Sociology of Sport and the Issue of Relevance: Implications for Physical Education

Susan L. Greendorfer
University of Illinois at Urbana-Champaign

Although Greendorfer's article reinforces several of Melnick's points, it focuses more on how the subdiscipline can or should meaningfully handle social data. Believing that the controversy is about the nature of knowledge (i.e., knowledge of what and for whom?), Greendorfer attempts to deal more directly with issues related to the dissemination and transfer of knowledge. This chapter discusses implication, application, and interpretation of findings from selected research studies in light of specific sport practices. The major contribution of this article is its attempt to demonstrate how issues pertaining to the "hidden curriculum," the impact of sport structure on behavior, and the problems of discrimination, culture clash, and gender stereotyping could be made more relevant to the practitioner.

For several years sport sociologists have made a deliberate effort to clearly differentiate the goals of science from those of education. Because application has been viewed as a mission of physical education, antithetical to the aims and objectives of the subdiscipline (Gruneau, 1978; Kenyon & Loy, 1965; Loy, McPherson, & Kenyon, 1980), issues of relevance and applied research have received minimal attention in the literature. Although separate concerns, relevance and application share some common elements. Both are concerned with the substance of subject matter and reflect a fundamental disagreement about the type of research questions that should be asked (the "knowledge of what?" issue) and for whom knowledge should be generated (the "knowledge for whom?" question) (Loy & Segrave, 1974).

Issues of application and relevance raise philosophical questions about the degree of responsibility researchers have for delivering information and insight that might

---

Paper presented at AAHPERD Convention, Cincinnati,OH, 1986.

be useful to others (Lueschen, 1979); they also raise ideological questions on the nature of knowledge and the relationship between practices in physical culture and social structural, historical, political, and economic influences. Although the philosophical concerns are the focus of several chapters in this anthology, some attention has been directed toward ideological ones. In a recent discussion on the professionalization of the academic, the scientization of politics, and the politicalization of science, Ingham and Donnelly (1990) address various aspects of the ideological issues. In arguing that sociological knowledge is practical knowledge, they distinguish the aim of those interested in the "amelioration of the human condition" from that of the technical intelligentsia who serve as brokers of "really useful knowledge." Thus the debate seems to have shifted over the past 25 years from a position that eschewed "mission-oriented" research (Kenyon & Loy, 1965; Kenyon, 1969) to a more sophisticated consideration of whose knowledge counts and what the connections are between knowledge production, knowledge application, and the political formulation of social policy (Ingham & Donnelly, 1990).

The emergent debate seems to revolve around three questions, each of which encompasses the "knowledge of what" issue: (a) whether practical relevance will be useful to the sociology of sport by furthering theoretical, substantive, and methodological progress (Chalip, 1990); (b) how social scientific research can enlighten by affecting decisions and policies (i.e., knowledge transfer) (Yiannakis, 1989); and (c) whether applied sociology of sport will merely serve the power elite (Ingham & Donnelly, 1990). The challenge posed by these questions resurrects and extends some longstanding criticisms of sport sociology. Although attention is again directed toward the quality and breadth of the body of knowledge (Rose, 1981), we can look forward to more sophisticated debates concerning sociology *through* sport rather than *of* sport as well as the extent to which the role of theory, ideology, and values needs to be reevaluated (Gruneau, 1976, 1978; Hall, 1982, 1984; Ingham, 1979).

Although the debate no longer seems to be whether sport sociologists should refuse to relate research to social problems or broader social contexts (Gruneau, 1976, 1978, 1983; Ingham, 1979; Melnick, 1975, 1980), discussion still focuses on how the subdiscipline *will be able to* or *should* meaningfully handle social data. The relationship between history and biography, personal milieu, and social structure continues to be at the core of the debate (Gruneau, 1978), but discussion has shifted from the isolation or separation of research from social practice to some acceptance that research *could* (should?) emanate from conceptions of social and cultural reality (Gruneau, 1978; Ingham & Donnelly, 1990). Finally, after 25 years, sociology of sport seems ready to come to grips with the issue of relevance.

Implications for Application or Relevance

Obviously, the relevance of knowledge in the existing literature is vast and multidimensional, and the purpose of this chapter is to identify and discuss a few topics with implications for either application or knowledge transfer (cf. Yiannakis, 1989). One of three criteria has been met by each topic: (a) It emanates from a rich theoretical framework, (b) there has been sufficient replication or similarity in empirical findings, or (c) the data themselves directly or indirectly relate to a "social problem" that has received considerable research attention.

Although social science research is rarely applied directly, even when research may be executed expressly for purposes of application (Chalip, 1990), various principles and insights can enhance analysis and understanding of physical education and sporting practices. This point has not escaped the attention of researchers in sport pedagogy, as much of what they study and discuss leans heavily on principles previously examined and discussed in sociology and psychology of sport.

In fact, many topics that comprise the essential foundation of knowledge in sport studies have been recognized as powerful influences in the teaching or learning of motor skills, behavior modification, teacher effectiveness, performance enhancement, and other related topics. Well over half of the articles published in the *Journal of Teaching Physical Education* have links with concepts and perspectives considered in sociology or psychology of sport. In many instances research questions have been quite similar, and the only distinction between sociological and pedagogical research seems to be the social context analyzed, or whether subjects were students and teachers or athletes and coaches! The examples cited here include topics of mutual concern to sport pedagogy and sport sociology.

During the past 25 years specialists have spent so much time and effort drawing boundaries and making distinctions that we have virtually ignored many subdisciplinary similarities and overlapping concerns. The next three sections provide examples from existing research that not only support this point but also suggest how sociocultural principles relate to and may operate in practical settings—thereby demonstrating relevance (i.e., readiness for knowledge transfer) in addition to implications for application.

Values, Expectations, and the Hidden Curriculum

One example of the ways in which social scientific research can be assimilated into policy and practice is in the realm of curriculum. Although the playing field and gymnasium have only recently been conceptualized as sites of ideological struggle (Sparkes, 1989), it would not be difficult to analyze the relationship between the context of the school and teachers' values, behaviors, and expectations. In her discussion of the "hidden curriculum," Bain (1985, 1989) considers "what is taught to students by the institutional regularities, routines and rituals of the teaching/learning setting" (1989, p. 289). This setting constitutes "lived culture," a powerful mechanism for transmitting values and beliefs to students. Pedagogical research focuses on systematic observation describing regularities of teacher behavior and class organization that communicate values and norms to students. Such research has revealed that patterns of behavior in physical education classes emphasize orderliness and achievement, conformity, inequality, and a movement standard that is masculine, athletic, and competitive (Bain, 1985; Kollen, 1981, 1983).

Knowledge transfer becomes quite powerful when specific research findings are integrated into teacher preparation courses. For example, research suggests that teacher and coach expectations are transmitted through subtle or overt forms of communication that convey implicit values learned in the physical education and sport setting (Bain, 1985; Dubois, 1986; Martinek, 1983). Various forms of communication may also influence student and athlete performance (Smith, Smoll, Hunt, Curtis, & Coppel, 1979; Martinek, 1981). Simple awareness of these facts points to application, particularly in the preparation of teachers and coaches, and the impact increases if teacher preparation courses can demonstrate through actual experience to the apprentice teacher or coach how what is said as well as how it is said conveys different meanings to students or athletes. Thus, training in delivery style and observation of how varying modes of communication (nonverbal as well as verbal) affect student learning become valuable experiences for those in teacher or coaching effectiveness preparation. Through training, practicing teachers would become more sensitive to the significance of value transmission by seeing how content and communication styles and behavioral mannerisms convey pertinent information as well as underlying values. This two-pronged example of relevance thus involves familiarization with social scientific findings and actual experiences that demonstrate how outcomes are effected once a teacher or coach understands the relationship between the dynamics of the message, the setting, style, and how value systems are transmitted.

Research pertaining to the context of the school environment itself can also provide information relevant to knowledge transfer. Factors relating to availability of space, central office policies, and unique qualities of multiracial urban settings have been found to influence much of what transpires during physical education class (Griffin, 1985). This research indicates that contextual factors exert such a powerful influence that they strongly affect what could be accomplished in physical education classes. In this instance knowledge transfer would take the form of conveying to apprentice teachers an understanding of the context of physical education class *within* the broader cultural context (e.g., machinations, policies, and constraints) of the school itself, the school district, and the demographics of the population.

When integrated, findings pertaining to lived culture, value transmission, teacher expectations, and contextual factors can affect specific teacher actions in a variety of ways. Transfer of knowledge can inform curriculum planners and influence the very structure and conduct of physical education classes and sport. Application can be general or specific; research findings can simply be conveyed to teachers or coaches to draw their own conclusions, or specific findings can be incorporated into learning experiences for teachers and coaches. In either case it is critical to recognize the active role that teachers and coaches play in conveying messages and setting the stage on the playing field and in the gym. The implication for application rests on an understanding of how conduct (i.e., specific values and norms) transmits subtle and open messages that accompany specific information about subject content (i.e., movement skills). Without this awareness, teachers and coaches may unknowingly undermine their course objectives. To date, implications from these studies have not been systematically teased out or explicitly conveyed to professionals.

Extending these principles of knowledge transfer to sport settings, research has shown that the degree of formalized, regulated competition influences not only children's orientations toward play and sport but also the quality of the experience and participant enjoyment (Dubois, 1986; Harris, 1983, 1984; Mantel & VanderVelden, 1974). However, philosophy and value structure of programs are not the only factors that influence the play experience. Studies have demonstrated that not only can coaches' values be effectively communicated to participants, but that they can influence participant perceptions of the sport experience. These findings are particularly relevant to program planning in youth sports, because researchers have found a relationship between high dropout rates and competitive emphasis (Dubois, 1986; Gould, 1987). Thus, application of these research findings could be directly related to modifying the organizational structure of sport programs so that less emphasis is placed on competition and winning and more on participation and sportsmanship. Obviously, a policy focused on retaining participants requires more than a shift of program objectives. To this end workshops and interventions could be designed to increase coaches' sensitivity to their coaching styles (the manner in which they transmit messages) as well as the content of what they transmit (e.g., instructional hints, gamesmanship hints, competitive values).

Whether it is through the teacher or the coach, the hidden curriculum or value structure and program philosophy, or physical education students or youth sport participants, social forces are impacting behavior in such a way that learning and play experiences are being affected. Thus the challenge for applied sport sociology is to demonstrate the connection between existing research and sport and physical education practice. Obviously, the implications for knowledge transfer are specifically related to the preparation of professionals.

Discrimination: Racial Stereotyping

Research on ethnic and minority group participation indicates that subtle forms of discrimination work in at least two ways: Sport skills have been stereotyped on the basis of race, and there has been a failure to understand the cultural basis for differing styles of playing games.

Racial stereotyping may operate when players are assigned playing positions; data reveal consistent patterns of black overrepresentation in noncentral positions (such as the outfield in baseball and speed positions in football) and underrepresentation in central positions like quarterback, catcher, and shortstop (Curtis & Loy, 1978; Loy & McEluoque, 1970). *Stacking*, the term for such patterns, refers to the linking of specific traits or skills to a minority group and treating all members of that group in the same fashion. If the prevailing ideology says that blacks are qualified to fill only limited positions, they may be grouped and thus forced to compete against one another for those positions, limiting their opportunities to make the team.

The point here is not to establish whether such discrimination exists in sport, but rather to demonstrate the importance of conveying to coaches and teachers how stereotypes and false beliefs can become embedded in sport and physical education practices. Coaches need to be sensitized to the subtleties of stereotyping so they do not assume that players possess or lack certain skills because of their skin color or ethnic background.

There is a twofold implication of research on ethnic and minority group participation. The most serious and compelling involves the failure of coaches to critically examine their own mind-set regarding race and ability. The second involves coaching practice directly. Once physical abilities are attributed to skin color, without the benefit of a truly open tryout, the discriminatory practice of stacking may result. Not only is racial stereotyping at the core of stacking, but racial stereotyping conditions teachers and coaches to expect to see certain skills in some players but not in others. In other words, coaches and teachers may see a pygmalion effect because player performance will match their expectations. By the same token racial stereotyping could condition coaches not to see that minority group players may possess a much more broad range of skills or abilities.

This knowledge transfer—increasing sensitivity toward possibly biased practices —could take place in coaching clinics, workshops, or coaching effectiveness classes, with participants comparing research findings to existing patterns of player distribution. Discussion could focus on comparisons of team statistics to what transpires during tryouts. Are players assigned to specific positions? If so, who and why? Can anyone try out for any position? If not, why not? Open discussion should enhance coaches' awareness of preconceptions about ability and race.

Discrimination and Culture Clash

Another topic indirectly related to discrimination has implications for application. There is a widely held belief that sport promotes good race relations and that cultural differences disappear on the playing field, but teachers and coaches need to know what impact cultural identity and values have on physical activity. Varying environmental and social conditions shape perceptions and symbolic meaning and give rise to different value systems and cultures. Evidence suggests that games and sport contests tend to serve as a forum for the expression of cultural values and that more than one cultural system may be operating when two groups play the "same" game (Allison, 1980; Carlston, 1983; Wyatt, 1976).

The implication from these research findings is that there is more to integration than simply having those of different cultures play in the same game, because players bring expectations, goals, and norms of their cultural and social backgrounds to the play setting. Cultural differences show themselves in playing styles (e.g., working the ball into the player who is in the best position to take the shot vs. using a running, dribble-and-shoot style) as well as in different game objectives (such as striving to win or achieve because the outcome is important vs. playing for fun without a concern for who wins).

Instead of integration, what often occurs when cultures meet during sport contests are arguments, disintegration of the game, fights, and even worse, de facto segregation. Thus, instead of fostering good intergroup relations, sport can also be a medium for perpetuating misunderstandings and disagreement. Teachers and coaches sensitive to the ways in which cultural and ethnic differences can influence sport and games could make appropriate choices about program planning, instructional activities, and the structure of competition. Such awareness would not only provide a consciousness raising experience, but taken one step further, practitioners would be taking overt steps to avoid culture clash by carefully evaluating the content of sport and activity programs.

Discrimination: Gender Stereotyping

In the same way that we may hold assumptions about racial or ethnic groups and performance, many professionals make assumptions about athletic ability on the basis of gender, expecting poorer performance from females than from males. Such an ideology may undermine the spirit of Title IX, legislation which mandates comparable opportunities for boys and girls in physical education and sport. Title IX clearly makes discrimination on the basis of sex in these activities illegal.

Although implementation of Title IX has resulted in coeducational physical education classes, little information has been offered to practitioners who must deal with discrepancies in skills between the sexes. A logical first step of knowledge transfer would be to make teachers and coaches aware of the precise nature of research findings and of the complexities of the sport socialization process.

For example, although research suggests differences in interest and performance levels in physical activity between boys and girls (e.g., boys generally tend to outperform girls in most motor skills), no research demonstrates that boys inherently move better or are more physically skilled than girls. Additional findings suggest that despite performance differentials between the sexes, performance levels can be improved because motor skills are learned activities. Support for this position has been clearly documented by the steadily improving performance levels of females since the implementation of Title IX, which suggests that better instruction, appropriate encouragement, and increased opportunities are strongly related to higher performance (Boutilier & San Giovanni, 1983).

These findings suggest that social learning may influence performance more than biology. A plethora of additional studies demonstrate that parents treat sons and daughters differently. This dissimilar treatment begins early in infancy and results in different exposure to a host of activities and experiences throughout childhood. For example, studies clearly demonstrate that parents act differently toward girls and boys in allowing early exploratory behavior (such as crawling and climbing), rewarding and punishing various styles of play, providing different kinds of toys, and giving encouragement for gross motor activity (Frish, 1977; Goldberg

& Lewis, 1969; Langlois & Downs, 1980; Lewis, 1972; Tauber, 1979). Boys are rewarded for being active and engaging in vigorous activity involving motor skills. But girls are punished for being active (Fagot, 1978a) and rewarded for playing passive nurturance games. Consequently, boys are directed toward sport and perceive it as a way to gain popularity, whereas girls are directed away from sport and do not rank physical activity very highly (Caplan & Kinsbourne, 1974).

Such parental practices affect the readiness, motivation, and expectations that boys and girls have for motor performance (Corbin, Landers, Feltz, & Senior, 1983). Research strongly suggests that girls and boys come to physical education classes not only with different perceptions about physical activity but also with different interests and motor skill levels. One sex is encouraged throughout early childhood to incorporate physical activity as a natural part of their lifestyle while the other is discouraged from such interests and involvement.

The task in knowledge transfer, then, is to dispel false assumptions about learning and performing motor skills. Application at this stage involves synthesizing research findings and "packaging" them so that knowledge can be useful and usable. Synthesis can provide the basis for change by offering practitioners information that explains reasons for differential learning and performance of males and females. Such knowledge could counteract teachers' and coaches' stereotypes and expectations in two ways: by making them aware of the fact that motor performance does not reside solely in biology, and by sensitizing them to the existence of an ideology that closely links the male gender role with sport and physical activity. Thus, practitioners should be taught that sex differences in childhood performance are not "natural" outcomes of biology but that as a consequence of socialization practices girls come to class with a very different and perhaps more limited movement repertoire than boys. Because gender role stereotyping continues to exist, females may need to be taught fundamental skills which boys of the same age have already mastered.

A second step of application would involve packaging findings so that specific strategies could be developed for overcoming or counteracting teachers', coaches', and even children's beliefs about sex differences in motor performance. One such strategy might be to provide a greater variety of play and game experiences that are less sex-typed. For example, more product-oriented games that stress mastery, competence, and elements of competition could be offered to females, while more process-oriented games that stress cooperation, expression, and intrinsic values could be provided for males. As a consequence, girls and boys could be offered more similar and comparable motor learning and game experiences, which in turn might equalize some of the social outcomes of participation (cf. Lever, 1976, 1978; Webb, 1969).

Although appropriate strategies and class experiences can counteract a void in learning, the practitioner's attitude is also important. Thus, some issues related to the hidden curriculum—particularly type and amount of feedback, transmission of values, and the subtler ways of conveying attitudes and normative expectations—are also pertinent. Research indicates that teachers as well as parents treat boys and girls differently (Fagot, 1978b, 1981), and that underlying messages as well as attitudes are communicated during the learning process. Therefore, not only are positive reinforcement, appropriate encouragement, and contingent feedback necessary for children of both sexes to learn motor skills, but these elements become more powerful when it comes to sex role stereotyping and physical activity.

Similar to the previous examples, the sport sociologist's role is to facilitate the transfer of knowledge by packaging research findings and principles of social behavior into a form that can be readily understood by teachers, coaches, and parents. But the task seems incomplete unless the sport sociologist also communicates specific suggestions for direct application, perhaps through workshops and clinics.

Conclusion

In sum, this chapter presented a brief overview of major points debated in the development of an applied sociology of sport. The chapter described specific topics of research that have implications for application and are relevant to teachers and coaches. Although the discussion demonstrates how research findings can provide insight and understanding beyond the pages of research journals to bridge the gap between knowledge and practical action, the reader should not ignore the fact that much of the research cited, although extremely relevant, was not undertaken with application in mind. It is more likely that the researchers' motives focused on knowledge for its own sake. Yet sport sociologists came to demonstrate the relevance of earlier findings by trying to synthesize and transfer knowledge to the practitioner. Such attempts, despite their rudimentary form and despite continuing debate over whose knowledge is more important, point to an undeniable acceptance that sport sociology can no longer ignore the domain of application.

References

Allison, M.T. (1980). *A structural analysis of Navajo basketball.* Unpublished doctoral dissertation, University of Illinois, Urbana-Champaign.

Bain, L.L. (1985). The hidden curriculum re-examined. *Quest, 37,* 145-153.

Bain, L.L. (1989). Implicit values in physical education. In T.J. Templin & P.G. Schempp (Eds.), *Socialization into physical education: Learning to teach* (pp. 289-314). Indianapolis: Benchmark Press.

Boutilier, M.A., & San Giovanni, L. (1983). *The sporting woman.* Champaign, IL: Human Kinetics.

Caplan, P.J., & Kinsbourne, M. (1974). Sex differences in response to school failure. *Journal of Learning Disabilities, 7,* 232-235.

Carlston, D.E. (1983). An environmental explanation of race differences in basketball performance. *Journal of Sport and Social Issues, 7*(2), 30-51.

Chalip, L. (1990). Rethinking the applied social sciences of sport: Observations on the emerging debate. *Sociology of Sport Journal,* **7**, 172-178.

Corbin, C.B., Landers, D.M., Feltz, D.L., & Senior, K. (1983). Sex differences in performance estimates: Female lack of confidence vs. male boastfulness. *Research Quarterly for Exercise and Sport,* **54**, 407-410.

Curtis, J.E., & Loy, J.W. (1978). Positional segregation in professional baseball: Replications, trend data and critical observation. *International Review of Sport Sociology,* **13**(4), 5-21.

Dubois, P.E. (1986). The effect of participation in sport on the value orientations of young athletes. *Sociology of Sport Journal,* **3**, 29-42.

Fagot, B.I. (1978a). The influence of sex of child on parental reactions to toddler children. *Child Development,* **49**, 459-465.

Fagot, B.I. (1978b). Reinforcing contingencies for sex-role behaviors: Effect of experience with children. *Child Development,* **49**, 30-36.

Fagot, B.I. (1981). Continuity and change in play styles as a function of sex of child. *International Journal of Behavioral development,* **4**, 37-43.

Frish, H.L. (1977). Sex stereotypes in adult-infant play. *Child Development,* **48**, 1671-1675.

Goldberg, S., & Lewis, M. (1969). Play behavior in the year-old infant: Early sex differences. *Child Development,* **40**, 21-31.

Gould, D. (1987). Understanding attribution in children's sport. *Advances in Pediatric Sport Sciences,* **2**, 61-85.

Griffin, P.S. (1985). Teaching in an urban, multiracial physical education program: The power of context. *Quest,* **37**, 154-165.

Gruneau, R.S. (1976). Sport as an area of sociological study: An introduction to major themes and perspectives. In R.S. Gruneau and J.G. Albinson (Eds.), *Canadian sport: Sociological perspectives* (pp. 8-43). Don Mills, ON: Addison-Wesley.

Gruneau, R.S. (1978). Conflicting standards and problems of personal action in the sociology of sport. *Quest,* **30**, 80-90.

Gruneau, R.S. (1983). *Class, sports and social development.* Amherst: University of Massachusetts Press.

Hall, M.A. (1982, November). *Towards a feminist analysis of gender inequality in sport.* Paper presented at the Third Annual Conference of the North American Society for the Sociology of Sport, Toronto.

Hall, M.A. (1984). Feminist prospects for the sociology of sport. *Arena Review,* **8**(2), 1-9.

Harris, J.C. (1983). Interpreting youth baseball: Players' understanding of attention, winning, and playing the game. *Research Quarterly for Exercise and Sport,* **54**, 333-339.

Harris, J.C. (1984). Interpreting youth baseball: Players' understanding of fun and excitement, danger and boredom. *Research Quarterly for Exercise and Sport,* **55**, 379-382.

Ingham, A.G. (1979). Methodology in the sociology of sport: From symptoms of malaise to Weber for a cure. *Quest,* **31**, 187-215.

Ingham, A.G., & Donnelly, P. (1990). Whose knowledge counts? The production of knowledge and issues of application in the sociology of sport. *Sociology of Sport Journal, 7*, 58-65.

Kenyon, G.S. (1969) A sociology of sport: On becoming a sub-discipline. In R.C. Brown & B.J. Cratty (Eds.), *New perspectives of man in action* (pp. 163-180). Englewood Cliffs, NJ: Prentice-Hall.

Kenyon, G.S., & Loy, J.W. (1965).Toward a sociology of sport. *Journal of Health, Physical Education and Recreation, 36*, 24-25, 68-69.

Kollen, P. (1981). The experience of movement in physical education: A phenomenology. Unpublished doctoral dissertation, University of Michigan, Ann Arbor.

Kollen, P. (1983). Fragmentation and integration in movement. In T.J. Templin & J.K. Olson (Eds.), *Teaching in physical education* (pp. 86-93). Champaign, IL: Human Kinetics.

Langlois, J.H., & Downs, A.C. (1980). Mothers, fathers, and peers as socialization agents of sex-typed play behaviors in young children. *Child Development, 51*, 1237-1247.

Lever, J. (1976). Sex differences in the games children play. *Social Problems, 23*, 478-487.

Lever, J. (1978). Sex differences in the complexity of children's play and games. *American Sociological Review, 43*, 471-483.

Lewis, M. (1972, December). Culture and gender roles: There is no unisex in the nursery. *Psychology Today*, pp. 54-57.

Loy, J.W., & McEluoque, J.F. (1970). Racial segregation in American sport. *International Review of Sport Sociology, S*, 5-24.

Loy, J.W., McPherson, B.D., & Kenyon, G.S. (1980). The emergence and development of the sociology of sport as an academic specialty. *Research Quarterly for Exercise and Sport, 51*, 91-109.

Loy, J.W., & Seagrave, J.D. (1974). Research methodology in the sociology of sport. In J.H. Wilmore (Ed.), *Exercise and sport science review* (pp. 289-333). New York: Academic Press.

Lueschen, G. (1979). Sociology of sport in the context of a sport science: Three issues of methodology. In M.L. Krotee (Ed.), *The dimensions of sport sociology* (pp. 19-23). Champaign, IL: Leisure Press.

Mantel, R.C., VanderVelden, L. (1974). The relationship between the professionalization of attitude toward play of preadolescent boys and participation in organized sport. In G.H. Sage (Ed.), *Sport and American society* (pp. 172-178). Reading, MA: Addison-Wesley.

Martinek, T.J. (1981). Pygmalion in the gym: A model for the communication of teacher expectations in physical education. *Research Quarterly for Exercise and Sport, 52*, 58-67.

Martinek, T.J. (1983). Creating Golem and Galatea effects during physical education instruction: A social psychological perspective. In T.J. Templin & J.K. Olson (Eds.), *Teaching in physical education* (pp. 59-70).Champaign, IL: Human Kinetics.

Melnick, M.J. (1975). A critical look at the sociology of sport. *Quest,* **24**, 34-47.

Melnick, M.J. (1980). Toward an applied sociology of sport. *Journal of Sport and Social Issues,* **5**, 1-12.

Rose, D. (1981, November). *Two steps toward eliminating chaos in the sociology of sport brickyard.* Paper presented at the Second Annual Conference of the North American Society for the Sociology of Sport, Forth Worth, TX.

Smith, R.E., Smoll, F.L., Hunt, E., Curtis, B., & Coppel, D.B. (1979). Psychology and the Bad News Bears. In G. Roberts & K.M. Newell (Eds.), *Psychology of motor behavior and sport— 1978.* (pp. 109-130). Champaign, IL: Human Kinetics.

Sparkes, A.C. (1989). Culture and ideology in physical education. In T.J. Templin & P.G. Schempp (Eds.), *Socialization into physical education: Learning to teach* (pp. 315-338). Indianapolis: Benchmark Press.

Tauber, M.A. (1979). Parental socialization techniques and sex differences in children's play. *Child Development,* **50**, 225-234.

Webb, H. (1969).Professionalization of attitudes toward play among adolescents. In G.S. Kenyon (Ed.), *Aspects of contemporary sport sociology* (pp. 161-179). Chicago: Athletic Institute.

Wyatt, D.L. (1976, November). *Pick-up basketball: A case study of clique behavior variation.* Paper presented at the 75th Annual Meeting of the American Anthropological Association, Washington, DC.

Yiannakis, A. (1989). Toward an applied sociology of sport: The next generation. *Sociology of Sport Journal,* **6**, 1-16.

SECTION 3

Types of Applied Sociology of Sport

Each of the nine research studies in this section represents a type of applied sociology of sport that was detailed in the conceptual model outlined in Section 1. To demonstrate the correspondence of these chapters with the theoretical framework, Section 3 is divided into three subsections, each reflecting one of the levels of abstraction described in the conceptual model outlined in chapter 1. Part I consists of five research articles representing the explanatory research phase. These articles were selected because they represent an intermediate level of theoretical abstraction. That is, although the studies were grounded in some type of theoretical framework, they addressed questions of practical significance and attempted to *explain* underlying causes or influential factors. Either the findings themselves or the generalizations obtained from these findings have implication for application because they in some way come close to social or empirical reality.

Although the link between explanatory research and application is not always apparent, we hope you will understand the connections between foundational knowledge and application. We challenge you to consider how research conceptualized from a narrow or focused perspective may help in designing and planning programs, making decisions, setting priorities, or identifying policy alternatives.

PART I

The Explanatory Phase

All five articles in Part I represent reports of social scientific research. However, the chapters by Snyder and Spreitzer (chapter 5), Sigelman and Bookheimer (chapter 6), and Marcum and Greenstein (chapter 7) differ slightly from those of Greendorfer (chapter 8) and Griffin (chapter 9). Chapters 5 through 7 address traditional research questions related to sport and physical activity, and their major focus is at the level of research reporting. The practical significance of these studies is left to your imagination, with no reference made to implications or practical application. In contrast, chapters 8 and 9 represent a slightly different level of abstraction. Although they also represent reports of research findings, their subject matter focus seems to be somewhat more amenable to application. Regardless of their differences, however, each article sheds some light on a research question that has practical relevance.

Chapter 5
Patterns of Adherence to a Physical Conditioning Program

Eldon E. Snyder and Elmer Spreitzer
Bowling Green State University

Although Snyder and Spreitzer examine adherence to a physical fitness regime, their analysis focuses on maintenance or dropout behavior—a phenomenon that can be generalized to a broad range of physical activities. The notable feature in their study is their attempt to develop a profile of the prospective dropout. Thus, the study represents a fact-finding basis from which special interventions could be suggested in order to enhance adherence. While it is not action research in and of itself, the policy implications of this study may be more recognizable than in some of the other articles in this section.

A serious concern of our society involves the maintenance of physical and mental health. Legislators develop proposals for public health programs, insurance companies charge higher rates to cover rising health costs, and physical therapists, educators, and medical specialists emphasize the need for increased attention to the prevention of physical and mental disabilities. These specialists emphasize the importance of exercise on a regular basis in order to enhance one's physical and mental health. In 1982 the National Academy of Sciences' Institute of Medicine estimated that 50% of the mortality from the 10 leading causes of death in the United States could be traced to life style (Federal Research Group, 1984, p. 31). Curiously, there is little research concerning the more important issues of (a) why some individuals prefer sedentary life styles, (b) why others choose to become physically active, and (c) why some individuals adhere to vigorous exercise programs once they are adopted whereas others discontinue (Morgan, 1977:236).

The scientific literature shows a clear relationship between regular physical activity and holistic health. The implications for preventive health are very evident.

Paper presented at the meeting of The North American Society for the Sociology of Sport, St. Louis, MO, 1983. This study has been supported in part by a grant from the American Heart Association, Northwestern Ohio Chapter, Inc. The authors are grateful to Dr. Richard Bowers, Director, Fitness and Sports Physiology Laboratory, Bowling Green State University, for providing the data and for his helpful consultation. *Note.* From *Sociology of Sport Journal*, 1(2), pp. 103–116. Reprinted by permission.

The literature shows that vigorous physical activity can reduce anxiety, depression, tension, and coronary risk factors such as obesity and hypertension (see Dishman, 1982, and Folkins & Sime, 1981, for a literature review). Unfortunately, adherence to a program of physical activity is relatively low. Organized exercise programs typically do not succeed in producing adherence to physical activity on an ongoing basis. The literature shows that about half the participants who begin an exercise program discontinue exercising within the first 6 months (Carmody, Senner, Malinow, & Matarazzo, 1980; Dishman, 1982; Morgan, 1977; Oldridge, 1979).

The present study, then, attempts to identify factors that affect both initial and continued participation by adults in physical fitness activities. An objective of our research was to analyze the values and meanings associated with involvement in physical activity as a part of a person's self-identity and life style. We view physical activity as one role within a person's total role configuration that involves competition for scarce time (e.g., spouse, parent, worker). We assume that discretionary time and energy are invested in activities that involve perceived social, intrinsic, and extrinsic rewards, that is, payoffs of one type or another. The challenge for directors of recreation programs, and for health educators, is to develop strategies to attract otherwise sedentary people to participate and to enhance their adherence to a physical regimen. An increased understanding of the factors associated with involvement and adherence in physical fitness activities is an important step in achieving these health care goals.

Most of the research on involvement in sport and physical activity focuses on the socialization processes affecting youth (Spreitzer & Snyder, 1976). Although these studies are enlightening, they address a truncated range of the life cycle. In the present study we extend the analysis of sport socialization into the adult stages of the life cycle. We shall attempt to explain the values and meanings associated with physical activity in lifelong activities. This study explores the ways by which physical participation becomes a part of one's identity, how it is socially reinforced, and the correlative aversive factors that may help explain the passive attitude of some adults toward physical activity.

This study draws upon two related perspectives. The first offers theoretical explanations of why people initially *become involved* in sport, while the second perspective attempts to explain *adherence* behavior in physical activities (Caplan, Robinson, French, Caldwell, & Shinn, 1976). Concerning the first question, several studies have demonstrated a positive relationship between the interest and encouragement of parents, siblings, and peers in childhood and the influence of participation in sports in adolescence and adulthood (Kenyon & McPherson, 1973; McPherson, 1972; Spreitzer & Snyder, 1976; Spreitzer & Snyder, 1983). However, we need to delve deeper into the explanations for participation in sport and related physical activities, particularly with respect to the question of why some show little continuing interest. In short, additional insights are needed into why some people continue to be involved (i.e., adherence behavior) in physical fitness activities throughout adulthood as part of their overall life style.

Independent and Dependent Variables

The rationale for emphasizing the particular clusters of independent variables is that the evidence from previous research suggests that variance within each of these clusters is relevant to participation in physical activity. One of the major objectives of our analysis is to incorporate social structural and psychological variables that have not previously been included in a single study. Furthermore, we need to investigate how these variables are associated with participation over a period of time. The causal linkages between the independent and dependent variables also need to be further explicated. We hypothesize that the dependent variables of participation in physical activity and adherence to it will be related to such variables as perceived physical ability, social influences, orientation toward work, and the perceived intrinsic and extrinsic rewards of physical fitness. Some of these variables may be both causes and effects of physical fitness. In this sense, an active life style may be viewed as both a dependent and independent variable. However, the primary focus of the analysis will be on adherence to a physical fitness regimen as the dependent variable.

Conceptualization and Measurement of Variables

Based on our earlier research and a review of other studies, we have organized the major variables into several categories. In the following discussion we outline the relevant variables with special emphasis on areas that we feel need greater clarification.

Demographics

These variables include age, income, and education. The type, degree, and continuation of participation may vary according to social background characteristics. Furthermore, these demographic variables will be used as control variables later in the analysis in order to test hypotheses.

Influence of Group Affiliations and Significant Others

One of the principal reasons for a commitment to physical activity among adults is the feeling of sociability, companionship, and social reinforcement. Social support and sentiments may be expressed in terms of friendship, loyalty, and mutual esteem. The social solidarity of some leisure sports groups may lead participants to feel a sense of loss when one of the participants is absent. Preliminary research indicates that family and friends are influential in becoming involved in sport (Spreitzer & Snyder, 1976), and we would hypothesize that continued participation is socially influenced in the same manner. Moreover, individuals have varying commitments within their set of roles. One's behavior will reflect the degree of commitment to, and negotiation between, the various expectations inherent in one's role cluster. In short, an analysis of initial participation in physical fitness by adults and its continuance must take into account the configuration of roles and the degree of identity invested therein.

Values and Meanings Attached to Fitness Activities

Recent research by Sonstroem (1974, 1978) is useful in the analysis of adherence to physical activity programs. Sonstroem posits that physical activity leads to improved physical fitness, resulting in increased estimation of physical ability (i.e., self-perception of athletic ability) that in turn is thought to increase one's attraction toward physical activity and self-esteem. While the present study does not measure physical fitness, it does tap self-perceptions of athletic ability and subjective meanings attached to physical activity and sport.

One aspect of the meanings attached to physical fitness involves the intrinsic and extrinsic rewards associated with the activity. Intrinsic enjoyment is based on the pleasure received from an activity itself rather than the expectation of an external reward (Deci, 1975). However, many of the meanings and values associated with organized sports are primarily product-oriented (Snyder, 1972; Snyder & Spreitzer, 1979:170-175; Webb, 1969). For many people, involvement is based on the fact that they excel and enjoy the extrinsic satisfactions of their competence. We do not know the relative importance of the intrinsic and extrinsic rewards in terms of encouraging lifelong involvement. Some research suggests that when extrinsic rewards are the primary form of motivation, the intrinsic gratification seems to recede (Deci, 1975; Greene & Lepper, 1974; Martens, 1976). In any event, most persons in the general adult population have not developed, or cannot maintain, the high level of athletic skill requisite for continued receipt of extrinsic rewards. Thus, we need to understand the relationship between perceived ability, social expectations, and intrinsic satisfactions.

Social Psychological Variables

Several social psychological variables have been analyzed in earlier research on factors associated with physical fitness activities. Specifically, Dishman and associates (Dishman, 1982; Dishman & Gettman, 1980; Dishman & Ickes, 1981; Dishman, Ickes, & Morgan, 1980) have shown that perseverance in preventive and rehabilitative medical programs is strongly related to the characteristic of self-motivation. Additionally, Rotter (1966) has postulated individual differences in the locus of control over one's behavior. For example, if one's behavior is primarily perceived to be attributed to personal actions (internal) rather than externally controlled, this characteristic might be particularly important for adherence to a physical fitness program.

From a health standpoint, perceived internal control should be associated with the desire to control one's health, as contrasted with a perception of health as determined by external or chance factors (Wallston, B.S., Wallston, K.A., Kaplan, & Maides, 1976). Moreover, some research suggests that individuals who are satisfied with their life (e.g., community, hobbies, health, job, and life in general) are more likely to maintain a positive attitude toward themselves and their bodies (Snyder & Spreitzer, 1974). Consequently, assessment of such social psychological dimensions may enable one to predict the probability of adherence to a fitness routine. Consequently, in this study we analyze several social psychological variables (including self-motivation, perceived internal-external locus of control over one's health, and life satisfaction) as possible predictors of physical activity.

A Theoretical Summary: Identity, Commitment, and Adherence

Physiological factors and age are commonly assumed to be the best predictors of the degree of involvement in physical activity by adults. However, involvement can be enhanced or limited by a variety of social and social-psychological factors. A theoretical summary of other possible factors is provided in the following paragraphs.

The extent of one's involvement in physical fitness activities is no doubt related to the degree of identity invested in such activities. The concept of identity is one's imaginative view of himself (or herself) as *"he likes to think of himself being and acting"* (McCall & Simmons, 1978:63, italics in the original). This imaginative view exerts an influence on our behavior and is important in the meanings we give to physical activities, our perceptions of fitness, and appraisal of our performances in this sphere of behavior. Additionally, the extent to which one's identity is invested in physical fitness reflects a level of commitment that in turn serves to maintain adherence to physical conditioning. Thus, the subjective meanings attached to physical ability are basic ingredients of one's identity. Furthermore, the more global social psychological variables of self-motivation, locus of control, and life satisfaction are also dimensions of one's self-concept.

Basic to the socialization process as viewed by the symbolic interactionists is the notion that one's identity reflects and filters the meanings that are transmitted by one's significant others. Therefore, one's identity and commitment to physical fitness will be influenced by one's group affiliations. Likewise, the rewards that one receives from others in terms of prestige, recognition, trophies, and other such extrinsic rewards, as well as the intrinsic enjoyment associated with physical movement, serve to maintain a commitment to physical activity.

In summary, the primary variables used to analyze adherence to physical conditioning in this study are embedded within a broader theoretical perspective. Specifically, the central line of thought in the symbolic interactionist perspective focuses on identity, the related concept of commitment, and social support factors including the intrinsic and extrinsic gratifications deriving from involvement in physical conditioning. In the following section we provide the operational definitions of these concepts and the research design. The scales that were used to quantify the social psychological variables discussed above are described in the appendix.

Method

Data for this study were collected through questionnaires, which were sent to persons who had voluntarily taken a physical fitness stress test at the Bowling Green State University Fitness and Sports Physiology Laboratory. These persons had taken the test over a period of approximately 5 years, and with the completion of the physical workup each individual was advised about the appropriate physical activity for his/her level of fitness. An important aspect of this study, as contrasted with some earlier research, is that the subjects in the present sample expressed their initial concern for physical fitness by making an appointment, paying a fee, and undergoing the physical test. In short, the respondents in this survey had been tested and prescribed an individualized physical regimen. The goal of this follow-up study was to analyze the variables associated with adherence to the prescribed program. The laboratory records indicate that 230 individuals with valid addresses took the test; the results of the data reported in this paper are based on 144 respondents, a return rate of 63%.

Items included on the questionnaires were compiled primarily from previous surveys; however, additional items were included expressly for the present study. The resources for the measures are noted below (and are given in more detail in the reference list at the end of this article):

- Satisfaction With Life—General Social Surveys;
- Attitudes Toward Work and Leisure—Neulinger and Breit (1971);
- Self-Motivation—Dishman and Ickes (1981);
- Health Locus of Control—Wallston, Wallston, Kaplan, and Maides (1976);
- Orientation Toward Sport. Attraction to Sport and Perceived Physical Activity—Carmack and Martens (1979); Sonstroem (1974); Spreitzer and Snyder (1975); Grove and Dodder (1979).

Findings

The first stage of our analysis involves a simple description of the current exercise pattern of our sample of respondents. It will be recalled that our sample is purposive in the sense of focusing on persons who had shown enough interest in physical conditioning to undergo a stress test and conditioning workup. In other words, this collection of respondents is not a cross-section of the adult population. Moreover, as will be noted later, the sample is somewhat homogeneous in terms of being well-educated, relatively affluent, and middle-aged.

The data pattern shown in Table 5.1 indicates that almost one-third of the respondents (31%) were essentially inactive in terms of daily exercise. On the other hand, 40% reported that they spend at least 5 hours per week in physical activity within an exercise context. The mean number of hours spent exercising per week was 5.12 hours, with a standard deviation of 2.35. Speaking in general terms of "adherence," we would conclude that a substantial proportion of this sample failed to comply with the conditioning regimen prescribed by the exercise physiologist at the time of the stress test. Unfortunately, we do not have access to the physiological measurements that were recorded at the time of the stress test, nor do we have access to the prescription for exercise that was recommended by the exercise physiologist.

Table 5.1   Hours Per Week Spent Exercising as Reported by Respondents Subsequent to a Stress Test

Hours	Frequency	Percent
0	44	31
1	1	1
2	15	10
3	15	10
4	12	8
5	19	13
6	13	9
7	5	4
8	5	4
9 or more	15	10
	(N = 144)	(100%)

Table 5.2 presents a correlation matrix that summarizes the interrelationships among the dependent variable of physical activity, three demographics (age, education, and income), and 11 social psychological variables. From the bottom row displaying the means and standard deviations for the respective variables, we can see that the average age was 42, with 17 years of education on the average, and a family income of some $43,000.

The three strongest predictors of hours of weekly exercise were an orientation toward sport as relaxation, perceived athletic ability, and intrinsic orientation toward sport as a human activity (.49, .46, and .40, respectively). Interestingly, the background characteristics of age, education, and income showed relatively weak correlations with hours of physical activity (−.12, .15, and .04, respectively). It is interesting to note that previous research (Dishman, 1982) had shown that global motivation was the single best predictor of adherence to physical activity. In the present study, this variable of motivation did not show a strong correlation ($r = .15$) with physical activity.

Table 5.2 Zero-Order Correlation Matrix for Variables Included in the Analysis[a]

Variable	Age	Educ.	Income	Par. encour.	Life satis.	Soc. inf.	Youth particip.	Work	Motivat.	Internal	Intrinsic	Extrinsic	Relax.	Ability
Hours exercise	-.12	.15*	.04	.19**	.24**	.23**	.03	-.23**	-.15*	-.13	-.40**	.32**	.49**	.46**
Age		.03	.27**	-.36**	.10	-.36**	.09	.06	-.13	-.13	-.22**	.05	-.18*	-.07
Education			.29**	.04	.06	.04	-.08	.17*	.21	.11	.11	.02	.22**	.14
Income				.05	.15*	-.09	.00	.14	.20**	.01	.02	.00	.12	.18*
Parental encouragement					.09	.83	.03	-.07	.33**	.12	.37**	.12	.34**	.36**
Life satisfaction						.15*	.16*	.00	.22**	.05	.15*	.22**	.17*	.35**
Social influence							-.10	-.16*	.26**	.22**	.56**	.06	.46**	.41**
Youth participation								.07	.13	.06	-.03	.15*	-.09	.06
Work orientation									.17*	-.11	-.25**	-.20*	-.09	-.11
Global motivation										.17*	.31**	.17*	.31**	.37**
Internal control											.18*	.17*	.17*	.30**
Intrinsic orientation												.19*	.68**	.56**
Extrinsic orientation													.25**	.25**
Relaxation orientation														.54**
Athletic ability														-
Mean	42.00	17.3	43,000.00	1.61	3.25	1.83	1.74	2.65	2.80	2.74	2.84	3.08	2.92	2.57
Standard deviation	9.8	3.4	6.3	.72	.41	.41	.30	.57	.40	.32	.49	.38	.58	.32

[a]Frequencies vary from 116 to 144 in terms of number of respondents.

*p < .05 level.

**p < .01 level.

In terms of interrelationships among the predictor variables, it is interesting to note a strong correlation (.83) between having been encouraged by parents as a child to participate in sports and enjoying the sociability aspects of sports as an adult. Similarly, there was a marked correlation (.68) between our scale for measuring an intrinsic orientation toward sport and a view of sports as a means of relaxation. More substantively, one's *self-perception of athletic ability* was clearly correlated with an intrinsic orientation toward sport (.56) but only weakly related to an extrinsic orientation toward sport (.25).

The multiple correlation coefficient between the dependent variable of hours of exercise and the 11 predictor variables shown in Table 5.2 was .57, which means that we were able to explain 33% of the individual differences in exercise among the respondents in our survey. In other words, about two-thirds of the variance is left unexplained. Clearly, other variables (and especially other theoretical models) need to be tested in future research. This level of predictability is not adequate to develop a screening instrument to identify prospective "dropouts" from a physical fitness program.

Our analysis of the data also included a calculation of partial correlations to determine whether the relative strength of the predictor variables was markedly altered when demographic characteristics and perceived athletic ability were introduced as control variables. Table 5.3 summarizes the pattern of zero-order and partial correlations concerning the number of hours spent per week in physical activity. The table shows that controlling on the background characteristics of

Table 5.3   Summary of Zero-Order and Partial Correlations Between Hours of Exercise as the Dependent Variable and a Series of Predictor Variables

Variable	Zero-order correlations	Partial correlations controlling for age, education and income	Partial correlations controlling for athletic ability
Age	−.12	−	−.03
Education	.15*	−	.12
Family income	.04	−	−.01
Youth participation	.03	.13	.10
Internal control	.13	.17*	.03
Global motivation	.15*	.05	−.06
Life satisfaction	.24**	.26**	.13
Parental encouragement	.19**	.13	.02
Work orientation	−.23**	−.34**	−.23**
Social influence	.23**	.24**	.08
Extrinsic orientation	.32**	.31**	.22**
Intrinsic orientation	.40**	.28**	.09
Athletic ability	.46**	.42**	−
Relaxation orientation	.49**	.38**	.23**

*Significant at .05 level.

**Significant at .01 level.

age, education, and income did not appreciably alter the findings observed at the zero-order level. The control variable of perceived athletic ability did introduce changes, however, in the basic pattern. Of the 10 predictor variables that were significant $p < .05$) at the zero-order level, only three of these variables were significant as predictors of physical activity after controlling for perceived athletic ability—work orientation ($-.23$), an extrinsic orientation toward sport (.22), and a relaxation motivation for exercise (.23).

The fact that one's self-assessment of athletic ability is directly related to one's subjective feeling of satisfaction from participation in sports has important implications for school physical education programs and community recreational sport programs. This correlation suggests that the emphasis in such noncompetitive contexts would be well placed on the *process* rather than the *product* of physical activity. In other words, there is a need to emphasize the *fit* between the particular individual and the channel of physical activity. When the emphasis is on the process of physical expression as an end in itself, every participant can be a winner. Consequently, it would seem important to link the individual's physical ability with an appropriate mode of activity if lifelong physical involvement is to be encouraged.

It is encouraging to note that perceived athletic ability was not strongly correlated ($r = .06$) with participation in sports as a youth (see Table 5.2). Perceived athletic ability did show a modest correlation, however, with parental encouragement ($r = .36$) and encouragement from friends ($r = .42$). Perhaps of most interest is the fact that an intrinsic orientation toward sport and a relaxation orientation toward sport were the two best predictors of perceived athletic ability ($r = .56$ and .54, respectively).

Summary and Conclusion

This paper basically attempted to identify factors that predict adherence to exercise subsequent to a physical fitness test. The policy implications involve the objective of being able to identify prospective dropouts in advance in order to permit special intervention to enhance the probability of adherence to an exercise program. The present study was only moderately successful in being able to identify dropout-prone participants in terms of demographic and social psychological characteristics. Our findings showed that 31% of the individuals in our sample who had undergone a physical fitness assessment and stress test were subsequently inactive in terms of regular exercise. On the more optimistic side, 40% reported that they engage in at least 5 hours of exercise per week.

The demographic variables of age, education, occupation, and income showed little correlation with adherence to an exercise program. The three strongest predictors of physical activity were perceived athletic ability, an intrinsic orientation toward physical activity as an end in itself, and an orientation toward sports as a means of relaxation. Our set of 11 predictor variables was able to explain 33% of the variance in physical activity.

Our research concurs with previous studies showing that most people do not exercise because it is good for them; rather, they exercise because it feels good (Morgan, 1977). In fact, some research suggests that participants can become emotionally dependent, even addicted, to regular exercise. William Glasser (quoted in Harris, 1978:53) suggests that physical activity can alter an individual's consciousness under the following conditions:

1. The activity must be noncompetitive and voluntarily selected.
2. It should be something that can be done easily and without much mental effort for at least an hour a day.
3. The activity should be one that can be done alone and does not depend upon the participation of others.
4. The activity must have some physical, emotional, or spiritual value for the participant.
5. The participant must believe that persistence will result in improvement.
6. The activity must be one that can be done without self-criticism.

The challenge, then, is to explain the process by which physical activity becomes assimilated into one's self-concept and lifestyle. Sonstroem (1974, 1978) has developed a theoretical model suggesting that physical activity leads to improved physical condition, resulting in a more favorable assessment of one's physical ability which in turn enhances one's overall self-esteem. Thus, as one's estimation of physical ability improves, one's attraction toward physical activity increases, which in turn reinforces ongoing physical involvement. In a similar vein, Becker "explains the most disparate life styles as variations around the single theme of self-esteem maintenance" (1968:329). In short, people like to feel good about themselves; they seek out situations that enhance their self-esteem, and they try to control the conditions that limit their self-worth.

Sample Items for Scales Used in the Analysis

Athletic Participation as a Youth (3 items in scale)

1. During your youth, did you participate in any sports activities as part of a formally organized program (e.g., high school teams, YMCA/YWCA, CYO, etc.)?
2. Did you participate in varsity sports in high school?

Perceived Athletic Ability (9 items in scale)

1. I'm a natural athlete.
2. When I participate in sports or physical activity, I often feel embarrassed by my performance.

Parental Encouragement for Sports Participation (3 items in scale)

1. When you were growing up, did your parents encourage you to participate in sports?
2. During your childhood, was your father interested in sports?

Social Influences for Participation in Sports (9 items)

1. When you were growing up, did your friends participate in sports?
2. Do you now have friends who encourage you to participate in sports?

Intrinsic Orientation Toward Sports (5 items)

1. I participate in sports and physical activity just for the enjoyment of the activity itself.
2. Participation in physical activities represents a type of beauty and artistic expression.

Relaxation Orientation Toward Sports (5 items)

1. Active physical participation provides me with a welcome escape from the pressure of everyday life.
2. Sports are a good way for me to relax.

Extrinsic Orientation Toward Sports (4 items)

1. I view participation in physical activity as primarily a means to improve one's health and physical fitness.
2. I participate in physical activity to help keep my weight down.

Internal/External Control Over Health (11 items)

1. I am directly responsible for my health.
2. Good health is largely a matter of good fortune.

Global Motivation (22 items)

1. I can persist in spite of pain or discomfort.
2. Whenever I reach a goal, I set a higher one.

Orientation Toward Work (4 items)

1. My personal identity is realized more in my work than in my leisure time activity.
2. I find that my leisure activities are more satisfying to me than my work.

Life Satisfaction (6 items)

1. In general, how satisfying do you find the ways you are spending your life these days?
2. Taking all things together, how would you say things are going these days?

References

Becker, Ernest
   1968   The Structure of Evil. New York: Braziller.
Caplan, R.D., E. Robinson, J. French, J. Caldwell, and M. Shinn
   1976   Adhering to Medical Regimens: Pilot Experiments in Patient Education and Social Support. Ann Arbor: Institute for Social Research.
Carmack, M. and R. Martens
   1979   "Measuring commitments to running: a survey of runners' attitudes and mental states." Journal of Sport Psychology 1:25-42.
Carmody, T.P., J.M. Senner, M.R. Malinow and J.D. Matarazzo
   1980   "Physical exercise rehabilitation: long-term dropout rate in cardiac patients." Journal of Behavioral Medicine 3:163-168.
Deci, Edward L.
   1975   Intrinsic Motivation. New York: Plenum Press.
Dishman, R.K.
   1982   "Compliance/adherence in health-related exercise." Journal of Health Psychology 1:237-267.
Dishman, R.K. and L.R. Gettman
   1981   "Psychobiologic influences on exercise adherence." Journal of Sport Psychology 2:295-310.
Dishman, R.K., W. Ickes and M.P. Morgan
   1980   "Self-motivation and adherence to habitual physical activity." Journal of Applied Social Psychology 10:115-132.
Dishman, R.K. and W. Ickes
   1981   "Self-motivation and adherence to therapeutic exercise." Journal of Behavioral Medicine 4:421-438.
Federal Research Group
   1984   Federal Research Report. "Social science research at NIH." January 27, p. 31.
Folkins, C. and W. Sime
   1981   "Physical fitness training and mental health." American Psychologist 36:373-389.
General Social Surveys
   1982   National Opinion Research Center, University of Chicago.
Greene, D. and M. Lepper
   1974   "How to turn play into work." Psychology Today 25:29-53.

Grove, S. and R. Dodder
   1979   "A study of functions of sport: a subsequent test of Spreitzer and Snyder's Research." Journal of Sport Behavior 2:83-91.
Harris, D.
   1978   "The happy addict." womenSports 5:53.
Kenyon, G. and B. McPherson
   1973   "Becoming involved in physical activity and sport: a process of socialization." In G. Rarick (ed.), Physical Activity: Human Growth and Development. New York: Academic Press.
Martens, R.
   1976   "Kid sports: a den of iniquity or a land of promise?" Proceedings of the National Physical Education Association for Men.
McCall, G.J. and J.L. Simmons
   1978   Identities and Interactions, New York: The Free Press.
McPherson, B.
   1972   Socialization Into the Role of Sport Consumer: A Theory and Causal Model. Doctoral dissertation, University of Wisconsin.
Morgan, W.P.
   1977   "Involvement in vigorous physical activity with special references to adherence." Proceedings of the Physical Education Association for Men.
Neulinger, J. and M. Breit
   1971   "Attitude dimensions of leisure: a replication study." Journal of Leisure Research 3:108-115.
Oldridge, N.B.
   1979   "Compliance in exercise rehabilitation." The Physician and Sportsmedicine 7:94-103.
Rotter, J.B.
   1966   "Generalized expectancies for internal versus external control of reinforcement." Psychological Monographs 80 (1, Whole No. 609).
Snyder, E.E.
   1972   "Athletic dressingroom slogans as folklore: a means of socialization." International Review of Sport Sociology 7:89-102.
Snyder, E.E. and E. Spreitzer
   1974   "Involvement in sports and psychological well-being." International Journal of Sport Psychology 5:28-39.
   1979   "Orientation toward sport: intrinsic, normative, and extrinsic." Journal of Sport Psychology 1:170-175.
Sonstroem, R.J.
   1974   "Attitude testing examining certain psychological correlates of physical activity." Research Quarterly 45:93-103.
Sonstroem, R.J.
   1978   "Physical estimation and attraction scales: rationale and research." Medicine and Science in Sports 10:97-102.

Spreitzer, E. and E. Snyder
   1975   "The psychosocial functions of sport as perceived by the general popu-
          lation." International Review of Sport Sociology 10:87-93.
   1976   "Socialization into sport: an exploratory path analysis." Research
          Quarterly 47:238-245.
Spreitzer, E. and E.E. Snyder
   1983   "Correlates of participation in adult recreational sports." Journal of
          Leisure Research 15:27-38.
Wallston, B.S., K.A. Wallston, G.O. Kaplan and S.A. Maides
   1976   "Development and validation of the health locus of control scale."
          Journal of Consulting and Clinical Psychology 44:580-585.
Webb, H.
   1969   "Professionalization of attitudes toward play among adolescents." In
          G. Kenyon (ed.), Aspects of Contemporary Sport Sociology. Chicago:
          The Athletic Institute.

Chapter 6

Is It Whether You Win or Lose? Monetary Contributions to Big-Time College Athletic Programs

Lee Sigelman and Samuel Bookheimer
University of Kentucky

This chapter examines the connection between athletic success or failure and voluntary financial contributions to universities and demonstrates the explanatory phase of applied research. Because the findings from this study are very specific, one must exercise caution in interpreting its results. Specifically, of all the factors considered relative to donations, success in football is the best predictor of contributions given *directly to the athletic department.*

A variety of practical issues are embedded in this seemingly simple research study. First, the examination of donations was limited to only big-time athletic departments, which limits the generalizability of findings. Second, the study (and hence the findings) focuses on some different issues than later research concerned with winning and giving. To truly provide explanatory value, the precise information conveyed as well as its meaning must be made clear (e.g., that the contributions related to football success are given directly to athletics, not to the university at large or to alumni associations). The use to which this knowledge is put, particularly with respect to administrative policy, may depend on how the findings are interpreted. For example, if it is widely thought that winning teams generate money for their universities, concessions might be made in admission standards for athletes (in order to have a "competitive" team).

Note. Reprinted from *Social Science Quarterly*, **64**(2), June 1983 by permission of the authors and of the University of Texas Press.

Recently there has been much public wringing of hands about the "shameful" state into which American intercollegiate athletics have fallen (Axthelm, 1980; Underwood, 1980). Skyrocketing budgets, multimillion-dollar coaching contracts, illegal "gifts" to star players, recurrent recruiting violations, illiterate "student-athletes," and other unsavory aspects of big-time college sports are all outgrowths of a pronounced desire on the part of coaches, administrators, faculty, students, fans, alumni, and public officials to be associated with a "winning program." Winning may not, however, simply be a psychological fixation. It may also be an economic necessity.

The ability of winning football and basketball teams to generate revenues for their universities and athletic departments is so widely taken for granted that it has become an integral part of the conventional wisdom concerning sport in America. This bit of conventional wisdom has some basis in fact, for ticket sales—easily the largest source of revenue for varsity sports programs—are correlated with on-field performance (Koch, 1971; Raiborn, 1978).

Increased ticket sales are, however, only one of the tangible benefits said to spring from football and basketball success—others being more favorable treatment at the hands of the legislature, increased student enrollments, and more generous voluntary financial contributions from alumni and others. However, empirical evidence concerning the impact of successful athletic programs on legislative appropriations and student enrollments is very scanty (see Beasley, 1974; Budig, 1976). Moreover, the connection between athletic success and alumni giving has recently been called into question (Sigelman & Carter, 1979), although Sigelman and Carter's findings have now been challenged by Brooker and Klastorin (1981), who claim that schools with successful football and basketball teams do indeed receive greater financial support from their alumni.

The purposes of the present study are twofold. First, we undertake another empirical analysis of the relationship between success in intercollegiate athletics and voluntary giving. Unlike the Sigelman-Carter and Brooker-Klastorin studies, both of which focus on donations to the university's annual fund, we examine donations made directly to the *athletic department*. Second, we undertake a parallel analysis of voluntary giving to the annual funds of the same schools, which allow us to determine whether the same factors which encourage generous outside contributions to the annual fund encourage generous contributions to the athletic department. The parallel analysis also provides a clearer perspective on the question—secondary in the present context but primary in the Sigelman-Carter and Brooker-Klastorin studies—of whether there is any connection between the success of a school's athletic programs and the size of its annual fund.

Private Giving and Big-Time Intercollegiate Athletics

In 1977, the most recent year for which data are currently available, outside contributions accounted for only about 10 percent of the revenues taken in by the typical big-time intercollegiate athletic program (Raiborn, 1978:15). This amount pales in comparison to the share of revenues generated by ticket sales, but the correlation between winning records and gate receipts means that some programs—the losing ones—can ill afford to rely on ticket sales alone, while at other schools the football stadiums and basketball arenas may be sold out years in advance, meaning that even unprecedented on-field successes cannot bring more customers through the turnstiles. Nor can ticket prices be raised indefinitely, especially in metropolitan areas, where the colleges face fierce competition for the entertainment and sports dollar (Atwell, Grimes, & Lopiano, 1980:31).

The limited ability of ticket sales to generate additional revenues becomes all the more pressing when the perilous financial condition of most athletic departments is taken into account. Even though total athletic revenues at schools which play big-time football schedules increased by almost 75 percent during the 1970s, expenditures more than kept pace. As a consequence, in 1977, 47 percent of the schools that played big-time football lost money doing so, and the situation was even bleaker in big-time basketball, where 54 percent of those that played lost money (Raiborn, 1978).

In these straitened circumstances, there is an understandable urgency about opening up new sources of revenue, and outside contributions loom large in the thinking of most athletic department officials. While such contributions constituted only one-tenth of athletic revenues in 1977, this was actually double their share of revenues in 1970 (Raiborn, 1978:15). The American Council on Education's Commission on Collegiate Athletics concluded after visiting 30 college campuses that "the prevailing attitude at all institutions included in this study is that the most probable source for increasing athletics revenues is private giving" (Atwell, Grimes, & Lopiano, 1980:33-34). In the words of the athletic director at the University of Kansas, "At one time fund raising was the icing on the cake; now it's the cake" (quoted by Novotny, 1980:7).

Is outside financial support for big-time athletic programs dependent upon a favorable win-loss ratio? To some, this connection seems self-evident. No less an authority than Norm Ellenberger (1982:21), who was convicted on 21 felony counts for his efforts to build a winning basketball program at the University of New Mexico, attests that intercollegiate sports "are the way they are because of the almighty dollar. We have to make money." Lewis Cryer (1981:5), Commissioner of the Pacific Coast Athletic Association, may sound as if he were about to disagree when he states that "a program can raise money whether or not it is winning," but he is quick to add that "it is just easier for a winner."

Others are less certain that there is any connection between winning and giving. Sociologist James Frey (1981:57-58) finds, based on surveys of Washington State University alumni, that the leaders of the alumni association place a much higher value on successful athletic teams than do alumni in general—a finding which, in Frey's view, "contradicts the ever-present myth and usual justification of athletics: 'The alumni demand winning and representative athletic teams.' " Maurice Mitchell (1982), former chancellor of the University of Denver and associate of that fabled foe of big-time college sports, Robert Hutchins, goes even further:

We are told that alumni contributions are important. Well, I have watched alumni, and my observation is that alumni are all talk and no money. The largest hot-air balloon that floats over the average university is the myth about alumni giving. If you need a new stadium, the alumni run around foaming at the mouth, promising you the sky if you build it, but giving you nothing. Alumni are good at threatening you with reprisals, but they don't even give you a chance to watch their checks bounce. Pleasing the alumni is the big excuse for having intercollegiate football, but it is not legitimate. (p. 23).

Is there a connection between the number of victories a team puts on the scoreboard and the number of contributed dollars that flow into the athletic department's accounts? Or are the skeptics correct when they call this bit of conventional wisdom into question? As athletic departments rely more and more heavily upon outside donations to carry them over the financial hump, this question becomes increasingly important.

Testing the Relationship Between Winning and Giving

Financial data on big-time intercollegiate athletics have always been in short supply, for many reasons, including sloppy accounting practices and the profusion of athletic funding sources, not to mention the fact that most athletic departments have not, as Atwell, Grimes, and Lopiano (1980:4) state so delicately, "been eager to share information." Studies published by the National Collegiate Athletic Association (Raiborn, 1970, 1978) have rectified this situation to some degree, but the NCAA studies present no financial data on an institution-by-institution basis. It thus came as a complete departure from precedent that the *Omaha World-Herald* was able to convince athletic personnel at more than 60 major universities to reveal how much they had received in voluntary donations during the 1980-81 school year. These data, reported in *The Chronicle of Higher Education* (Middleton, 1982), are to the best of our knowledge the first institution-by-institution figures on contributions to athletic departments that have ever been made public. They must be approached with caution, for they are subject to unknown amounts of error, inadvertent or otherwise; one obvious area of concern is the possibility that ". . . a considerable portion of private-giving income may not be reflected in the revenue data because it never reaches institutional accounts. It could reasonably be hypothesized that a portion of recruiting costs . . . may be hidden in this manner" (Atwell, Grimes, & Lopiano, 1980:35). Nonetheless, these are the most accurate and most comprehensive data to which we are likely to enjoy access in the foreseeable future; despite our reservations, they provide a firmer basis for analysis than the rank speculations, unsubstantiated rumors, and isolated examples that have heretofore dominated discussions of the connection between winning and giving in big-time college sports.

The *World-Herald* surveyed the athletic department of members of the Atlantic Coast, Big Eight, Big Ten, Pacific 10, Southeastern, and Southwest conferences, several leading "independent" powers (Florida State, Notre Dame, Penn State, Pittsburgh, South Carolina, Tulane, and West Virginia), and a few members of others conferences of lesser athletic stature. Our analysis focuses on all these schools except the final group and those that did not supply the requested information to the *World-Herald* (Auburn, Notre Dame, Tennessee, Texas, and Wisconsin). In all, then, we have data on 57 big-time athletic programs, whose 1980-81 voluntary contributions are shown in Table 6.1.

Table 6.1   Outside Contributions to Intercollegiate Athletic Programs, 1980-81

School	Athletic donations	School	Athletic donations
Stanford	$4,000,000	Alabama	$1,200,000
Oklahoma	3,500,000	Arizona State	1,200,000
Clemson	3,140,000	Texas Tech	1,200,000
North Carolina	3,000,000	West Virginia	1,140,000
Georgia	2,700,000	Louisiana State	1,100,000
South Carolina	2,300,000	Duke	1,000,000
Florida State	2,100,000	Purdue	1,000,000
California	2,000,000	Michigan State	965,000
Washington	2,000,000	Oregon State	955,000
Iowa	1,900,000	Georgia Tech	945,000
North Carolina State	1,900,000	Iowa State	900,000
Southern Methodist	1,900,000	Colorado	862,000
Florida	1,750,000	Kentucky	850,000
Texas A&M	1,800,000	Arizona	800,000
Houston	1,600,000	UCLA	800,000
Southern California	1,600,000	Oregon	765,000
Virginia	1,600,000	Mississippi	700,000
Arkansas	1,500,000	Pittsburgh	657,000
Kansas State	1,500,000	Washington State	602,000
Missouri	1,500,000	Mississippi State	600,000
Oklahoma State	1,500,000	Rice	575,000
Vanderbilt	1,500,000	Minnesota	550,000
Wake Forest	1,500,000	Tulane	525,000
Penn State	1,470,000	Nebraska	462,000
Illinois	1,350,000	Baylor	450,000
Indiana	1,350,000	Texas Christian	450,000
Maryland	1,300,000	Michigan	400,000
Ohio State	1,250,000	Northwestern	300,000
Kansas	1,240,000		

Source: Survey of athletic departments by the *Omaha World-Herald*, summarized in Middleton (1982).

In order to test the proposition that there is a positive correlation between contributions to the athletic department and success in football and basketball, we calculated a "success score" for each football and basketball team. These scores are based on the percentage of games won per year (with a tie counting as half a win) during the four-year period which culminated in 1980-81; instead of figuring simple four-year averages, we used a linear decay function to weight the four yearly percentages, on the assumption that how well a team had done three years ago, for example, would matter considerably less than how well it did this year. Accordingly, a school's 1980 football winning percentage was weighted by a factor of 4, its 1979 record by 3, 1978 by 2, and 1977 by 1, with the sum of the weighted percentages divided by 10 so that the "football success score" would be bounded by 0 and 1; the same procedure was used to calculate "basketball success scores."

In addition to success in football and basketball, several other factors might help to explain the variance among schools in total contributions to the athletic program—factors whose impacts on voluntary donations are interesting in and of themselves and may also clarify the relationship between winning and giving. These include:

1. *The Size of the Institution.* Teams representing larger schools may simply have more followers, and thus more potential contributors; other factors remaining equal, a larger pool of potential contributors should produce a larger pool of contributions. Of all the available indicators of institutional size, the most appropriate for our purposes is the total number of living alumni as of 1980-81 (Council for Financial Aid to Education, 1982).

2. *Public or Private Control of the School.* It may be easier for teams representing public schools to attract a mass following, for the man on the street can more readily identify with an LSU than a Tulane. Accordingly, outside support for the athletic program might be higher at public than private schools. To check on this possibility, we coded a dummy variable which indicated whether each school is privately (0) or publicly (1) controlled.

3. *The Academic Quality of the School.* Winning football and basketball teams are supposed to put a school "on the map," but schools that are more prestigious academically may be less concerned about winning football and basketball games. If they are, we might expect contributions to the athletic program to be relatively low at schools known for their academic excellence and presumably less concerned about the public relations value of sports. There is no ideal measure of academic quality, but for our purposes a composite scale designed by *Barron's Profiles of America Colleges* (1980) will serve; the *Barron's* index ranges from a low of 1 ("noncompetitive") to a high of 9 ("most competitive"). As such, the index is a measure of admissions selectivity rather than academic quality, and thus may underrate the quality of a few of the large land-grant universities in the sample; more generally, however, admissions selectivity and academic quality, however measured, seem certain to be very highly correlated.

4. *The "Hotbed" Factor.* The areas of the United States which are the most conspicuously "college basketball–crazy" or "college football–mad" seem to

share certain characteristics. More than anything else they tend to be rural and noncosmopolitan (e.g., Arkansas, Nebraska, and Texas in football, Indiana, Kentucky, and North Carolina in basketball). In such settings, virtually the entire state may join together in celebrating a victory or mourning a loss. As a rough gauge of this "hotbed" factor, we employed three indicators: the percentage in agriculture of the population of the state in which the school is located; the median educational attainment of the state's adult population; and median family income in the state.

5. *The Prevailing Ethos*. Closely related to the "hotbed" factor is the idea that certain cultures tend to place relatively heavy emphasis on civic responsibility, good works, and the ethic of noblesse oblige. In such settings we might anticipate higher rates of alumni giving to the university annual fund. More speculatively, these may also be the very settings in which the lowest value is placed on inter-collegiate athletics, and in which, by extension, contributions to the athletic program are lowest. The best available indicator of this ethos factor is the Sharkansky-Elazar political culture index (Sharkansky, 1969), which ranges from a score of 1 for the most "moralistic" states to 9 for the most "traditionalistic."

6. *"The Only Game in Town" Factor*. College football and basketball may find themselves competing for fan interest and consumer dollars with professional franchises located nearby—a perennial problem for schools like Southern Methodist University, whose football team plays in the shadow of the vastly more popular professional Dallas Cowboys. It is by no means impossible for such schools to raise large amounts of money for their athletic programs (witness the $4 million contributed to Stanford, which lies just down the road from the San Francisco Forty-Niners and the Golden State Warriors), but it is a good deal more difficult to raise money in the face of direct professional competition. For this reason, we coded a dummy variable for each school to indicate whether a professional football or basketball franchise is located within two hours' driving time (0) or whether the teams representing the school play "the only game in town."

Finally, so that we could present parallel analyses concerning the determinants of giving to athletic programs and to university annual funds, we also employed a second dependent variable. As in the Sigelman-Carter (1979) and Brooker-Klastorin (1981) studies, our data source was a biennial publication of the Council for Financial Aid to Education (1982), which indicates, on an institution-by-institution basis, the total volume of alumni giving to the university annual fund, 1980-81. This variable is thus perfectly parallel to but entirely separate from the *Omaha World-Herald's* figures on outside contributions to intercollegiate athletic programs.

Findings

As can be seen in Table 6.2, part A, the correlation between donations to the athletic program and alumni giving to the university annual fund during the

1980-81 academic year is nonsignificant. This means that for all intents and purposes we are working with two separate dimensions of financial support, whose relationships with the predictors introduced in the preceding section are summarized in the remainder of part A of Table 6.2.

Table 6.2   Relationships Between Athletic Contributions, Alumni Giving, Athletic Success, and Various Other Predictors

	A. Simple correlations	
Predictor	Athletic contributions	Alumni giving
Alumni giving	.160	–
Number of alumni	−.013	.068
Private vs. public control	.069	.034
Barron's rating	.112	−.040
Percent rural	−.057	.094
Median education	−.060	.065
Median income	−.093	.034
Traditionalism	.242*	−.220
No professional competition	.067	.140
Basketball success	.092	.076
Football success	.335*	−.073

B. Regression summary

Athletic contributions = 699,989 + 1,251,600* (football success)
(474,600)

$N = 57$

*$p < .05$

In only two instances did we encounter a statistically significant correlation between any of these predictors and donations to either the intercollegiate athletic program or the university annual fund. A school's number of living alumni, public or private control, and academic quality turned out to be unrelated to either form of voluntary giving, as did most of the state-level factors—percentage, rural, median education, and median income. Nor does the presence or absence of professional sports franchises exert a significant impact on financial support at the collegiate level.

The first significant relationship revolves around the tendency for donations to college athletic programs to be high in traditionalistic cultures and low in moralistic cultures. The impact of political culture actually reverses from one dimension of financial support to the other, to the extent that the correlation involving alumni giving to the university's annual fund (−.220) is virtually the mirror image of the correlation involving outside contributions to the university's athletic program (+.242). The correlation between political culture and alumni giving to the university annual fund falls just short of statistical significance at the .05 level, but the *difference* between the coefficients for donations to the annual fund and the athletic program is easily significant ($p < .05$). Thus, just as we had anticipated, donations to the sports program tend to be highest in traditionalistic cultures, but donations to the university's annual fund tend to be highest in moralistic cultures.

The remaining significant correlation involves athletic success. Both correlations involving success in basketball are positive, but both are of a magnitude far too modest to permit the conclusion that there was any real connection between winning in basketball and attracting outside financial support. In the case of football success, the correlation involving alumni donations to the annual fund is nonsignificant but negative, which means that if anything it was the schools with poorer football records that received more generous gifts to their annual funds. But this is most distinctly not the case with respect to outside donations sent directly to the school's athletic program. The correlation of .335 between football success and athletic donations allows us to say with considerable confidence that the more successful the football team, the greater the outside financial support for the intercollegiate athletic program.

We also undertook several sets of multiple regression analyses designed to isolate the unique impact of winning on giving, holding constant the effects of the control variables. In one set of regressions, contributions to the athletic program and to the university annual fund were regressed in turn on all the predictors introduced earlier. However, the relatively large number of predictors in our analysis, combined with the relatively small number of cases at our disposal, made for a fairly severe degrees of freedom problem, which led us to experiment with two other regression-based approaches. Given our central interest in the impact of basketball and football success, the two athletic success ratios were used as predictors of the two forms of giving in separate equations, always accompanied by a single one of the remaining predictors; thus we had a series of three-predictor models, with the latter variables brought in one at a time as controls. Finally, we tried a stepwise approach, with variables being allowed to enter only if they brought about a significant increase in variance explained. All three of these approaches led to the very same set of conclusions, which we will report here within the context of the findings based on the stepwise analyses.

Given the absence of significant correlations involving alumni giving to the university's annual fund, the stepwise analysis of this dimension of financial support never got off the ground (the parallel in the full model being an extremely low coefficient of determination and an absence of any significant effects of individual predictors). With respect to contributions to athletic programs, once the football success score has been entered, no other predictor was able to meet the entry criterion (see Table 6.2, part B). Still the unstandardized regression coefficient for the football success score provides some interesting new information. A one-unit increase in the football success score is associated with an increase of $1,251,600 in donations to the athletic program. This means that if one big-time college football team lost all the games it played over a four-year period while another team was winning all its games, the latter would be expected to have taken in $1.25 million more than the former in voluntary donations during 1980-81. This is an extreme example, but even in less extreme cases the dollar differentials are by no means trivial; indeed, for every 10 percent improvement in football success, the unstandardized regression coefficient leads us to anticipate an increment of $125,160 in outside donations to the athletic program.

Conclusion

These findings allow us to speak to two separate sets of issues. First, they open up a fresh perspective on the disagreement between Sigelman and Carter (1979) on the one hand, and Brooker and Klastorin (1981) on the other, as to whether alumni giving to university annual funds varies as a function of athletic success or failure. Second, they provide an answer to the separate but related issue of whether there is any connection between athletic success and donations intended specifically for the intercollegiate athletic program.

Before we can speak to the first issue, we need to review the manner in which the Sigelman-Carter and Brooker-Klastorin studies were conducted. Sigelman and Carter analyzed data on approximately 100 schools that maintained NCAA Division I football programs, undertaking separate cross-sectional regressions for each of the 14 years for which data were available. They found no relationship whatsoever between alumni giving and athletic performance. Brooker and Klastorin, however, argue that the 100 or so schools in the Sigelman-Carter analysis are too heterogeneous to permit valid conclusions to be drawn; not all Division I schools play "big-time" football in the truest sense of the term, and even if they did, Sigelman and Carter's failure to take account of such factors as the public or private control of the schools, their size, and the like "masks important differences that could affect the conclusions drawn" (Brooker & Klastorin, 1981:745). Based on these criticisms, Brooker and Klastorin analyzed separate subsets of as few as 10 schools at a time, but pooled 10 separate years of data on each school into each analysis. Both basketball and football performance turn out, in these analyses, to have significant positive effects on alumni giving. Thus, Brooker and Klastorin conclude that Sigelman and Carter's failure to control for the nature of the institutions being studied led to the wrong conclusions about the relationship between athletic success and alumni giving.

In the present study, we have attempted to institute statistical controls for a far more extensive set of institutional and environmental factors than did Brooker and Klastorin, and we have confined our attention to schools whose status as "big-time" participants in intercollegiate athletics is not open to serious question. If Brooker and Klastorin were correct, these features of our study should lead us to conclude with them that there is indeed a connection between athletic success and alumni giving to the annual fund. But what we have found is totally inconsistent

with such a conclusion, though it is perfectly in tune with the conclusion that
Sigelman and Carter drew.

How can this discrepancy be explained? We think that the answer may lie in
the way that Brooker and Klastorin conducted their data analysis. As noted above,
their analysis consisted of several regression runs on *pooled cross-sectional time-
series data sets*. Pooling greatly increases the number of cases being analyzed:
10 Big Ten schools observed 10 times apiece become, in effect, 100 Big Ten
schools. This multiplication of cases naturally makes it easier to uncover "significant" effects, as Brooker and Klastorin did. Still, pooling is not objectionable
in and of itself, although time-series data typically lead to violations of one of
the most crucial assumptions of ordinary least-squares (OLS) regression analysis,
that of uncorrelated error terms. In the case of a pooled cross-sectional time-
series data set, use of the OLS model puts one in the uncomfortable position of
having to assume that over time errors in prediction are uncorrelated within each
unit (in this case, schools). There are several standard ways to deal with this
problem, all of which involve the abandonment of the OLS model and the substitu-
tion of more complex statistical models. Brooker and Klastorins' decision to
employ the OLS model to analyze a pooled cross-sectional time-series data set
is thus extremely problematic—so problematic, we believe, that their conclusion
simply cannot be taken at face value.

This bring us to the second issue, which is more central in the context of the
present study. Even though we have been unable to find any connection between
athletic success and alumni giving to the university annual fund, we are certainly
not prepared to conclude that athletic victories are inefficacious as a means of
attracting voluntary contributions. There is in fact a fairly strong linkage, which
comes in the form of the correlation between success in football and contributions
made directly to intercollegiate athletic programs. It is worth repeating that success
in basketball does not have the same sort of impact—a finding which bears out
the widespread impression that most gifts to athletic departments are made by
football fans (Atwell, 1979:368).

What are the implications of this relationship between donations to the athletic
program and gridiron success? When winning or losing a football game has such
direct financial repercussions on the economic viability of the athletic program,
college football ceases to be a sport in the classical sense and becomes a battle
for financial survival instead. The resulting "win-at-all-costs" ethic must bear
much of the responsibility for the ills besetting big-time college sports.

It should also be recognized that the ability of a successful football program
to bring in sizable contributions to the athletic department is by no means an
unmixed blessing from the institution's perspective. As a quid pro quo for this
outside support, some schools have had to relinquish much internal control over
"their" athletic programs, often with less than salutary results; indeed, Atwell,
Grimes, and Lopiano (1980:54) observed some institutions that were hesitant to
encourage outside donations to their athletic programs precisely because they
feared that such donations would "bring more external influence to bear on a
program which already has a lot of such influences." The recent abandonment

of the varsity basketball program at the University of San Francisco is likely to make other schools even more anxious about outside influences, which were largely responsible for the demise of the USF program. Athletic fund raising is also very likely to compete with general university fund raising, thus draining off much-needed revenues which might otherwise be used in conjunction with the university's primary mission of educating students (Atwell, Grimes, & Lopiano, 1980:55). This does not show up very clearly in our cross-sectional data, where the correlation between the two forms of giving is, as we noted earlier, mildly positive ($r = .16$); however, there is still a fairly widespread fear that over time, a greater emphasis on athletic fund raising could detract from non-athletic fund-raising efforts. In sum, the increasingly precarious financial situation in which most athletic programs find themselves is apt to beget an emphasis on winning which has many unfortunate consequences, and also to set into opposition the economic interests of the largely independent athletic program and those of the rest of the campus.

Finally, the link between winning and giving helps to perpetuate the "inner circles" of intercollegiate sports (Crase, 1972). Every game won by a traditional powerhouse like Nebraska, Ohio State, or Texas is also a game lost by a traditional doormat like Kansas State, Northwestern, or Rice. Success brings in money, money makes it easier to succeed, and success brings in more money still; as the process feeds upon itself, the rich get richer and the poor get poorer. Seen in this light, it is altogether fitting that it was a graduate of Vanderbilt, long the weak sister of the Southeastern Conference, who authored those immortal lines, "When the One Great Scorer comes to call your name, He asks not whether you won or lost, but how you played the game." Had Grantland Rice attended any other school in the conference, he might not have ended up writing poetry, but he almost certainly would have gained some sharper insights into what really matters in big-time college sports.

References

Atwell, Robert H. 1979. "Some Reflections on College Athletics" *Educational Record*, 60 (Fall):367–73.

Atwell, Robert H., Bruce Grimes, and Donna A. Lopiano. 1980. *The Money Game: Financing Collegiate Athletics* (Washington, D.C.: American Council on Education).

Axthelm, Pete. 1980. "The Shame of College Sports," *Newsweek*, 22 September, pp. 54–59.

Barron's Educational Series, Inc. 1980. *Barron's Profiles of American Colleges, Vol I: Description of the Colleges* (Woodbury, N.Y.: Barron's Educational Series, Inc.).

Beasley, Jerry. 1974. "The State Politics of Intercollegiate Athletics," in George Hanford, *An Inquiry into the Need for and Feasibility of a National Study of Inter-*

collegiate Athletics (Washington, D.C.: American Council on Education): Appendix C.

Brooker, George, and T.D. Klastorin. 1981. "To the Victors Belong the Spoils? College Athletics and Alumni Giving," *Social Science Quarterly*, 62 (December): 744-50.

Budig, Jeanne E. 1976. "The Relationships among Intercollegiate Athletics, Enrollment, and Voluntary Support for Public Higher Education." Ph.D. dissertation, Illinois State University.

Council for Financial Aid to Education. 1981. *Voluntary Support of Education*, 1980-1981 (Washington, D.C.: CFAE).

Crase, Darrell, 1972. "The Inner Circles of Intercollegiate Football," *Sport Sociology Bulletin*, 1 (Fall):7-11.

Cryer, Lewis, A. 1981. Introduction to *NCAA Fund Raising Manual* (Shawnee Mission, Kans.: National Collegiate Athletic Association): pp. 5-6.

Ellenberger, Norman, 1982. "Tell It Like It is: We have To Make Money." *The Center Magazine*, 15 (January/February):21-22.

Frey, James H. 1981. "The Place of Athletics in the Educational Priorities of University Alumni," *Review of Sport & Leisure*, 6 (Summer): 48-64.

Koch, James V. 1971. "The Economics of 'Big-Time' Intercollegiate Athletics," *Social Science Quarterly*, 52 (September):248-60.

Middleton, Lorenzo. 1982. "Large Expenses for Sports Programs Lead More Colleges to Seek Funds from Donors," *Chronicle of Higher Education*, 3 March, pp. 5-6.

Mitchell, Maurice. 1982. "Big-Time Sports Should Be Banished from Campus," *The Center Magazine*, 15 (January/February):22-24.

Novotny, John. 1980. "Athletic Fund Raising," in *NCAA Promotion Manual* (Shawnee Mission, Kans.: National Collegiate Athletic Association): pp. 7-9.

Raiborn, Mitchell H. (1970). *Financial Analysis of Intercollegiate Athletics* (Shawnee Mission, Kans.: National Collegiate Athletic Association).

_____. 1978. *Revenues and Expenses of Intercollegiate Athletic Programs: Analysis of Financial Trends and Relationships 1970-1977* (Shawnee Mission, Kans.: National Collegiate Athletic Association).

Sharkansky, Ira. 1969. "The Utility of Elazar's Political Culture: A Research Note," *Polity*, 2 (Fall):66-83.

Sigelman, Lee, and Robert Carter. 1979. "Win One for the Giver? Alumni Giving and Big-Time College Sports," *Social Science Quarterly*, 60 (September):284-94.

Underwood, John. 1980. "Student-Athletes: The Sham, the Shame," *Sports Illustrated*, 52 (19 May):36-72.

Chapter 7

Factors Affecting Attendance of Major League Baseball: A Within-Season Analysis

John P. Marcum
University of Mississippi

Theodore N. Greenstein
University of Texas at Arlington

Marcum and Greenstein's examination of game attendance represents still another type of applied sport sociology. Although a number of factors may explain variations in sports attendance, their significant findings (that quality of an opponent and/or promotional product is less influential for a winning team than for a losing team) relates specifically to sport administrative policy. Knowledge about the relationship between team success, promotions, and attendance patterns could be invaluable to owners, general managers, and executives whose administrative philosophy is determined by profit-making ability.

Every year millions of Americans attend professional and amateur sporting events. A recent nationwide survey (Miller Brewing Company, 1983) found that 79% of those polled had attended at least one sporting event during the previous year, and a majority of men (as well as 48% of women) reported attending six or more events during that period. Despite the pervasiveness of this spectator role in American society, the forces that affect sports attendance are not completely understood. Why do some events attract more fans than others?

A variety of factors have been proposed to explain variation in sports attendance, from team quality (Demmert, 1973; Canes, 1974) to population size of the host

Paper presented at the meeting of the American Sociological Association, San Antonio, TX, 1984. The authors wish to acknowledge the assistance of Dave Fendrick of the Texas Rangers and Marty Hendin of the St. Louis Cardinals for providing some of the data reported herein, and Kofi Benefo (now of the University of Michigan) for his help in constructing the database. *Note.* From *Sociology of Sport Journal*, 2(4), pp. 314–322. Reprinted by permission.

community (Demmert, 1973; Noll, 1974) to the vagaries of weather (Siegfried & Hinshaw, 1977). In a previous paper (Greenstein & Marcum, 1981), we suggested the factors that affect attendance at sports events fall into three broad categories. The first category consists of *sociodemographic* characteristics such as population composition (age-sex structure, size, distribution), social status, and economic conditions. Also included would be the presence of competing recreational and cultural activities, such as another professional sport team (Demmert, 1973). A second group of factors concerns the *accessibility* of the event, to include relatively permanent factors such as seating availability, location of the event, and transportation facilities as well as more transient factors such as day of the week (Jones, 1969) and weather (Siegfried & Hinshaw, 1977). The third category, *performance*, includes indicators of team quality such as won-lost record and relative position in league standings, as well as individual achievement such as the presence of a star player (Davenport, 1969; Scully, 1974).

Studies of attendance at sporting events have examined a variety of professional sports: basketball (Noll & Okner, 1972), cricket (Schofield, 1983), football (Federal Communications Commission, 1978), and hockey (Jones, 1969). However, disproportionate attention has been directed at baseball (e.g., Demmert, 1973; Scully, 1974; Davenport, 1969; Becker & Suls, 1983; Hunt & Lewis, 1976; Greenstein & Marcum, 1981) for a variety of reasons. First, its form has remained largely unchanged for decades, in contrast to other popular American professional team sports (Demmert, 1973:55). Combined with the fact that the baseball season has many more contests than any other professional sport, the result is an extremely large data base for analysis. Second, there is, in Guttman's words, "the tendency of baseball toward extremes of quantification" (1978:100). Baseball officials and fans both seem to have a mania for record-keeping; statistics are readily available (e.g., Reichler, 1985) on every team and individual ever to play in the major leagues. Third, baseball tickets are typically lower than those of other professional sports, making attendance financially practical for virtually anyone. Fourth, season ticket sales in Major League Baseball comprise a relatively small proportion of total ticket sales, thus allowing greater variability in attendance levels.[1] Finally, a relatively large share of the American population is fascinated with baseball. Even though football seems to have surpassed baseball as the favorite sport of Americans, 28% of those polled in a national survey reported that they "always or usually are interested" in baseball (Miller Brewing Company, 1983).

The emphasis in previous research has been on the effect of performance on attendance. Despite a variety of measures, studies of Major League Baseball uniformly reveal a strong, positive relation between success on the field and attendance when the entire season is the unit of analysis. Demmert (1973:64-66), using data for 16 clubs from 1951-1969, found that the number of games a team finished behind the divisional leader was negatively associated with home attendance even when a variety of sociodemographic factors had been controlled. On average, teams had 25,000 fewer paying fans over the course of a season for each game they finished behind the division leader. Similarly, in an examination of major league records for 1920-1968, Canes (1974) found that a one-place rise in the standings was accompanied by an average increase of 84,000 fans in combined road and home attendance. Noll (1974) found attendance for the 1970 and 1971 seasons positively associated with the number of recent pennants won, number of star players on the team, and closeness of the pennant race (Scully, 1974; Becker & Suls, 1983; Davenport, 1969).

Our own previous research (Greenstein & Marcum, 1981) documented the importance of won-lost record for attendance using season-long performance and home attendance measures for all teams in the National League of Professional Baseball Clubs from 1946-1975 (a dataset of 282 cases in which each team-season constituted an observation). Multiple regression analyses predicting proportion of seats filled indicated that linear composites representing offense (team doubles, triples, home runs, batting average, slugging average, and stolen bases), defense (team errors, fielding average, and double plays) and pitching (team complete games, walks, strikeouts, shutouts, saves, and earned-run average)—along with won-lost percentage—accounted for about 27% of the variation in attendance. Surprisingly, however, *only* won-lost percentage had a significant direct effect on attendance. It alone accounted for just over one-fourth of the variation in attendance.

Fans, of course, do not attend "seasons," they attend individual games, and season-long attendance is a sum of the drawing power of individual games. As we noted previously (Greenstein & Marcum, 1981), many variables (e.g., weather, day of the week, promotions) likely to affect attendance fluctuate throughout the season, and to study their effects on attendance requires game-by-game information. Yet, except for the occasional study of a star pitcher's effect on attendance at those games he starts,[2] game-by-game analyses of baseball attendance have been lacking. This omission has been attributed both to the difficulty of acquiring data for each game (Davenport, 1969) and to the need, once acquired, of "laboriously analyzing attendance for every team for every game during the season" (Scully, 1974:918). Although we are unable to overcome these problems entirely in the present research, we undertake a beginning step toward narrowing the focus (and unit of analysis) from the *season* to the individual *game*.

We analyze game-by-game records for two teams from the 1982 season— the Texas Rangers of the American League and the St. Louis Cardinals of the National League. The research is exploratory, and we make no formal hypotheses. While it would be unwise to generalize from this limited dataset, the Cardinals and Rangers had very different seasons in 1982, and a comparison of the relative effects of different factors on these two teams' home attendance should tell us a great deal. The Cardinals won their division by three games and defeated Milwaukee in seven games to win the World Series,[3] while Texas lost 98 games and finished 29 games out of first place. Perhaps even more important in an analysis of attendance, the Cardinals were in first place for over three-fourths of their home openings in a hotly contested race whereas the Rangers were never competitive.

The data for this study comes from a variety of sources. Some of the data— attendance figures and information on team promotions—was provided by the club offices. Team performance information was gathered from published box scores and league standings. Weather information was obtained from the official NOAA [National Oceanic and Atmospheric Administration] publication *Local Climatological Data* (1983).

We have selected a variety of independent variables based on previous research (see especially Demmert, 1973; Noll, 1974; Jones, 1969; Greenstein & Marcum, 1981). Some variables that might otherwise have been included were omitted due to practical considerations, mainly difficulty of measurement. A good example would be other events taking place in the metropolitan area that might siphon off potential baseball fans. However, Noll (1974) notes that population provides a proxy for competing entertainments. Because the populations of Dallas-Fort Worth and St. Louis are so similar in size—3,821,622 and 3,684,727, respectively, based on 1980 census data (U.S. Bureau of the Census, 1981) for counties within a 100-mile radius of Arlington and Busch Memorial stadiums—this factor is unlikely to differ significantly for the two clubs. Further, local television coverage of road games, a practice found by Demmert (1973:69) to be associated with lower home attendance, was similar for the two clubs during the 1982 season in that both clubs televised about half of their away games via commercial television.

Method

The data for this research consists of one observation for each home opening for the Texas Rangers (78 openings) and the St. Louis Cardinals (80 openings) for the 1982 regular season.[4] Measures of 10 factors that could reasonably be expected to affect attendance were gathered: day of the week,[5] type of team promotion, opposing team, opponent's won-lost percentage, opponent's games behind first place, home team's won-lost percentage, home team's games behind first place, home team's record over the previous 10 decisions, weather conditions, and whether the opening involved a doubleheader.

The dependent variable in these analyses is attendance, which, by necessity, is operationalized in slightly different ways for the two teams. American League attendance data are reported in terms of total ticket sales (i.e., those who purchase tickets but are not present in the stadium are included in the attendance total), while National League figures are for turnstile count only (no-shows are not included in the attendance total even though they may have purchased a reserved seat ticket). This difference should not present a major problem for interpretation, however; inspection of data available from the Rangers organization (not reported here) indicates that the American League attendance figures overstate turnstile count data only slightly.

To allow for direct comparisons between the two ballclubs' data, we standardized the attendance figures by dividing by stadium capacity. This is especially important because Busch Stadium in St. Louis officially seats 50,222 in its baseball configuration while Arlington Stadium seats 41,284.

Dummy-variable coding was used for categorical variables such as day of the week, opponent, and so forth. Weather conditions were coded as 0 = bad (temperature 5 degrees lower than normal in April and September, 5 degrees higher than normal in other months; rain or other inclement weather), and 1 = other. Promotions were classified into two categories: major promotions involved major giveaways such as Cap Night or Bat Night; minor promotions were all others. The Cardinals held 8 major and 36 minor promotions; the Rangers, 7 major and 34 minor promotions.

Results

Table 7.1 presents data on the distribution of the attendance variable for both ballclubs. The median proportion of seats filled was .499 for St. Louis and .310 for Texas, with means of .526 and .358, respectively.

Table 7.1   Distribution of Proportion of Seats Filled, 1982 Season

Percentile	Cardinals	Rangers
90	.773	.705
75	.630	.419
50 (median)	.499	.310
25	.396	.220
10	.314	.205

Table 7.2 presents results of the multiple regression analyses for both clubs. These are unstandardized multiple regression coefficients; because the dependent variable has been rescaled as the *proportion* of seats filled, the coefficients are interpretable as the increase in proportion of seats filled attributable to a specific factor, controlling for the effects of all other factors in the model. For example, Table 7.2 shows that the unstandardized regression coefficient for the weather factor had a value of .052 for the Rangers' data. This means that there was an increase of 5.2% in seats filled on days with good weather as opposed to days with poor weather. The asterisk next to this value indicates that the significance test for this particular coefficient shows that it is significantly different from zero at the .05 probability level.

It is interesting to note that only two of the factors (in addition to the intercept value) are significantly different from zero for both ballclubs: Saturday attendance and major promotions. If the opponent variable is coded into a single factor, it also shows a significant coefficient although it is not directly interpretable and

Table 7.2   Unstandardized Regression Coefficients Predicting Proportion of Seats Filled, 1982 Season

Factor	Cardinals	Rangers
Intercept	.458*	.320*
Sunday	.086	.106**
Monday	.024	.051
Tuesday	.003	–
Wednesday	–	.036
Thursday	.066	.033
Friday	.083	.093*
Saturday	.220***	.157***
Games behind	.008	−.001
Percentage	−.611*	−.111
Last 10	.316*	.114
Opponent's record	−.013	−.429*
Opponent's behind	−.002	−.007
Weather	.008	.052*
Twinbills	.325*	.076
Minor promotions	.049	.060*
Major promotions	.277***	.471***
R^2	.66	.88

*$p < .05$.

**$p < .01$.

***$p < .001$ for test of significance from zero.

so is not included here. The net increase in attendance attributable to opponent is about 3% for the Cardinals and just over 6% for the Rangers.

The overall fit of the model to the data is quite good for both ballclubs[6]; the 10 factors account for 66% of the variation in Cardinal attendance and 88% of the variation in the Rangers' data. Both of these values are significantly different from zero. To get a better idea of the relative effects of these factors, Table 7.3 presents the results of the multiple regression analyses in a different way. The entries in this table represent the proportion of variation in attendance attributable to a particular factor. For example, a little over 14% of the variation in Cardinals' attendance is accounted for by the opponent factor (after controlling for the effects of other factors in the model), while opponent accounts for about twice that amount —28.7%—of the variation in Rangers' attendance. Table 7.3 shows that three factors—day of the week, opponent, and type of promotion—account for the bulk of the explained variation in attendance for both clubs. Nearly 60% of the variation

Table 7.3   Proportion of Variation in Attendance Explained by 11 Major Factors, 1982 Season

Factor	Cardinals	Rangers
Opponent	.143	.287
Day of the week	.289	.211
Games behind	.000	.015
Percentage	.004	.004
Last 10	.045	.004
Opponent's record	.001	.010
Opponent's behind	.008	.005
Weather	.000	.011
Twin bills	.030	.003
Minor promotions	.005	.005
Major promotions	.147	.335
Total variation explained (R^2)	.66	.88

in Cardinals' home attendance and over 80% of the variation in Rangers' home attendance is attributable to just these three factors.

Discussion

Perhaps the most interesting finding in these data is that most of the variation in attendance can be attributed to three factors: opponent, day of the week, and promotions. While the order of effects is different—promotions are the single most important factor in the Rangers' data whereas day of the week contributes the most in the Cardinals' analysis—nearly all the explained variation in both datasets can be attributed to these three variables. None of the other factors accounts for as much as 5% of the variation in either dataset.

In comparing the differences in effects for the two clubs, we find that promotions and opposing team have far more effect on attendance for the Rangers. Considering the poor season that the Rangers had, this is not unexpected. As Canes (1974) has observed, quality of the visiting team likely also relates positively to attendance, and for a poor home team the visitors' won-lost records may take on greater importance in fans' decisions about whether to attend particular games. Similarly, performance over the previous 10 decisions had a significant effect on Cardinal attendance, but not for the Rangers, suggesting that nonperformance measures have much more effect on attendance for losing teams than for winners. When a team is doing well, attendance will be good regardless of which club is in town or what the management is giving away at the ballpark. When a team is doing poorly, however, fans need an extra incentive to show up; thus, giveaways and first-place opponents increase attendance.

Another interesting point is the difference in total explained variation for the two ballclubs. The 10 factors account for nearly 90% of the variation in Ranger attendance but less than 70% for the Cardinals. Again, we believe the difference in team performance may explain this finding. In particular, some writers (Davenport, 1969:6-7; Demmert, 1973:14-15) have argued that the existence of a close pennant race, independent of won-lost record, increases attendance. While prior empirical evidence is mixed (Demmert, 1973:67, fails to find support for this hypothesis while Davenport, 1969:6-7, does), our results seem consistent with this argument: Notice how much larger the intercept term is for the Cardinals' data than for the Rangers'. At the same time, past performance may be more important for Cardinals' as opposed to Rangers' fans. With its longer and more successful history, St. Louis may attract fans based on memories of past Cardinal championships, a memory Ranger fans do not have (Becker & Suls, 1983).

We advise caution in extrapolating these findings to other teams because there are major differences between the Cardinals and the Rangers beyond won-lost percentage. For example, differences in importance of day of the week are probably better understood in terms of the Cardinals' greater regional following. For many fans, distance from the ballpark precludes attending any games except on weekends, and such long excursions to St. Louis are often planned well in advance of the actual game and hence are relatively unaffected by current won-lost record or weather at game time.

One other issue is raised by the rather high values of explained variation for these data. We are already accounting for well over 60% of the variation in the Cardinals' attendance and nearly 90% for the Rangers'. Such high values lead us to suspect there are probably few, if any, other variables we could add to this model that would produce an appreciable increase in explained variation. Adding such esoteric factors as whether a star player is nearing a record or who the starting pitchers are will not likely increase the amount of explained variation appreciably. Rather, our future analyses will focus on interactions among these variables. Such analyses must await larger datasets, however, because even a limited study of interaction effects will require a model with a large number of terms and a corresponding decrease in the degrees of freedom term.

In our future research on this topic, we would like to study the effects of sociodemographic factors on attendance. How have population shifts affected attendance of Major League Baseball? What about changes in ethnic and racial composition, both in the stands and on the playing field? What is the role of economic factors such as ticket prices and unemployment? How does accessibility to the stadium affect attendance? Finally, while research suggests that Major League Baseball attendance is not unique (Jones, 1969; Noll & Okner, 1972), amateur and minor league professional sports have yet to be subjected to the same scrutiny. It would be useful to extend this research to all levels of sport.

References

Becker, M.A. and J. Suls
    1983   "Take me out to the ballgame: the effects of objective, social, and temporal performance information on attendance at Major League Baseball games." Journal of Sport Psychology, 5:302-313.

Canes, M.E.
    1974   "The social benefits of restrictions on team quality." Chapter 3 in R.G. Noll (ed.), Government and the Sports Business. Washington: The Brookings Institution.

Davenport, D.S.
    1969   "Collusive competition in Major League Baseball: its theory and institutional development." The American Economist, 13:6-30.

Demmert, H.G.
    1973   The Economics of Professional Team Sports. Lexington, MA: D.C. Heath.

Federal Communications Commission
    1978   The Effect of the Sports Anti-Blackout Law. Fifth Annual Report. Washington: Government Printing Office.

Greenstein, T.N. and J.P. Marcum
    1981   "Factors affecting attendance of Major League Baseball: I. team performance." Review of Sport and Leisure, 6:21-33.

Guttman, A.
    1978   From Ritual to Record. New York: Columbia University Press.

Hunt, J.W. Jr. and K.A. Lewis
    1976   "Dominance, recontracting, and the reverse clause: Major League Baseball." The American Economic Review, 66:936-943.

Jones, J.C.H.
    1969   "The economics of the National Hockey League." Canadian Journal of Economics, 2:1-20.

Miller Brewing Company
    1983   The Miller Lite Report on American Attitudes Toward Sport. Milwaukee: Miller Brewing Company.

National Oceanic and Atmospheric Administration
    1983   Local Climatological Data. Washington, DC: Government Printing Office.

Noll, R.G.
    1974   "Attendance and price setting." Chapter 4 in R.G. Noll (ed.), Government and the Sports Business. Washington: The Brookings Institute.

Noll, R.G. and B.A. Okner
  1972 Professional Basketball. Testimony before the subcommittee on Antitrust
        and Monopoly of the Committee on the Judiciary, United States Senate
        5:2373, A Bill to Allow the Merger of Two or More Professional Basket-
        ball Leagues. September 21, 1971. Washington: Government Printing
        Office.
Reichler, J.L. (ed).
  1985 The Baseball Encyclopedia (6th edition). New York: Macmillan.
Schofield, J.A.
  1983 "The demand for cricket: the case of the John Player League." Applied
        Economics, 15:283-296.
Scully, G.W.
  1974 "Pay and performance in Major League Baseball." The American
        Economic Review, 64:915-930.
Siegfried, J.J. and C.E. Hinshaw
  1977 "Professional football and the anti-blackout law." Journal of Communi-
        cation, 27:169-174.
U.S. Bureau of the Census
  1981 Census of Population and Housing, 1980: Summary File 1C
        (microfiche). Washington: U.S. Bureau of the Census.

Notes

[1] Jones (1969) reports that the Toronto and Montreal National Hockey League teams sell out their respective arenas year after year, and attendance at professional football games is so high that studies have focused on "no-shows" rather than on attendance per se (Siegfried & Hinshaw, 1977).

[2] Davenport (1969), for example, found that during the 1966 season Sandy Koufax (with a 27-9 record) increased attendance by an average of 6,000 at home and 7,000 on the road per game.

[3] Our analysis is limited to regular season play.

[4] An opening is a game or pair of games for which a separate admission is charged. Most openings are single games, and most doubleheaders are a single opening.

[5] Time of game (day or night) was excluded because of potential multicollinearity problems with day of the week. Texas plays few day games and, for both clubs, day games were concentrated on weekends.

[6] The opponent variable does not appear in this table due to the noncomparability of opponents for the two teams. Opponent was coded as a series of dummy variables for each team and included in the analysis, however, so the effects reported in Table 7.2 control for the effects of opponent. See Table 7.3 for an estimate of the amount of variation in attendance attributable to the opponent variable.

Chapter 8

Differences in Childhood Socialization Influences of Women Involved in Sport and Women Not Involved in Sport

Susan L. Greendorfer
University of Illinois at Urbana-Champaign

Using a social learning paradigm to better understand female socialization into sport, Greendorfer identifies the type of reference group influence that determines whether women become involved in sport. If family encouragement and positive influences during early childhood have long-lasting effects on participation, then the absence of encouragement or negative influences could lead to a life of noninvolvement in physical activity. Although the connection between this study and application may seem obscure, a closer look suggests that female nonparticipation is viewed as a "social problem," and findings from this study can provide practitioners with valuable information for overcoming barriers to nonparticipation. For example, those interested in broad-based participation of all children in physical activity may learn that careful publicity needs to be directed to individuals and groups who provide social support for female participation. Thus, in addition to appealing to the clients themselves (in this case, young females), practitioners may have to educate parents to encourage their daughters' participation.

Female sport socialization has been a relatively neglected area of study in sociology sport. Consequently, very little is known about the process by which women do or do not become involved in sport. Not only is there a dearth of empirical data pertaining to factors which influence active sport participation of women,

Note. From "Differences in Childhood Socialization Influences of Women Involved in Sport," by S.L. Greendorfer. In *The Dimensions of Sport Sociology* (pp. 59–72) by M. Krotee (Ed.), 1979, Champaign, IL: Leisure Press. Reprinted by permission.

111

but those social learning factors which may contribute to female nonparticipation have been virtually unexplored.

To date there are two research traditions which could be of assistance in filling this knowledge gap. The first involves the women and sport literature of the early 1970s in which several theoretical notions were hypothesized relative to the role and sex of siblings, presence of role models, and birth order (Hauge, 1973; Portz, 1973; Zoble, 1973). To some extent these hypotheses suggested sex-typing; however, focus for the topic more often focused on masculinity-feminity dimensions or self-concept and attitudes (Ziegler, 1973). Despite the absence of empirical data as well as any type of socialization framework relative to these notions, current thinking about female sport participation continues to be dominated by beliefs which arose from this tradition.

The second research orientation has been more substantive since it has placed equal emphasis on theory as well as empirical evidence. Most work from this perspective has utilized a social learning paradigm in order to investigate specific factors which influence active sport involvement (Kenyon, 1969, 1970; Kenyon & McPherson, 1973, 1974). Unfortunately, the majority of such research has focused on the male athlete. Only to a limited extent have theoretical notions from this paradigm been utilized to study female sport participation (Greendorfer, 1974, 1976; Snyder & Spreitzer, 1973, 1976). Despite a recent shift toward a social-role social-system approach to the study of sport socialization, there has not been a break with the social learning tradition, in that major concepts— such as significant other influence, value structure, and similar notions borrowed from role theory—still retain a primary focus. This approach simply represents a more dynamic conceptualization of the complex social system interactions which may influence sport involvement.

It would appear, then, that one means by which this knowledge gap pertaining to female sport socialization can be filled would be to build upon the existing work from the social learning perspective as well as incorporating the most valuable notions available from the women and sport literature. Although there is an unevenness in research, certain predominant themes can be clearly identified from both perspectives. One such theme focuses on significant other influence, particularly the role of the family. According to both Malumphy (1970) and McPherson (1978) family support would be essential for female athletes. Some empirical data are available; however results are not clear, since specific findings differ from study to study. Perhaps the inconsistency is a consequence of the nature of the questions asked, the nature of the population sampled, or the type of statistical treatment performed on the data.

For example, Malumphy's data indicated that family influence was a major factor in college women's competing in sport (1970). Not only did the typical female athlete have family approval for her participation and competition, but there was a history of family participation in sports as well. Similarly, in a study of physical activity among Canadian women Hall (1976) found that two major determinants of activity level when younger were enjoyment of school physical education experiences and involvement of previous significant others. In addition she found that adult or present active involvement was a function of activity level when younger as well as *present family* involvement. This finding suggests another aspect of family influence—spouse's participation level—which should also be included in research approaches. Furthermore, Hall concluded that in order for a woman to become involved in and to continue in sport she had to have been continually in an environment which was highly supportive of her activities (Hall, 1976).

Additional descriptive data from two investigations of female intercollegiate sport participants also tend to support the notion that family is a primary agent of socialization (Greendorfer, 1974, 1976). In the first study family was reported as the original stimulus for sport involvement by 39.5% of the women (another 31% indicated neighborhood, whereas 23.6% mentioned the school). In the second, 46.5% indicated that family was responsible for initial sport interest (21% indicated school). More interesting, however, is the fact that upon more powerful statistical treatment the family was not a primary socialization agent. Specifically, in the first investigation peers as well as family accounted for childhood sport involvement (and this as the only life cycle state in which family was a significant influence); whereas the follow-up study revealed that family was not a significant factor during any of the three life cycle stages (Greendorfer, 1976).

In contrast, in their analysis of family influence as a predictor of sport involvement Snyder and Spreitzer (1973) discovered a positive linear relationship between parental encouragement and most indicators of sport involvement for both sexes. Also, there was a tendency for like-sexed parents to have greater influence on respondents' behavioral involvement than opposite-sexed parents. It should be kept in mind that this inconsistency in results may be a function of the sample frame.

Another relevant consideration of female sport involvement concerns childhood socialization into sport and the social milieu in which the child is socialized. According to McPherson, Guppy, and McKay (1976), regardless of motor talent, unless children are exposed to social systems in which they have the opportunity to engage in sport and receive positive sanctions, it is unlikely that games and sport will become a salient aspect of lifestyle (McPherson, Guppy, & McKay, 1976:161). Similarly, a child must interpret the sport situation as having positive consequences if she or he is to become involved in sport (Orlick, 1974). Unfortunately very little research attention has focused on children's sport socialization. Orlick (1972) identified three factors which may be responsible for learning sport roles: role models, expectancies, and sport-related reinforcement. More specifically, Orlick found that boys who began to participate in organized sports at an early age had parents who were or had been effective role models. These boys came from an environment in which parents actually participated in sport. Similarly, Watson (1975) noted that children perceive their parents as being an important reference group for sport involvement.

Childhood environmental settings of females who participate in intercollegiate sport reflect a similar orientation. For example, Greendorfer (1974) found that during childhood a majority of the girls' fathers (81%) and mothers (70%) actively participated in sport; however, as the girls grew older parental participation declined. This pattern was also found in the replication study; data indicated that 88% of both parents participated in sport when the female participants were children. Data from a recent exploratory study of children's socialization into sport further support the strong family environment hypothesis, particularly when active participation of parents and their participation with their children is concerned (Greendorfer & Lewko, 1978).

However, the family is composed of a variety of relationships and social interactions. Nevertheless, the absence of specific family members or siblings, or of one parent for that matter, has received minimal empirical attention. In contrast, theoretical consideration of sibling-sex, birth order, and family size has received much attention in the women and sport literature. Limited evidence from Landers (1970, 1971) and Sutton-Smith, Roberts, and Rosenberg (1964) suggests that the influence of siblings is an important family structural variable for sport participation, since siblings close in age interact in play groups throughout the socialization years. Unfortunately, the disproportionate amount of attention focusing on the role of siblings may have too easily convinced sport scientists that at least one, if not all three, of the available hypotheses would be of critical importance in explaining female sport involvement (Hauge, 1973; Landers, 1970; Portz, 1973; Zoble, 1973). The use of modeling theory (in which sibling-similarity and sibling-opposite hypotheses are advocated), structural balance theory (which incorporates a sibling-parental influence contingency), and the conformity hypotheses (in which parental treatment, not sibling sex, is considered) assures the researcher that his or her data can be logically explained regardless of outcome.

Despite the popularity of these various notions, evidence for the sibling-similarity hypothesis is not consistently supportive (Portz, 1973), nor is that for the sibling-opposite hypothesis (Gould & Landers, 1972). More recently, an explicit linkage with modeling concepts has been made. Specifically, McPherson (1978) has suggested that a female may become involved in sport by seeing her mother or older female siblings participate or compete in sport. Yet a recent exploratory study on children's sport socialization revealed that parents rather than siblings were predictors of girls' sport participation (Greendorfer & Lewko, 1978). Moreover, a detailed analysis indicated that the father was the sole family member accounting for girls' sport participation, whereas fathers and brothers were significant influences on the boys.

Thus, the nature of influence as well as specific identification of socializing agents appears quite ambiguous where female sport involvement is concerned. Rather than continue in past research traditions, there seems to be a need for consistency in investigating significant other influence relative to female sport involvement. Furthermore, the time has come to conceptually discard those notions which clutter the literature and confuse understanding. The use of a theoretical framework along with a comparative research design would be of great assistance. However, sport scientists have not made ample use of a comparison group in the examination of either male or female socialization into sport. How do we know that family influence and ordinal position data obtained on athletes are any different from that of nonathletes?

Therefore, the purpose of the present study is to examine childhood socialization experiences of two distinct groups of women; those who were involved and those who were not involved in intercollegiate sport. Several hypotheses were generated in order to make comparisons. Specifically:

1. The influence of family is greater for athletes than nonathletes.
2. The influence of parents is greater for athletes than nonathletes.
3. The influence of father is greater for athletes than nonathletes.
4. The influence of peers is greater for athletes than nonathletes.
5. There is no difference in mother's influence between athletes and nonathletes.
6. There is no difference in sibling influence between athletes and nonathletes.
7. There is no difference in teacher influence between athletes and nonathletes.
8. There is no difference between athletes and nonathletes in birth order or ordinal position in the family.
9. There is no difference in the sex of siblings of athletes and nonathletes.

Definition of the Sample

The total population of female intercollegiate participants at the University of Illinois[1] was selected as subjects for this study. Data were obtained from 110 athletes, which represented a 92.5% response. For the noninvolved women, a purposive stratified sampling technique was used in order to strive for a balanced number of women enrolled in various colleges at each undergraduate year level at the University.[2] Data from 224 women were obtained.

Although it is not the primary intention of this paper to challenge existent definitions of sport and athletics (Loy, 1968, 1978), some critical clarification is necessary with reference to the samples. The criterion for involved women was membership on one of several intercollegiate teams. However, institutionalized sport can be represented by more than one form or type of organized activity; membership in one domain does not preclude membership in another. Consequently, despite the noninvolvement classification of one sample, analyses of the data revealed that these women were actively participating in some sort of physical activity they considered to be sport. Thus, definition of the sample frame eliminated a more thorough consideration of the participation phenomenon that exists for women. This presents two conceptual implications for sociology of sport: 1) a need to define a term such as noninvolvement more sociologically, and 2) a need to broaden current conceptualizations which now exist—namely, sport and athletics. This existing terminology is narrow in scope and represents a rather ethnocentric approach. That is, it is a male elaboration of a more general social phenomenon and as such it considers only males and elite female athletes. Current definitional notions have extremely limited or omitted completely those forms of institutionalized physical activity of young girls and many women. Unless a more broad conceptualization of the participation phenomenon is considered, the bulk of female sport participation (which may be greater than existing research suggests) will continue to be ignored.

The Questionnaire

A modified version of an instrument designed to tap sport socialization concepts was used in this investigation (Greendorfer & Lewko, 1978). Questions dealt with active sport involvement during childhood as well as at the present time. Additional questions focused on specific agents of socialization (i.e., mother, father, sisters, brothers, peers, teachers, etc.), the nature of their influence, and their interactions with the subjects when the subjects were children relative to sport behaviors. Theoretical constructs were organized according to the social systems of family, peers, and school as well as their derivatives (i.e., parents, siblings, etc.) In addition values toward sport construct along with a construct referring to individual agents were created. These constructs represented summed totals of appropriate responses in each question category. Values of items were scaled so the more active the child the higher her sport involvement score; the stronger the influence from particular agents the higher the construct score for these agents.

Results

The descriptive data depict underlying patterns of differences between the two groups. Moreover, such data are of assistance in suggesting in-depth understanding of the sport socialization process. Ultimately, the goal is to move toward explanation and prediction through utilization of existing or new conceptual frameworks.

As observed in Table 8.1, both groups appear quite similar relative to general characteristics.

Likewise, the data pertaining to family background characteristics also reveal similarity (see Table 8.2). Whereas both groups represent a middle class or above socio-economic background, a tendency toward upper class overrepresentation is accentuated in the group composed of athletes. This pattern supports previous research concerned with social class backgrounds on both male (Kenyon & McPherson, 1973) and female athletes (Greendorfer, 1976). Moreover, data relating to religious background supports notions suggested by Luschen (1970) and Seppanen (1970). Specifically, there appears to be a disproportionate representation of Protestants among athletes.

The data in Table 8.3 reflect group responses to specific questionnaire items. (In each case the percentages indicate total responses from the "very much" and "a lot" categories.)

As observed in the first few items as well as in the ability and values categories,

Table 8.1   General Characteristics of the Two Samples

Characteristic	Athletes ($N = 110$)	Nonathletes ($N = 244$)
Age range	17-23 years	17-26 years
Mean age	19.3 years	19.3 years
Year in school		
Freshman	40%	32%
Sophomore	18%	25%
Junior	19%	21%
Senior	21%	20%
Major field (top 5)		
Physical education	23%	8%
Business	11%	13.5%
Leisure studies	9%	1%
Education	4%	9%
English/language	2%	7%
Biological science	7%	7%

Table 8.2   Family Background Characteristics of the Two Samples

Characteristic	Athletes ($N = 110$)	Nonathletes ($N = 244$)
Religion		
Catholic	40%	43%
Protestant	53%	38.5%
Jewish	2%	12%
None/other	5%	4%
Father's education		
Below high school	3%	4%
High school graduate	13%	15.5%
Beyond graduation	83%	67%
Missing data	1%	13.5%
Father's occupation		
Duncan SE 1		
Low (9-40)	3.5%	16%
Medium (41-67)	12%	33.5%
High (68-96)	81%	36.5%
Missing data	3.5%	13%

there are some distinct differences between groups. In contrast, the agency of first involvement reflects a more balanced pattern. Yet, it could be hypothesized that when the family is low in influence another social system takes on greater importance; in this case it would be the school. Verification of such a hypothesis

Table 8.3   Comparison of Childhood Influences*

Category	Athletes ($N = 110$)	Nonathletes ($N = 244$)
Amount of games played	92%	75%
Learned skills easily	90%	67%
Sports as very important	91%	70%
Agency of first involvement		
Family	38%	27.5%
Peers	41%	45%
School	13%	24%
Park/recreation	5.5%	3%
Ability in sports		
Very good	88%	59%
Not good at all	2.7%	7.4%
Values toward sport		
Self	83%	63%
Father	30%	20%
Mother	33%	12%
Brothers	30%	24%
Sisters	23%	15%
Friends	40%	41%
Teachers	21%	22%
Encouragement to participate		
From father	50%	30%
From mother	43%	18%
From brothers	43%	26%
From sisters	26%	19%
From friends	52%	47.5%
From teachers	66%	55%
Person who most discouraged		
Father	7%	7%
Mother	19%	28%
Brothers	2%	7%
Sisters	5.5%	4%
Friends	15.5%	4%
Teachers	19%	16%
P.E. teachers	7%	10%

*Percentages based on "very much and a lot."

could lead to further notions relative to the "completeness" of the sport socialization process under such circumstances. For example, previous research on female athletes indicates that between 55% and 60% of the women had no school sport program (Greendorfer, 1977). Could the existence of noninvolved women be attributed to one or both of these factors?

Further examination of the data indicates childhood presence of a strong value structure toward being good in sport for the athletes. With the exception of sisters and teachers, a moderately positive value structure toward sport appears to characterize the athletes' socializing agents. Such is not the case for the nonathletes. Of interest, the strongest encouragement or value orientation toward sport for this group comes from peers.

Identification of the significant others who most discouraged these women is also of interest. Although mothers represent a fairly strong negative influence in both groups, they appear to be disproportionally so for the nonathletes. Also, the physical education teacher is not necessarily a positive influence for either group. Another obvious fact is that female athletes are not totally surrounded by positive influences. There is ample evidence here to suggest that some socializing agents discourage their participation. Perhaps under such circumstances certain agents become more prestigious or counterbalance the negative influence of other agents. There is evidence, for example, that the father may be more important than the mother (Lamb, 1976); and as mentioned earlier this has been verified in children's sport socialization research (Greendorfer & Lewko, 1978).

Data in Table 8.4 relate to the first four hypotheses which predicted that family, parents, father, and peer influence will be greater for athletes than nonathletes. Several t-tests were performed to test these hypotheses. Relative to the first hypothesis, there was a significant difference in mean family influence of athletes as compared to nonathletes. Comparison of mean parental influence between groups revealed a significant difference in the hypothesized direction for Hypothesis Two also. The mean influence of fathers was also significantly greater for athletes. Thus, the first three hypotheses were not rejected. However, Hypothesis Four which predicted significant differences between groups relative to peer influence was rejected, since the t-tests indicated no statistically significant differences. In summary, athletes receive significantly greater influence from family, parents,

Table 8.4 t-Test Data Related to Hypotheses One, Two, Three, and Four

Variable	Sample	N	Mean	SD	SE	t-Value	df	Probability*
Family	Athletes	110	60.42	12.91	1.23	3.32	189	$p < .0000$
	Nonathletes	244	55.14	11.42	0.73			
Parents	Athletes	110	28.83	7.10	0.68	3.32	176	$p < .0005$
	Nonathletes	244	26.27	5.77	0.37			
Father	Athletes	110	13.77	3.85	0.37	1.89	180	$p < .03$
	Nonathletes	244	12.97	3.22	0.21			
Peers	Athletes	110	19.17	3.65	0.35	−1.15	352	$p < .267$ NS
	Nonathletes	244	19.66	3.82	0.24			

*One-tail probability.

and father than do nonathletes. However, peer influence among athletes and nonathletes does not differ significantly.

Hypotheses Five, Six, and Seven predicted no significant differences between
groups relative to influence from mothers, siblings, and teachers, each individually
considered. Results of the t-tests from these hypotheses were contained in Table
8.5. Hypotheses Five and Six were rejected since the t-tests indicate significant
differences between groups; namely, athletes receive greater influence from
mothers and siblings than do nonathletes. Hypothesis Seven was not rejected since
differences between the groups relative to teacher influence were not statistically
significant.

Table 8.5 t-Test Data Related to Hypotheses Five, Six, and Seven

Variable	Sample	N	Mean	SD	SE	t-Value	df	Probability*
Mother	Athletes	110	15.05	4.26	0.41	3.79	179	$p < .000$
	Nonathletes	244	13.29	3.54	0.23			
Siblings	Athletes	110	31.21	8.12	0.77	2.73	352	$p < .007$
	Nonathletes	244	28.60	8.40	0.54			
Teacher	Athletes	110	11.955	2.49	0.24	0.48	352	$p < .630$ NS
	Nonathletes	244	11.82	2.41	0.15			

*Two-tail probability.

Perhaps one factor contributing to rejection of Hypothesis Five (mother influence) was the amount of discouragement enhibited by mothers in the nonathletes
group. Such an explanation needs further investigation, however. Nevertheless,
the mother certainly seems to be a significant socializing agent who may partially
account for differences in the sport socialization of women.

In order to examine the relationship between birth order and female sport participation a preliminary set of categories was established. The groups were compared
according to whether they were an only child, first born, middle born, or youngest
child. The chi-square analysis in Table 8.6 indicates that there is a nonsignificant
relationship between ordinal position and sport involvement. The results of this
comparison should strongly suggest that patterns found or hypothesized from the
literature may be "red herrings" as far as female sport participation is concerned.
To suggest a tendency toward significance regarding this relationship would require
a lowering of critical values beyond traditional statistical interpretation. Therefore,
the null hypothesis of independence between variables is accepted.

Hypothesis Nine predicted no differences between the groups relative to the
sex of siblings. The chi-square analysis in Table 8.7 reveals a nonsignificant
relationship between sport involvement and presence of only brothers, only older
brothers, only sisters, only older sisters. Further analysis seems unwarranted

Table 8.6   Comparison of Samples Relative to Ordinal Position

	Percentage				
Subjects	Only child	Firstborn child	Middle child	Youngest child	Total
Nonathletes	83.3	78.5	61.4	68.0	68.9
Athletes	16.7	21.5	38.6	32.0	31.1
Total	100.0	100.0	100.0	100.0	100.0
	(N^56)	(N^579)	(N^588)	(N^5181)	(N^5354)

Note. $\chi^2 = 6.378.$ $df = 3.$

$*p < .094$ NS.

Table 8.7   Comparison of Samples Relative to Sex of Siblings

	Percentage				
Subjects	Brothers only	Older brothers only	Sisters only	Older sisters only	Total
Nonathletes	72.7	76.5	75.0	79.2	75.5
Athletes	27.3	23.5	25.0	20.8	25.5
Total	100.0	100.0	100.0	100.0	100.0
	(N^544)	(N^551)	(N^536)	(N^524)	(N^5155)

Note. $\chi^2 = 0.388.$ $df = 3.$

$*p < .943$ NS.

considering nonsignificance of the relationship. Again, these data suggest that certain notions regarding siblings and female sport involvement should probably be discarded.

Although this paper covers much ground, albeit rather superficially, it is hoped that some points will be considered in greater depth in future research. Some of the following concerns are offered as suggested research directions:

1. There is a need to re-evaluate existent definitions of sport and athletics in order to incorporate the social phenomenon of physical activity that applies to both sexes. A more broad-based definition might be adopted (Lueschen, 1970).
2. There is a need to employ comparative research designs, specifically those which focus on nonathletes or the noninvolved. To better understand sport involvement it would seem there is a need to understand the reciprocal phenomenon as well.

3. More in-depth analysis of female socialization into sport is needed. It is imperative to utilize a theoretical framework and operate from an empirical knowledge base rather than an untested belief system.
4. There is a need for continued growth in theory building. Sociology of sport cannot afford to mechanically accept without challenge those notions or concepts which are relatively static or lead to conceptually blind alleys. Challenge of existing paradigms and focusing on more dynamic models will improve the state of the field and increase the knowledge base, particularly where female sport participation is concerned.

References

Gould, D., and Landers, D. Dangerous sport participation: A replication of Nisbett's birth order findings. Paper presented at the annual meeting of the North American Society for the Psychology of Sport and Physical Activity, Houston, March 1972.

Greendorfer, S. The nature of female socialization into sport: A study of selected college women's sport participation. Unpublished doctoral dissertation, University of Wisconsin, 1974.

Greendorfer, S. A social learning approach to female sport involvement. Paper presented at American Psychological Association Convention, Washington, D.C., September 1976.

Greendorfer, S. Sex differences in sport involvement: A case of nonconscious inequity. *Sex Equity in Illinois Schools: Problems, Research, and Remedies.* Springfield, IL: Illinois Office of Education, 1977, pp. 93-121..

Greendorfer, S., and J. Lewko. The role of family members in sport socialization of children. *Research Quarterly*, 1978, 49, 146-152.

Hall, M.A. Sport and physical activity in the lives of Canadian women. In R. Gruneau and J. Albinson (Eds.), *Canadian Sport: Sociological Perspectives.* Don Mills, Ontario: Addision-Wesley (Canada Ltd), 1976.

Hauge, A. The influence of the family on female sport participation. In D. Harris (Ed.), *DGWS Research Reports: Women in Sports.* Vol 2. Washington, D.C.: AAHPER Publications, 1973.

Kenyon, G. Explaining sport involvement. Paper presented at Fall Conference of Eastern Association of Physical Education for College Women, Lake Placid, New York, October 1969.

Kenyon, G. The use of path analysis in sport sociology with special reference to involvement socialization. *International Review of Sport Sociology.* 1970, 5, 191-203.

Kenyon, G., and McPherson, B. Becoming involved in physical activity and sport: A process of socialization. In G. Rarick (Ed.), *Physical Activity: Human Growth and Development.* New York: Academic Press, 1973.

Kenyon, G., and McPherson, B. An approach to the study of sport socialization. *International Review of Sport Sociology.* 1974, 9(1), 127-138.

Lamb, M. *The Role of the Father in Child Development*. New York: John Wiley and Sons, 1976.

Landers, D. Sibling-sex status and ordinal position effects on females' sport participation and interests. *Journal of Social Psychology*, 1970, 80, 247–248.

Landers, D. Sibling-sex and ordinal position as factors in sport participation. Paper presented at Third International Symposium on Sociology of Sport, Waterloo, Ontario, Canada, August 1971.

Loy, J. The nature of sport: A definitional effort. *Quest*, 1968, Monograph 10, 1–15.

Loy, J., McPherson, B., and Kenyon, G. *Sport and Social Systems*. Reading, Mass.: Addison-Wesley. 1978.

Lueschen, G. The interdependence of sport and culture. In G. Leuschen (Ed.), *The Cross-Cultural Analysis of Sport and Games*. Champaign, Ill.: Stipes Publishing Co., 1970.

Malumphy, T. The college woman athlete—Questions and tentative answers. *Quest*, 1970, Monograph 14, 24–26.

McPherson, B., Guppy, L., and McKay, J. The social structure of the game and sport milieu. In J. Albinson and G. Andrew (Eds.), *The Child in Sport and Physical Activity*. Baltimore: University Park Press, 1976.

McPherson, B. The child in competitive sport: Influence of the social milieu. In R. Magil, M. Ash, and F. Smoll (Eds.), *Children in Sport: A Contemporary Anthology*. Champaign, Ill.: Human Kinetics Publishers, 1978.

Orlick, T. Family sports environment and early sports participation. Paper presented at Fourth Canadian Psychomotor Learning and Sports Psychology Symposium, University of Waterloo, Waterloo, Ontario, Canada, 1972.

Orlick, T. Sport participation—A process of shaping behavior. *Human Factors*, 1974, 5, 558–561.

Portz, E. Influence of birth order, sibling sex on sports participation. In D. Harris (Ed.), *Women and Sport: A National Research Conference*. Penn State HPER Series No. 2, 1973.

Seppanen, P. Sport success and the type of culture. Paper presented at First International Seminar on the History of Physical Education and Sport, Wingate Institute, Netanya, Israel, April 1968.

Snyder, E., and Spreitzer, E. Family influence and involvement in sports. *Research Quarterly*, 1973, 44(3), 249–255.

Snyder, E., and Spreitzer, E. Correlates of sport participation among adolescent girls. *Research Quarterly*, 1976, 47(4), 804–809.

Sutton-Smith, B., Roberts, J., and Rosenburg, B. Sibling association and role involvement. *Merrill-Palmer Quarterly*, 1964, 10, 25–38.

Watson, G. Sex role socialization and the competitive process in little athletics. *The Australian Journal of Health, Physical Education and Recreation*, 1975, 70, 10–21.

Ziegler, S. Self-perception of athletes and coaches. In D. Harris (Ed.), *Women and Sport: A National Research Conference*. Penn State HPER Series No. 2, 1973.

Zoble, J. Femininity and achievement in sports. In D. Harris (Ed.), *Women and Sport: A National Research Conference.* Penn State HPER Series, No. 2, 1973.

Notes

[1]The author wishes to acknowledge Dr. Karol Kahrs and the Women's Athletic Association at the University of Illinois, Urbana-Champaign, without whose assistance this project could not have been completed.

[2]The sampling technique was accomplished by placing interviewers in central campus locations in which it was felt a rather varied population would be crossing in order to reach lecture halls. Interviewers were instructed to collect information from at least one freshman, sophomore, junior, and senior.

Chapter 9

Teaching in an Urban, Multiracial Physical Education Program: The Power of Context

Patricia S. Griffin
University of Massachusetts, Amherst

Griffin's article is one of the few examples of the explanatory level within physical education. Finding that the quality and content of physical education classes is influenced by the availability of outdoor activity space, central office policies, professional support, and degree of understanding of the unique features in an urban multiracial setting, Griffin concludes that much of what goes on in physical education class lies beyond the control of the teacher. This research has far-reaching philosophical overtones as well as practical suggestions. Although those who prepare new teachers can help them establish more realistic objectives in light of actual constraints in the practical setting that make teaching and learning difficult, not everyone might agree with Griffin that attention should shift from pedagogical to political strategy. Regardless of one's position on this issue, the relevance of such research should be apparent.

Several national reports on the status of education in the United States focus on the inadequate preparation of teachers and the failure of education to attract better teachers (National Commission on Excellence in Education, 1983). No doubt there is justification for these criticisms, but to blame teachers for the inadequacies in education ignores many other factors that affect the quality of instruction in schools.

Physical education, like any other discipline, has its share of incompetent or uncaring teachers, but it also has other teachers who work hard at providing the best possible physical education program within the limitations imposed by school policies, facilities, and resources. Yet many of these energetic and talented teachers

Note. From *Quest*, 1985, **37**, pp. 154–165. Reprinted by permission.

125

ultimately fail to achieve measurable changes in student achievement in physical skills or knowledge.

More than dedicated effort is required to produce good education. Although individual teacher actions are important in determining the quality of instruction, there are other factors impinging on a teacher's ability to consistently achieve excellence, or even adequacy, in the instruction provided and the outcomes accomplished. Most studies of teaching in physical education focus on intraclass phenomena: teacher and student behavior and attitudes. Such variables as student academic learning time (Dodds & Rife, 1983), teacher-student interactions (Lombardo & Cheffers, 1983), instructional strategies (McKenzie, Clark, & McKenzie, 1984), and aptitude treatment interactions (Griffey, 1983) are frequently studied. While investigations of intraclass events yield important information about teaching, their ultimate utility is limited because they do not consider the extraclass (contextual) factors indigenous to individual schools. It is the school environment itself that often restrains teachers' capacity to use research-based information about effective teaching these studies provide.

Contextual factors are systemic characteristics of the community, school district, or school. In examining these factors, the investigation focuses on such variables as physical plant, rules, policies, or informal norms rather than individual teachers, students, or intraclass interactions. Sarason (1982) and Heckman, Oakes, and Sirotnik (1983) have used the phrase "culture of the school" to describe the behavioral and programmatic regularities that define the contextual factors at work in a particular school. Using this perspective to examine physical education requires the consideration of contextual factors that can affect how teachers conduct their classes. The purpose of this report is to identify contextual factors that affected the physical education program in an urban, multiracial junior high school. The focus question for this study was: What contextual factors affected the instructional quality of the physical education program?

Information Gathering and Review

The study spanned a year from September to September. From September through December, weekly on-site observations were conducted. The investigator then withdrew from the school to begin intensive data analysis from January through June. Additional observation days in the school during February and June focused on confirming patterns identified in preliminary data analysis.

During school visits, both in-class and out-of-class interactions were observed among teachers and students. Through numerous informal discussions between classes, over lunch, and before and after school, the physical education teachers shared their thoughts about teaching physical education in their school. Other teachers were occasionally included in these discussions. Informal conversations with students walking to and from class supplemented discussions with teachers. One physical education teacher, who served as a primary focus for observations and discussions, was formally interviewed in December, June, and September. Each interview was audiotaped and lasted approximately an hour.

A total of 84 hours were spent at the school. In addition, two half-day visits to other schools in the city provided background comparisons among different schools in the same district. Teachers were told that the study was being conducted to describe teaching physical education in an urban, multiracial school setting. Students in physical education classes were told that the observer was a visitor from the university who wanted to see what their school was like.

Data analysis began after the first school visit and continued into December of the next school year, following the final visits and interview. Initially, a domain analysis was conducted to begin organizing field notes into categories (Spradley, 1980). As categories and subcategories of data were identified, these initial groups were used to focus subsequent observations. Checklist matrices (Huberman & Miles, 1984) were used to help identify relationships among the domains and to indicate where more data were needed.

Strategies used for confirming findings included cross-checking observations with both teachers and students. In particular, the investigator actively sought differing perceptions among teachers or negative evidence to disconfirm themes which had been identified (Huberman & Miles, 1984; Patton, 1980). Finally, a preliminary account of findings was submitted to the primary focus physical education teacher for verification and correction prior to preparation of the final manuscript.

Description of the Context

Central City

Central City, a city in New England, had a population of 160,000, of which approximately 76% were white, 16% were black, and 8% were Hispanic. The economic range of the residents varied from upper middle-class professionals to unemployed welfare recipients.

The Central City school system included four high schools, six junior high schools, and several elementary schools. An elected school board and an appointed school superintendent controlled the functioning of the schools from offices located in the center of the city. Teachers used the term "Central Office" when speaking of Central City school administrators. Central City schools had been desegregated since 1972, when the city voluntarily developed a plan to redistribute the student population in the junior high schools. The elementary schools in Central City were desegregated by court order in 1974. Students chose which of the four high schools they wanted to attend.

The community surrounding Central City Junior High had undergone many changes during the last 15 years. Until the early 1960s the community was primarily white and upper middle class, but since that time more black and Hispanic families settled in the community and the economic level had become more diverse.

Central City Junior High School

Built in the early 1900s, Central City Junior High comprised grades 7, 8, and 9. According to the 1983 Individual School Report required by the state, 881 students (497 boys and 384 girls) were attending Central City Junior High during the year of the study. Of the total number of students, 191 were black, 5 were Asian, 129 were Hispanic, and 456 were white. There were 10 students for whom English was a second language. Some 532 students were from low-income families. Of the 57 teachers at Central City Junior High, there were 38 white men, 4 black men, 14 white women, and 1 black woman. The school enjoyed a reputation of being one of the better junior highs in the city. There had been few racial conflicts in recent years, and the teachers interviewed regarded the principal as a strong administrator.

The Central City Junior High Physical Education Program

Physical education was the only subject that all students at Central City Junior High were required to take. Each student had physical education for one 90-minute period each week. Student-teacher ratios averaged 25:1 per class. Activity units typically lasted for 3 or 4 weeks. Activities observed were soccer, flag football, physical fitness testing, floor hockey, volleyball, wrestling, track, gymnastics, and softball. Students received grades in physical education. There were approximately 10 class meetings in physical education during each marking period. Students were grouped in classes by academic performance and scheduled for physical education with their academic group. Consequently, physical education teachers referred to classes as "highs," "mediums," and "lows" according to their academic division.

Facilities at Central City Junior High were limited. Its basketball court-sized gym could be divided into two teaching areas when a motorized flexible partition was lowered from the ceiling. A small bare room adjacent to the boys' locker room was used as the other indoor teaching station. Students also were rotated into a classroom health unit for one marking period each year, which helped alleviate indoor crowding.

There were no outdoor activity facilities, but there was a city park across the street from the school. By agreement with the city park department, physical education classes were taken across the street to use the park fields. This was a 15-minute walk and involved crossing a busy four-lane highway each way.

The physical education staff also walked students to nearby bowling lanes for bowling classes and to a local health club for weight training classes. Until a state tax-cutting measure eliminated the funding, a church pool was used for swimming classes. Physical education classes at Central City Junior High had been coed since 1970, when the staff received money to purchase equipment as an incentive to integrate the sex separate classes.

The Physical Education Staff

There were two male (Mike and Tom) and two female (Karen and Joan) physical education teachers at Central City Junior High, all of whom were white and had several years' teaching experience. Karen, who headed the department, taught seven activity classes (90 minutes per class) and five health classes (45 minutes per class) each week during the year of the study. Her schedule was similar to those of the other staff members.

Karen was the primary focus teacher in this study. Her classes were observed most frequently and she served as an important source of information about Central City, Central City Junior High, and the physical education program. She grew up in Central City and had attended Central City Junior High. After completing her undergraduate work in physical education at a small college in the Southeast, Karen returned home to accept a position teaching physical education at Central City Junior High.

She was beginning her 20th year of teaching as the study began, and therefore had seen many changes in the school over the years. When she began teaching, Central City Junior High was a neighborhood school serving primarily white middle-class students. She taught girls only. Now, however, it was a multiracial school with students from low- and middle-income families. Many black and Hispanic students were bused to Central City Junior High from their homes in other parts of the city. All of Karen's classes now were coed.

Contextual Factors Affecting the Instructional Quality of the Physical Education Program

Four contextual factors were identified as exerting a limiting effect on instructional quality in the physical education program: (a) outdoor activity space, (b) central office policies, (c) school-based professional support for teaching, and (d) the unique qualities of urban, multiracial schools.

Outdoor Activity Space

The lack of outdoor activity space prompted the physical education staff to persuade the principal to schedule physical education once a week for a double period rather than the regularly scheduled 45-minute class twice a week. This change gave classes time to walk across the street and use the athletic fields in the city park. Since this was a 15-minute walk each way, using the park would have been impossible during a 45-minute class.

However, there were two disadvantages to this solution to the outdoor facility problem. First, having classes meet only once a week limited the amount of learning that was carried over from one class to the next. Second, and perhaps more immediately frustrating to the physical education staff, was their lack of control over the park fields they were using. During fall and spring all the classes used the park fields rather than the gym. During winter several classes each day used the park fields for cross-country skiing. At least once during each observation day there was some misunderstanding with the park personnel about the physical education classes using the fields.

When the teachers first took students to the park in September, they discovered they couldn't use the fields because of reseeding operations. Instead, they had to use grass areas that were not officially marked athletic fields. Consequently, Karen taught her soccer class on a patch of grass beside the park road, an area much smaller than a regulation soccer field. On the first day of observation, a huge truck was pouring asphalt for a curb in the road next to the field. Karen spent the class period trying to shout encouragement and instructions over the drone of the truck.

There were no lines or goals (piles of sweat shirts and cones served as goal-posts) and the grass area was not rectangular. The ground sloped unevenly toward the road (students had to chase the ball across the road several times). A large thick bush at one end of the field and a small indentation with a rose bush in it at the other end compounded the problem, for the ball often rolled into the large bush. Whenever this happened, the game stopped while a student disappeared into the bush to retrieve the ball. At one point during the game there was a question about whether a goal had been scored, but the goalie assured Karen that it had. The ball had gone into the rose bush hole and was kicked out of the hole into the goal by an offensive player.

During one class a man driving a park department truck told Karen the area they were using was not a designated play area, so Karen had to take time from her class to explain the situation to him. Several days later students informed Karen that recreation league soccer teams were using the park athletic fields. Employees of the park work crew told her that only small groups could use the fields, and that was why the rec league teams could use the fields but not the physical education classes. Karen felt this was unfair, so she decided to use the park soccer field for class that day. Immediately after class the park superintendent called Karen to say that no one could use the fields.

Yet, people had use of the park fields all day on Saturday. When Karen called the park department to find out why, she was told the department could not control Saturday use of the fields but that she should keep her classes off the fields during the school week. Karen called Central Office to see if there was any way she could use the fields. A park official came to her next class and told her to stay off the fields and that from now on the fields would be closed to the public on weekends. Karen's reaction was, "Well, the only thing I accomplished is getting everyone kicked off the fields."

After class, all four teachers got together and agreed the playing areas they were using were unsafe and inadequate. Yet they knew if they complained to Central Office they'd only be told to stay off the small areas they had, and then there would be no outdoor areas for classes at all. To add to this frustration, the teachers also had to contend with the recreation department's using the school gym during the winter for evening programs. The recreation people left soda cans, food wrappers, and other trash on the gym floor; in addition, some physical education equipment in the gym had been vandalized. Complaints to Central Office and to the park department failed to alleviate the problem. Finally, the principal intervened to end the recreation department's use of the gym.

Because of limited facilities, they physical education staff tried to adapt the program to make the most of their situation. But the lack of control over facilities had a detrimental effect on the quality of instruction they could offer.

Central Office Policies

Policy decisions made by administrators in the central offices also limited the ability of the physical education staff at Central City Junior High to provide quality instructional programs. In 1975 a district-wide grading policy had been approved by the school committee and distributed to all physical education teachers in the system. Physical educators were not consulted about this policy before its implementation.

The policy required that physical education students be graded on "attitude, improvement in skill, and knowledge of the rules of the activity." The first criterion included "attitude toward program, participation, other pupils, and preparedness." The policy also stated, "When student attitude is satisfactory, it is understood that no grade should be less than 'B'." The section on skill improvement stated, "When students participate with a proper attitude, it is reasonable to expect skill improvement. Improvement in skills should be stressed more than the ability to achieve definite standards. Improvement will be achieved if attitude is satisfactory." Karen said, "The school committee decided that if a student has good rapport with the teachers and students, they must get a 'B'. A school committee member's daughter was kept off the honor roll with a 'C' in gym, so they changed the rule."

Even if the teachers at Central City Junior High had the class time and facilities to make skill improvement a reasonable program goal, the grading policy mandated by the school committee would prevent them from evaluating students on anything more than their attitude and compliance with regulations.

The physical education teachers were also required to administer physical fitness tests each fall and submit the results to Central Office. The AAHPERD test including sit-ups, shuttle run, standing long jump, pull-ups, arm hang, 600-yard run, and the 50-yard dash was used. Fitness report cards for each student were due to be returned to each school in April but usually were not returned until June, which meant the teachers received the previous year's results in September. The scores were not used at Central City Junior High to plan programs or to help individual students improve their scores. Mike, one of the P.E. teachers, summed up his perceptions as, "They make us do it to keep federal and state funds, that's all."

The Central Office policy on granting teachers time to attend professional conferences or inservice workshops placed Central City's 40 physical education teachers in competition with each other for one or two slots. Teachers had to apply to attend these programs and only two or three were chosen, which meant that opportunities to attend professional meetings with other physical educators were few. During the year of this investigation no district-wide professional development programs were planned for physical educators in Central City. Thus, physical educators at Central City Junior High rarely had professional contact with other colleagues in the city.

Over the years, Central Office had turned down requests from the physical education staff for funds to support facility improvement, equipment acquisitions, and curriculum innovation. For example, the Central City Junior High physical education staff had requested money to develop a Project Adventure Urban Modification component in their curriculum and had identified a teacher from another city who would help them build the equipment and train them to use it. However, the funding was not approved.

When two gym classes were being held simultaneously, separated only by the "mat" divider, the noise was deafening. Floor hockey sticks slapping each other, sneakers screeching on the floor, high-pitched yells, shouted instructions from the teacher, and clapping hands all echoed from the brick and cement walls and ceilings. Karen commented,

> We asked for acoustical tile. Central Office laughed at us. They thought it would be too unreasonable, it would just get broken. We did have a better divider that helped the acoustics, but it broke. We could still pull it shut by hand though. They replaced it with this thing, much worse. I couldn't believe it when they brought it in.

The Central Office policy that students be assigned to classes by academic performance had a pervasive effect on physical education. The "high" classes were predominantly white and middle class, the "low" divisions were mostly black, Hispanic, and low income, and the "medium" classes were of mixed race and economic level.

Most of the obstacles to providing instruction occurred in the low division classes, which also tended to have the highest absentee rate. On some days so few students were present in a low division class that the teacher was hard-pressed to field two volleyball teams. There were also many transitory students in the low divisions. "You can start out with a class and by the end of the semester, the whole class will be new kids," said Joan. Another problem with the lowest divisions was that students who failed to advance to the next grade were automatically put in the lowest academic division to repeat a grade. Consequently, there were some students in the lowest seventh grade division who had failed two or three times. This presented teachers with some extreme differences in physical size, such as 15- and 16-year-old young men in a flag football class with 12-year-old boys and girls.

Karen and her colleagues did not view Central Office as a resource to help them do their jobs better, but rather as an obstacle to their ability to do a good job. City-wide grading policies and physical fitness testing requirements formulated without teacher input limited the control teachers had over their programs. The district's policies on professional development did not make it easy or attractive for teachers to expand their teaching skills. The perceived lack of Central Office responsiveness to teacher requests for facility and program innovation discouraged teachers from implementing new ideas or requesting help from Central Office.

Professional Support for Teaching

The principal of Central City Junior High was very supportive. He arranged for the physical education classes to be double sessions to accommodate the walk to and from the park. He got cross-country skis for the new winter unit in the park. In addition, he allowed physical education classes to go off school grounds regularly to bowl, weight train, and use a ropes course at local organizations in the area. Despite the principal's support, there were no professional development programs to help teachers evaluate or improve their teaching skills. P.E. teachers Joan and Tom needed help with class organization and management. To compound the problem, they were assigned to team-teach several low division classes. Two excerpts from field notes illustrate some of their problems:

> During a low division track class, the 31 students have walked 15 minutes to a dirt strip between the park tennis courts and some trees. This area will serve as the "track" for learning starts. Apparently they have already learned the technique; they begin practicing the start and racing as soon as we get there. The two teachers divide the 31 students into two lines, a girls' line and a boys' line. One teacher gives the starting command over and over as each pair (a girl and a boy) race to a line drawn in the dirt approximately 50 yards away. The other teacher stands at the finish line. Neither teacher comments on student performance. After about 1 minute of this process, the 29 students not racing begin to talk, wander out of line, begin small group conversations, or start pushing and shoving each other. The students who are paying attention to the racers laugh at their running style or make fun of the boys who are beaten by girls. Five girls, two white and three black, refuse to take a turn at all. They walk to the other end of the dirt strip after everyone else has taken a turn. There are several time-consuming interruptions as Joan and Tom yell at disruptive students or try to regroup lines. The students complete two sprints in this fashion before the teachers tell them to line up for the return walk to the school.

During a volleyball class in the gym, the 21 students in attendance in a low division class have just completed a circle drill passing the ball around the circle to see how long they can keep the ball up. Practically every hit is an underhand slap or carry; the ball rarely goes above head level. The teachers stand and watch the groups from the center of the gym. Tom then announces that they will begin to play a game as soon as there have been "10 perfect serves" back and forth over the net by the two teams on each of the two courts. "If someone misses, start over." For 15 minutes the students unsuccessfully attempt to get 10 consecutive serves in the court. One court gets eight before a white girl hits the ball into the net. There is a collective groan as they begin again. After several times of starting over, some students are sitting down against the wall, a black boy and a Hispanic boy are trading shoe laces, a black girl hits the ball into the net twice in a row and begins to suck her thumb. Two black boys start break dancing on the court. Finally, Tom announces that they can begin playing even though they haven't made 10 serves. By now, many of the students are not paying attention. The game begins with Tom standing beside the center pole officiating. One black boy punches the ball as hard as he can. It caroms wildly off the wall. Students punch and tease each other; one black girl rolls on the floor complaining to Tom about a call. Tom does not react to any of this behavior, but keeps officiating the game.

These vignettes were typical of the observed classes taught by Joan and Tom, who tended to blame students for the problems they were having. "Common sense is not a priority in this class." "Look at this attendance. Most of them will fail because they don't bother to come to class."

The other two teachers, Karen and Mike, did not have such class management and organization problems but they were both aware that their colleagues were struggling. Mike (whose office window looks out into the gym) said he left his office during his planning period one day because he could not stand to watch the class Joan and Tom were teaching in the gym. Mike occasionally stepped in to discipline students for the other teaching team, but he never discussed those incidents with Joan and Tom as problems with their teaching methods. No norms were established for these teachers to help each other. It was clear that none of the four felt comfortable with the situation, but neither did they feel comfortable about addressing the problem directly.

School administrators were of little help, though they were aware of the problem. Karen said Mike had been transferred to Central City Junior High from another junior high school partly because he would provide a "strong male teacher role model" for Tom. This indirect strategy was the only attempt made to help Joan and Tom. Karen did not have the authority to intervene; her responsibilities as department head did not include supervision or evaluation of her colleagues. She was concerned about the situation, but there simply was no school procedure to help teachers improve their teaching skills.

Unique Qualities of Urban, Multiracial Schools

Several unique aspects of teaching in an urban, multiracial school became apparent during school observations and interviews. Teachers were faced with a wide range of diversity among students, the more salient differences being racial, cultural, economic, and academic. All of these differences interacted with the problems that plague many cites: crime, poverty, residential racial segregation, racism, and violence. Though the same problems probably existed in schools surrounding Central City, the comparative lack of racial and economic diversity in these suburban schools tended to make such problems less obvious. Teachers in Central City, however, were forced to deal with the problems of urban life every day because they affected the lives of many students and ultimately their performance and behavior in school.

Since most of the teachers were white and middle class, there were differences not only among students but also between teachers and many students. Because academic grouping by the previous year's grades resulted in highly segregated class compositions, there was potential for reinforcing racial stereotypes already held by teachers (e.g., that black and Hispanic students are poor, uninterested in school, and have a disrupted family life whereas white students are middle class, motivated for academic achievement, and have secure families). How each teacher interpreted student behavior depended on his or her own attitudes and experiences. There were no professional development programs to help teachers understand either their own prejudices or the dynamics of racial and economic discrimination in schools (Griffin, 1985). Karen described her thoughts on this topic:

> The biggest injustice done to teachers is not to prepare them for what students are like in multiracial schools. The city made the same mistake with Hispanic students [as it made with black students]. They never sent anyone here to teach me about Hispanic students. They're different from black students. Now we're getting Asian students. I don't know anything about Asian culture.

Teachers had to respond daily to cultural differences in dress, language, inter-action patterns, and perceptions of physical activity that affected student participa-tion in physical education. Some black students referred to cross-country skiing and tennis as "white people's sports" and did not want to participate. Many Hispanic girls came to school dressed "like I would go to church," Karen said. They wore makeup, jewelry, hosiery, and high heels, and were often reluctant to participate in any physical activities. Many white girls tended to hang back in team games, gathering in small groups around the fringes of activity.

Black girls were more assertive both in their game participation and in their interactions with boys who tried to tease them. Hispanic students were bilingual, sometimes speaking Spanish to their friends in class. Black students often were loud, and black boys and girls interacted with each other more frequently than did white students, often using nonstandard or black English. Many white boys participated in out-of-school football or ice hockey programs and hung out with their teammates in school. Black boys were much more careful about their clothes than white boys were. As one black boy said, "People will crack on you if you aren't dressed with style."

This mix of cultural, racial, and sexual differences presented teachers with patterns of student behavior far more complex than those encountered in schools with less heterogeneous populations.

Trying to be fair to all students, respect cultural differences, and avoid stereotyping students presented teachers with daily challenges to their white, middle-class backgrounds. Students from low-income families needed some flexibility in dress requirements and restricted special programs that meant students had to pay for use of nonschool facilities. Furthermore, the hardships some students faced at home made the physical education program requirements seem absurd at times.

Karen learns that someone has been threatening to kill the mother of one of her students. His older brother has been arrested for robbery. During the walk back from the park after class, this 8th grade student demonstrates how people steal gold chains and earrings in New York and asks if we know what a "piece" is [a gun]. After we return to the gym office, Karen turns to me and says, "With the problems that poor kid has, I'm asking him where his gym uniform is?"

Discussion

The examination of systemic contextual factors affecting the conduct of the physical education program shows there are many important outside considerations when assessing the quality of instruction inside the gym. At Central City Junior High, the interaction of outdoor activity space, Central Office policies, professional support for teaching, and the unique qualities of urban, multiracial schools limited what teachers could accomplish in their classes. This limit was far below the idealistic goals outlined in most curriculum guides or professional journals. Given the present conditions at Central City Junior High, instruction for improving the activity skills or physical fitness of students would be an impossible goal.

Placek (1983) described teachers whose primary goals in physical education were to keep students busy, happy, and good. Given the contextual restraints at Central City Junior High, keeping students busy, happy, and good are far more reasonable goals than attempting to provide instruction and evaluation of student achievement in sport and activity skill learning.

The corrosive effect of contextual factors on the design and content of the physical education program at Central City Junior High was evident. The effect of these same factors on the teachers was less immediately apparent but equally serious. Teachers were isolated not only from physical education teachers in other schools but also from colleagues within the school. Though Karen, Tom, Mike, and Joan spent time together between classes, at lunch, and even teaching together, there were no established norms for talking about improving teaching performance or understanding the complexities of student diversity.

Teachers felt powerless to control several important aspects of their teaching. The city recreation and parks departments, Central Office, and the School committee made decisions about facility use, grading, curriculum change, and fitness testing without teacher input. Yet, when asked what she perceived to be the biggest obstacle to a high quality program at Central City Junior High, Karen answered, "Me. My own lack of knowledge of new activities and methods." Even after a year of close observation and shared experience, this response was unexpected. Given the problems she faced, Karen, an energetic and caring teacher, blamed herself for not being able to implement the kind of program she would like to have. Perhaps after being so long in this environment she felt the only thing she could change was herself.

This report is a detailed description of contextual factors affecting physical education in one school. The issue is not whether Central City Junior High was typical of urban, multiracial schools, or whether we can generalize from this description to other schools. The issue is how readers can integrate the description into their own experiences and thereby gain a greater understanding of the complexities of school physical education and the lives of teachers who work there.

For the sake of discussion, however, if we speculate that the contextual factors affecting physical education at Central City Junior High are accurate representations of conditions in other urban settings, and perhaps some suburban schools as well, what does this portend for the future of physical education? For teachers in these schools, the contextual factors described probably are not surprising. They have learned to adjust their professional goals, whether consciously or not, to match what they perceive is possible in their schools.

For teacher educators who have not spent much time in schools recently, however, or for physical educators who have spent time only in schools where contextual factors are more favorable, there is more to learn. Professional leaders must eliminate the gap between the idealistic rhetoric that is typical of so many of our publications and the contextual realities of schools. Researchers must expand their concept of what constitutes important and interesting questions to include consideration of systemic variables in schools as a significant addition to the investigation of intraclass events. Finally, state and district supervision personnel, as well as teacher educators working in outreach programs, must find ways to work with teachers in the schools to address some of the contextual factors that affect the conduct of physical education.

To the extent that the school described in this report is representative of other schools, physical education has a serious problem. Not that the program described was somehow dishonorable: To the contrary, the teachers at CCJH worked hard and within the constraints of the program, most students were probably getting the most possible from their P.E. classes. Rather, the problem lies in our failure to acknowledge and act on the gap between our professional ideals and the day-to-day reality of life in many school gyms.

Imagine the following scene: The teacher is teaching a flag football class; there will be four class meetings in this unit. Her class is held on a strip of dirt punctuated with occasional islands of grass. They are outside the fence that protects the park baseball field, a well kept skinned infield and closely cropped green outfield. The teacher gathers the students around her and begins to go over the fundamentals of passing. She demonstrates with one of the boys in the class. The class divides into pairs, two lines facing each other to pass the footballs back and forth. The teacher walks up and down the lines giving feedback, instruction, encouragement, and an occasional warning about off-task activity.

What will these students remember next week when they meet again? How much practice will they get in four classes? Will they really understand the game by practicing on this dirt strip instead of a marked field? At least they are all busy passing, most of them seem to be enjoying the class, and there are few discipline problems. The students are busy, happy, and good, but is this really physical education?

What more can teachers in situations like this realistically expect to achieve, given the contextual factors impinging upon their programs? Probably nothing whatever: Perhaps it is time to face the fact that systemic constraints can make teaching and learning impossible goals to achieve. Perpetuating the myth that we can improve the quality of physical education in the schools by focusing on better instructional skills or more exciting activity units does a disservice to teachers who are doing the best they can, given the contextual factors at work in their schools. If there is to be real hope for change, it lies not in finding the right pedagogical stuff but in acting on the right political stuff. By focusing on and developing strategies for addressing the systemic constraints that teachers work against, we may begin moving toward real change in the teaching of physical education.

References

Dodds, P., & Rife, F. (1983). Time to learn in physical education. *Journal of Teaching in Physical Education, Monograph I.*

Griffey, D. (1983). Aptitude × treatment interactions associated with student decision making. *Journal of Teaching in Physical Education,* **2**(2), 15-32.

Griffin, P. (1985). Teaching in an urban, multiracial junior high school: The experiences of a white teacher. Manuscript submitted for publication.

Heckman, P., Oakes, J., & Sirotnik, K. (1983). Expanding the concepts of school renewal and change. *Educational Leadership,* **40**(7), 26-32.

Huberman, M., & Miles, M. (1984). *Qualitative data analysis*. Beverly Hills, CA: Sage.

Lombardo, B., & Cheffers, J. (1983). Variability in teaching behavior and interaction in the gymnasium. *Journal of Teaching in Physical Education*, 2(2), 33-48.

McKenzie, T., Clark, E., & McKenzie, R. (1984). Instructional strategies: Influence on teacher and student behavior. *Journal of Teaching in Physical Education*, 3(2), 20-28.

National Commission on Excellence in Education. (1983). *A nation at risk: The imperative for educational reform*. Washington, DC: U.S. Department of Education.

Patton, M.Q. (1980). *Qualitative evaluation methods*. Beverly Hills, CA: Sage.

Placek, J. (1983). Conceptions of success in teaching: Busy, happy and good? In T. Templin & J. Olson (Eds.), *Teaching in physical education* (pp. 46-56). Champaign, IL: Human Kinetics.

Sarason, S. (1982). *The culture of the school and the problem of change*. Boston: Allyn & Bacon.

Spradley, J. (1980). *Participant observation*. New York: Holt, Rinehart, & Winston.

PART II

The Operational Phase

Each of the three articles in Part II is an example of the operational research phase as conceptualized in Yiannakis's model of an applied sociology of sport. Unlike the explanatory phase, which is more reflective of research findings that have implications for application, operational research attempts to provide rather narrow technical or practical solutions to significant problems. In other words, researchers at this level take findings and go a step beyond explanatory research to propose solutions. Researchers may test findings in applied settings to determine their use or effectiveness. Chapters 10, 11, and 12 all suggest ways in which a particular type of program or method has been tested in a realistic context.

Chapter 10

Effects of a Transition Program on Student Athletes' Academic Success: An Exploratory Study

Larry Weber and Thomas M. Sherman
Virginia Polytechnic Institute and State University

Carmen Tegano
University of Tennessee

In their article, Weber, Sherman, and Tegano compare achievement scores of freshman football players who enrolled in a summer transition program with those who did not. Their finding that a summer transition program can contribute to the academic success of athletes can lead to specific implementation: Programs that provide a sense of academic security and support can assist athletes in adjusting to a new environment.

Athletic scholarships afford an opportunity for a college education to some individuals who otherwise may not be able to attend an institution of higher learning. Regrettably, the proportion of athletes who graduate has declined steadily over the last 30 years (Shapiro, 1984), particularly among players "in those sports which receive national recognition" (Henschen & Fry, 1984:55). In addition, black athletes were reported to have lower graduation rates than white athletes in a study at Michigan State University (Shapiro, 1984). According to an NCAA [National Collegiate Athletic Association] report (Advanced Technology, 1984), only 27% of white and 14% of minority male student athletes receiving scholarship assistance graduate after 4 years.

Student athletes present unique challenges to both the athletic and academic facets of college life (Snyder, 1985). Some observers have been harsh in their criticism of how each has responded to these challenges. Ross (1983), for example, reported that "many athletes are filing court suits because schools have exploited their athletic abilities and ignored their educational needs." Phelps (1982) pointed out that some athletic departments have been perceived to use athletics during their college years and then dump them on society without any marketable skills.

Note. From *Sociology of Sport Journal*, 1987, **4**, pp. 78–83. Reprinted by permission.

In support of this view, Purdy, Eitzen, and Hufnagel (1982), in a study of major sport athletes over a 10-year period at one state university, found that athletes were less prepared for college and achieved less academically than the general student population. Purdy et al. (1982) also found that of athletic scholarship holders, blacks and football and basketball players had the "poorest academic potential and performance." Other studies by Purdy, Hufnagel, and Eitzen (1981) and Warfield (1983) support the conclusion that revenue-sport and black athletes are likely to fare worse as students.

Unquestionably, many factors contribute to athletes' academic problems and some institutions have initiated steps to address the unique needs of these students. However, current NCAA policies and regulations may preclude implementing academic assistance services that could provide poorly prepared student athletes with programs designed to help them perform at an acceptable academic standard. For example, the NCAA prohibits granting financial aid to student athletes to attend summer school unless there is evidence of prior matriculation at the institution (NCAA, 1985). That is, incoming freshman athletes are not permitted to receive scholarship aid to attend summer school. The research in this paper reports the results of student athlete participation in a summer transition program over a 2-year period.

Methodology

Many colleges and universities throughout the United States have established summer programs to assist incoming freshmen with low admission qualifications in making the transition to the university environment. We investigated the results of student athletes' participation in a summer transition program (STP) at a land grant university with an enrollment of 22,000. The STP is designed to serve all admitted students with low admission qualifications. Student athletes receiving grants-in-aid are eligible for the STP if they meet the criteria used to invite other students. During the summers of 1983 and 1984, 28 entering freshman varsity football players were eligible to enroll in the STP: Of that number, 13 chose to do so, and 15 declined.

The achievement of these two groups was compared and analyzed using a simple one-way analysis of covariance design. Incoming Scholastic Aptitude Test (SAT) scores were used as the covariate, and cumulative grade point average (GPA) following the winter 1984 quarter served as the dependent variable. This included the cumulative GPAs for two academic terms for the '84 group and five terms for the '83 group.

Findings

SAT scores and cumulative GPAs for the two groups of students are shown in Table 10.1. After conducting a one-way analysis of variance test to assure

Table 10.1   SAT and Cumulative Grade Point Averages for Students Who Did and Did Not Attend the Summer Transition Program

	Attended ($n = 13$)		Did not attend ($n = 15$)	
	SAT score	GPA	SAT score	GPA
	500	1.70	640	1.50
	620	1.45	640	1.40
	700	1.75	600	1.50
	500	2.20	700	1.70
	900	3.20	710	2.20
	720	2.20	900	1.77
	650	2.50	550	1.75
	630	1.00	740	2.10
	640	1.25	630	2.50
	800	2.60	600	1.00
	720	1.60	630	1.20
	800	2.20	650	1.00
	860	2.30	550	0.73
			500	0.75
			480	0.90
M	695	2.00	635	1.47

equivalence of the two groups on the covariate measure, SAT scores (see Table 10.2), a simple one-way analysis of covariance test was performed. The mean adjusted cumulative GPA[1] for student athletes choosing to enroll in the STP prior to their freshman year was 1.90 (4.0 = A, 3.0 = B, 2.0 = C, 1.0 = D). Their unadjusted GPA was 2.0, a C letter grade. For the students not electing to attend the STP, the adjusted cumulative grade point average was 1.55 (the unadjusted GPA was 1.47, about a D+ and below the academic eligibility cutoff). The F value for the ANCOVA test (see Table 10.3) was 3.51 ($p = .07$), which we

Table 10.2   Analysis of Variance Results for SAT Scores of Student Athletes

Source of variation	Sum of squares	Degrees of freedom	M square	F value	Probability $> F$
Treatment	256	1	256	1.99	$p > .10$
Within	3342	26	128.54		
Total	3598	27			

Table 10.3   Analysis of Covariance Results on Student Athletes Enrolled Under
Two Conditions of Attendance

Source of variation	Sum of squares	Degrees of freedom	M square	F value	Probability $> F$
SAT scores	2.77	1	2.77	11.96	$p < .01$
Attendance	.81	1	.81	3.51	$p < .073$
Within	5.79	25	.23		

believed was at a probability level sufficient to raise suspicion about the positive effects of the STP—especially considering the exploratory nature of this study and the number of students involved.

Consequently, we investigated further the differences in academic standing between the two groups. Because students must maintain a minimum of 1.50 to continue their studies at the university, we compared the frequencies of students below 1.50 in the two groups. The STP group included three students (23%) below the academic eligibility level; the nonparticipant group included seven students (46%). A second important measure is the number of students who have achieved the 2.0 GPA necessary to graduate. The STP group included seven students (53%) while the nonparticipants included three (20%). A simple chi-square indicated that these differences were significant ($\chi^2 = 6.4$, df $= 1$; $p < .025$). Thus, it appears that participation in the STP is an important factor in maintaining academic eligibility and achieving a GPA equal to or above that required to graduate.

Discussion

The findings of this study indicate that a summer transition program can contribute to the academic success of athletes. Grade point averages for those who enrolled in the transition program were higher, their athletic and academic eligibility was more secure, and their potential to graduate was greater than similar student athletes who did not attend the STP. Many colleges and universities have recognized for years that a transition experience assists students with low admission qualifications and helps them adapt to the new responsibilities of higher education (Grant & Hoeber, 1978). These data appear to indicate that regulations prohibiting such programs for athletes may be unwise, particularly when the added stresses of athletics are added to this adjustment process.

Aside from the other advantages that athletics can provide the athletically gifted, Hanks (1979) and Ballantine (1981) found that participation in athletics facilitated the formation of educational goals for athletes and had a positive effect on their aspirations. However, they reported that athletes got "better grades once the sport season was over.'' Unquestionably, the heavy demands on time and energy required during the season mitigate against some students devoting sufficient effort to maintain satisfactory academic progress. Knowing this is the case, it appears that athletic and academic decision-makers should initiate actions to facilitate academic success. One reasonable approach might be summer transition programs designed to help poorly prepared freshman student athletes develop the skills and attitudes necessary to handle the academic rigors of college life.

And finally, what impact could a summer transition program have with respect to Proposition 48? The answer is speculative but it appears that, overall, the likely effect is minimal. As Sojka (1985) pointed out, the history of college athletics has been one of calls for reform that went unheeded. Yet, within the confines of the athletic enterprise itself, an emphasis on the often competing roles of athletes may help students make more informed choices. Snyder (1985) proposed four types of commitment to the dual roles of athlete and scholar:

1. Scholar-athlete: The individual receives gratification from both roles and has a high commitment to each.
2. Pure scholar: The individual is highly committed to the scholar role and gains little gratification from the athlete role.
3. Pure athlete: The individual is highly committed to the role of athlete and devotes little energy to the scholar role.
4. Nonscholar-nonathlete: The individual has no serious commitment to either role.

Most student athletes verbalize an idealized version of Type 1 when entering college as freshmen. They are unlikely, however, to recognize the demands that college athletics place on their time and energy. Rhatigan (1984) estimated that college athletes may miss as much as 17% of their classes. Less academically qualified students may have problems defining their roles as academic and athletic demands increase during their first term. It is possible that a summer transition program could help students develop secure role identities by providing opportunities for academic successes early in their college careers without the pressures of athletic practice and performance. These programs also may provide a sense of academic security and support, which can be helpful in adjusting to a new environment.

Clearly, this study does not answer all questions about transition programs. For example, we would be remiss if we failed to mention that students *elected* to participate in the STP; this may have contributed to the favorable results. Regrettably, it was impossible to control for such motivational factors in this study. On the other hand, to attribute the results solely to selection factors would entail some problems of conjecture, since some students *not* participating in the STP program chose not to do so for reasons other than what might be interpreted as academic motivation. Nonetheless, this study does provide evidence that students who have low admission qualifications can be successful as student-athletes. The data also support the contention that a summer transition program may be an important factor in these students' academic success.

References

Advanced Technology
   1984   Study of Freshman Eligibility Standards: Executive Summary, Report submitted to the National Collegiate Athletic Association, Mission, KS.
Ballantine, R.J.
   1981   What Research Says: About the Correlation Between Athletic Participation and Academic Achievement. (ERIC Document Reproduction Service No. ED 233994)
Grant, N.K. and D.R. Hoeber
   1978   Basic Skills Programs: Are They Working? Washington, DC: The American Association for Higher Education. AHE-ERIC/Higher Education Research Report No. 1.
Hanks, M.
   1979   "Race, sexual status in athletics and the process of educational achievement." Social Science Quarterly, 60:482-896.
Henschen, K.P. and D. Fry
   1984   "An archival study of the relationship of intercollegiate athletic participation and graduation." Sociology of Sport Journal, 1:52-56.
National Collegiate Athletic Association
   1985   Constitution. Mission, KS: National Collegiate Athletic Association.
Phelps, N.O.
   1982   "The student athlete: a proposal." College Board Review, pp. 27-28.
Purdy, D.A., D.S. Eitzen and R. Hufnagel
   1982   "Are athletes also students? The educational attainment of college athletes." Social Problems, 29:439-448.
Purdy, D.A., R. Hufnagel and D.S. Eitzen
   1981   "Educational attainment and collegiate athletes: intra-group analysis and comparison to the general student population." Paper presented at the annual meeting of the American Alliance for Health, Physical Education, Recreation and Dance, Boston.
Rhatigan, J.J.
   1984   "Serving two masters: the plight of the college student athlete." Pp. 5-11 in A. Shrifery and F.R. Brodzenski (eds.), Rethinking Services for College Athletes. San Francisco: Jossey-Bass.
Ross, C.T.
   1983   "Is student athlete a contradiction in terms? how universities deny student athletes an education." Update on Law-Related Education, 7:6-9.
Shapiro, B.J.
   1984   "Intercollegiate athletic participation and academic achievement: a case study of Michigan State University student-athletes 1950-1980." Sociology of Sport Journal, 1:46-51.

Snyder, E.E.
  1985   "A theoretical analysis of academic and athletic roles." Sociology of
         Sport Journal, 2:210-217.
Sojka, G.S.
  1985   "The evolution of the student-athlete in America: from the divinity to
         the divine." Pp. 17-33 in D. Chu, J.O. Segrave and B.D. Becker (eds.),
         Sport and Higher Education. Champaign, IL: Human Kinetics.
Warfield, J.L.
  1983   "Sport and social mobility research: the role of race." Paper presented
         at the Annual Convention of the Association for the Study of Afro-
         American Life and History, Detroit.

Notes

[1]Adjusted mean GPAs are corrected group means computed by eliminating the effects of initial differences between the groups on SAT scores.

Chapter 11

Applying Theory Y in Sport Sociology: Redesigning the Off-Season Conditioning Program of a Big Ten Swim Team

Timothy Jon Curry
Ohio State University

This article is an excellent example of accomplishing goals for athletes and coaches as well as the researcher through applied research. Using a particular set of theoretical assumptions about behavior—namely, that if individuals are committed to a set of goals, such goals can be achieved through self-direction and self-control—Curry demonstrates how the use of various types of data (photographs, interviews, and a sport identity questionnaire) led to a more humanistic off-season conditioning program for swimmers. Not only were the data useful in improving and revising the conditioning program, but they also served as the basis for providing feedback to coaches and swimmers while monitoring changes in athlete behaviors and expectations.

The summer "off-season" poses a difficult conditioning challenge for the college swim coach and his or her athletes. Most swimmers recognize the need to maintain conditioning in the summer. Yet for many student-athletes, the summer also represents a welcome break from the routine of nine long months of training and competing in the pool and in the classroom. It may also be a time of gainful employment where working takes precedence over training, or a period of rest and recuperation from injuries. The summer can represent a prolonged period of unsupervised "play time" for athletes, and coaches may well fear and resent any loss of conditioning.

This applied research was directed at finding an approach to the off-season conditioning program that would appeal to both the coach and the athlete. The particular Big Ten team involved was typical in several ways of many other swim teams in the nation. It had a few swimmers of talent and physique who were capable of competing at a national level. A majority, however, were athletes who were not so exceptional and who had to train hard and well to place in the conference competition.

Perhaps not so typically, the team did not have in place a workable plan for off-season training. Some swimmers would report back to practice in the fall heavier and with more body fat than when they left in the spring; both the coach and the swimmers were distressed at this loss of conditioning. Moreover, the dissatisfaction felt by the team and the coach over this problem was compounded by a lack of clear expectations. The coach had never clarified in his own mind, nor conveyed to the swimmers, exactly in what shape they were to report back to practice. While the problem of overweight might have affected just a few of the team members, the lack of clear off-season guidelines made it difficult to determine who was "too fat" and who was not.

Then there was the equally difficult problem of motivating and monitoring athletes during the off-season. During these 3 months, the athletes were following different schedules and were geographically dispersed.

The following sections outline the theoretical elements that emerged as critical to redesigning the program; the data concerning the effect of the new design are presented after that.

The Theory X Style of Coaching

Like many other coaches, the swim coach managed his team with a "Theory X" set of beliefs (Curry & Jiobu, 1984). This style of management is guided by certain assumptions. As applied to athletes, the set of beliefs may be paraphrased from McGregor (1960) as follows: The average athlete dislikes intensive training and will avoid it if possible. Because they dislike training, athletes must be carefully monitored, even coerced at times, to achieve their training objectives. The average athlete prefers to be directed, wishes to avoid responsibility, and is probably not able to devise his or her own training schedule.

During the regular season, team rules and practice sessions gave the swimmers little leeway in how they went about practicing and participating in their sport. Typical, for example, was this rule, which the coach had instituted concerning missing practice: "Attendance at every practice is mandatory and punctuality for every practice is of extreme importance . . . [For the] first miss, you automatically miss the next practice; third miss—off the team." Weight training and conditioning also were monitored closely during the season; failure to show up at a weight training session was considered the same as missing practice. The training programs were compulsory, and the individual swimmer had no say in the design of the program or practice routines. His responsibility was to do the work the coach had specified.

Not surprisingly, the coach also attempted to use the same Theory X approach to training during the 3-month off-season. A contract was prepared for each swimmer that specified in detail a rigorous swimming and exercise program to be followed during the summer. The minimum requirements called for 7 hours per week of swimming, along with 4 hours per week of weight training. Each swimmer was also asked to begin a running and endurance lifting program 3 weeks before practice began. The last item on the contract was a note that quoted from an authoritative source saying that while "Breaks in training are essential to the conditioning process . . . long layoffs are detrimental to performance and cannot be recommended." The contract was signed in the presence of the coach before the athlete left for the summer.

The problem with Theory X style management is not that it doesn't work. It does work under some conditions, but not all (McGregor, 1960). Specifically, it requires the presence of a supervisor who will exert managerial control, organize the daily activities, and dispense sanctions for good or poor performance. In the case of the swim team, these conditions did not apply to the summer off-season. Hence, if a swimmer did not seek out a local coach to monitor his behavior, he was left on his own. In addition, not all of the swimmers were near a pool, meaning some could not follow the prescribed training schedule even if they had wished to. Clearly, these conditions called for a different style of management with a different set of assumptions.

Theory Y and the Sociology of Motivation

Another possible approach to the off-season challenge was the "Theory Y" strategy. Theory Y assumes that external control and the threat of punishment "are not the only means for bringing about effort toward organizational objectives" (McGregor, 1960, p. 47). Theory Y assumes

> that people will exercise self-direction and self-control in the achievement of organizational objectives to the degree that they are committed to those objectives. If that commitment is small, only a slight degree of self-direction and self-control will be likely, and a substantial amount of external influence will be necessary. If it is large, many conventional external controls will be relatively superfluous, and to some extent self-defeating. (p. 56)

Therefore, the committed person can be trusted to assume responsibility for the achievement of organizational objectives because these objectives are similar to his or her goals. When Theory Y is applied to sports, the coach using this style of management is more a teacher and counselor than an authoritarian taskmaster. He or she works with the athlete to help set goals and suggests strategies that might be followed, but leaves much of the implementation to the creativity and ingenuity of the individual athlete.

Theory Y is not a soft or permissive style of management. The objectives must still be met. Sanctions still follow success or failure. The difference is that the individual athlete plays a much larger role in determining the objectives and the manner in which they may be met.

In articulating the psychological foundation for Theory Y, McGregor (1960) relied heavily on Maslow's (1954) hierarchy of needs. McGregor claimed that individuals would want to work diligently for the satisfaction of ego and self-actualization needs, such as the needs for self-esteem, achievement, competence, and the "deserved respect of one's fellows."

The sociological approach to motivation, at least according to symbolic inter-actionists (McCall & Simmons, 1978; Stryker, 1980), is characterized by its emphasis on internalized role-identities and the social relations dependent on those role-identities. Unlike the psychological emphasis on inner states, the prime socio-logical motivators are other persons as role-audiences and their imagined or actual approval. Even so, the sociological motivators are similar to some of the psycho-logical needs mentioned by McGregor. Self-esteem, achievement, competence, and respect of one's peers are often determined socially: They are in fact the outcomes of superior performance in a role.

It is possible, in other words, to use a Theory Y style of management without assuming a psychological hierarchy of needs. In sports, a coach may expect that an individual who has internalized an athletic role-identity will work hard to be successful in that role even without direct supervision. Athletes who are deeply committed to their sport should be coachable under a Theory Y style of manage-ment when that style is appropriate, such as during the summer off-season. Specifi-cally, a coach should be able to assume that his swimmers will want to maintain their conditioning, not because the coach says so, but because it is important to them *as swimmers*.

Data Gathering Procedures

Not all athletes are committed equally to the sport role-identity, however. In the case of the swimmers, it seemed appropriate to gather some baseline data before a shift in styles was attempted, since Theory Y requires a strong personal commit-ment to the objectives of the program.

Sport Identity

The instrument used to measure the commitment of swimmers on this Big Ten team to their role-identities was the *Sport Identity Index* (Curry & Parr, 1988; Curry & Weaner, 1987). Briefly, the SII was used to compare the importance of the sport, academic, kin, peer, religious, and romantic identities of each swim-mer as well as to measure the involvement of self in the sport role, the number of persons known through the sport role, and other variables theoretically important to sport identity.

Sport identity was defined on the questionnaire as a label that described "your sports participation," and included swimming as an example. Peer identity was defined by a label describing "relationships you have with people your own age," and included teammates in the example. The other identity descriptions were similar.

The SII asked the swimmers first to think about the six identities, and to ask themselves, "How important is each identity in my life from week to week?" Then each swimmer was to rank the identities from 1 to 6 (1 being the most important and 6 being the least). Next the swimmers were asked to reorder the identities in response to the question, "If for some reason I had to give up my identity in one of these categories, would I do so in the order listed here? That is, would I give up the one at the bottom first, then the next one, and so on up the line, giving up last the one at the top of the list?" If not, the swimmer was told to change the order of the identity categories so that it was correct. Following that, the swimmer was asked to rate the importance of each identity on a scale from 0 to 100, with 0 being of "no importance" and 100 "as important to me as I can imagine."

The identities were measured three times—once near the peak of the season (end of February 1985), once near the end of the season (end of May 1985), and the third time in an interview session that occurred a month into the following season (October 1985). The data are reported in Table 11.3a-b, and in Hall, 1986. During the interview, the swimmers were also shown a set of photos taken of themselves and asked about the effectiveness of the previous year's off-season training contract. These photographs are described in more detail later.

Satisfaction

A simple measure of the satisfaction or dissatisfaction of each swimmer toward his or her own weight, strength, and endurance was also gathered at two different time periods, once at the beginning of the 1984 season and again near the peak of that same season. A scale of 1 = satisfied and 2 = dissatisfied was used (Table 11.2).

Physical Measurements

The third type of data was physical measurements. The assistant coach had taken weight and body-fat measures for the 1984-1985 team members (Table 11.1). An additional body-fat measurement was made in autumn 1986. Tape measurements of the chest, waist, hip, thigh, and body fat were made in spring and autumn of 1986 (Table 11.4). (Since team membership changed considerably from 1984 to 1986, the data were reported as team averages and as averages for the same specific swimmers, when possible.)

The Photographs

The final type of data collected was visual records, made at or near the same time the body-fat compositions were being taken. For the first three photo sessions (autumn 1984; winter 1985; spring 1985), swimmers were asked to flex their back, chest, and arm muscles. For the spring 1986 photographs, only a frontal view of the swimmer was taken.

The photographs served different purposes during the study. Initially, they were an interview stimulus to elicit comments from the swimmers regarding both the shape in which they reported to practice in autumn 1984 and the effects their weight training program had on them through spring 1985 (Curry, 1986). Copies of these photographs were given to the swimmers and the coach as a visual record of each swimmer's progress before and after the season's conditioning. Slides of the same photographs were shown at the team banquet in spring 1985 as a way of showing parents and guests the progress the team was making in its weight training program, and as a subtle reminder to the swimmers to stay in shape during the off-season.

By spring of the following year, it had become apparent that a photograph taken of a swimmer could be used as a prod toward self-motivation. Hence, the spring 1986 photographs were taken for the purpose of inclusion on "The Body Firm Form," described later.

Initial Findings

Table 11.1 lists the weight and body-fat measures for the team, taken during the 1984-1985 season. The first part of the table is for the whole team at the time of its arrival (September 24, 1984), during the peak of the season (March 11, 1985), and at the beginning of the next season (October 8, 1985). The second part of the table contains similar data for the same 10 swimmers at these points. The data in this table support the coach's concern over his team's lack of off-season conditioning. Body fat and weight both declined during the peak of the season, only to rise again by the start of the next season. Additionally, while norms for body fat are difficult to establish for competitive swimmers, a team average greater than 12% seemed high; the coach himself wanted his swimmers to swim at 10% or less during the season. Ten of 17 team members were over that mark on the March 11, 1985, measurement.

The swimmers' own assessments of their physical condition upon arrival in the fall was negative. Table 11.2 indicates the mean satisfaction/dissatisfaction scores for the same 17 swimmers in September 1984 and at the peak of the season, in March 1985. As might be expected upon arrival, the swimmers were mostly dissatisfied with their endurance, but they were also relatively unhappy with their strength and weight in September. They became more satisfied with these as the season progressed.

Table 11.1   Changes in Body Fat and Weight

Characteristic	Sept. 24, 1984	March 11, 1985	Oct. 8, 1985
	Team average		
Weight (lb)	175.74	174.07	175.66
Body fat (%)	12.66	10.82	12.94
N	22	17	19
	Same 10 swimmers		
Weight (lb)	180.25	178.32	182.45
Body fat (%)	11.93	11.39	12.61

Note. Body fat was measured by underwater weighing.

Table 11.2   Team Average Satisfaction/Dissatisfaction With Physical Condition

Characteristic	September 24, 1984	March 8, 1985
Weight	1.57	1.28
Strength	1.64	1.28
Endurance	1.71	1.57

Note. 1 = Satisfied; 2 = Dissatisfied; $N = 17$.

The interviews held with the team members in November 1985 concerned the effectiveness of the off-season contract in motivating them. Of the 14 swimmers interviewed, only about a third fulfilled the terms of the contract. For some, the necessity of work had intervened; for others, injury; and for others, the need for a break from swimming. Moreover, the majority of swimmers were resentful about the tone of the contract. One expressed the resentment with a statement to this effect:

> I thought that it was a joke, I mean I thought it was good for the people that he didn't think would swim, but I'm not going to go home and not do anything over the summer. I want to improve so I'm not going to have to sit around. I don't think that I should sign a contract saying that I'm going to have to do much yardage, when I didn't even do the yardage. I did work out, but I didn't think too much of the contract.

The data on the role-identities from these swimmers also provided some insight into the problem. The sport identity of the swimmers was ranked fairly low; it would be given up after religion and romantic identities, but before kin, academic,

Table 11.3a   Mean Rankings of the Six Role Identities Across Three Points of Time for the Same 14 Swimmers

| Role identity | Mean rank | | | |
	Feb. 1985 Time 1	May 1985 Time 2	Nov. 1985 Time 3	Average
Kinship	2.21	1.86	1.57	1.88
Peer	3.64	2.43	3.36	3.14
Academic	3.21	3.79	3.00	3.33
Sport	3.21	3.93	4.07	3.74
Romantic	4.06	4.00	4.43	4.16
Religion	4.93	5.00	4.57	4.83

Note. 1 = Most important; 6 = Least important.

and peer identities (Table 11.3a). Considering the amount of time the swimmers spend performing the sport role during the academic year, it should have been ranked at least second by the swimmers (Curry and Weaner, 1987). From some swimmers' point of view, however, competitive swimming was one role that they were going to have to give up fairly soon, anyway. Here is a typical remark of a swimmer about his sport:

> I'm going to go on living if I don't have swimming. . . . I always put it last 'cause, I mean it is important to me, but it isn't as important as any of the other things you have listed there. If someone came in and said you had to do without one of them, I'd say, OK, I won't swim anymore.

The rankings of the sport identity were stable throughout the data collection period; the α reliability coefficient of the ranked sport identity was .90 for the 14 swimmers who provided completed data sets (Hall, 1986). By comparison, the reliability coefficients for the other identities were .87 for kinship, .86 for religion, .83 for romantic, .67 for academic, and .39 for peer.

Comparison of the rating (100 to 0) of the sport identity to the other identity ratings was more encouraging (Table 11.3b). The mean rating of the sport identity was 76.29 across the three time periods. This was quite close to the mean ratings for the peer (77.74) and academic (76.36) identities. Hence, even though the swimmers ranked swimming fairly low among the six identities, they rated it about the same as their academic and peer identities.

Interpreting the Initial Findings

As we have seen, the swimmers were not maintaining condition in the off-season. While the coach had an idea as to what exercise and swimming routines he wanted

Table 11.3b   Rating of the Six Role Identities Across Three Points of Time for the Same 14 Swimmers

| | Mean rating | | | |
| | Feb. 1985 | May 1985 | Nov. 1985 | |
Role identity	Time 1	Time 2	Time 3	Average
Kinship	83.36	86.00	92.07	87.14
Peer	76.21	79.64	77.36	77.74
Academic	77.07	71.50	80.50	76.36
Sport	80.43	76.93	71.50	76.29
Romantic	69.79	70.21	66.79	68.93
Religion	51.70	51.43	53.64	52.25

Note. Range of rating scale is 100 (high) to 0 (low).

the swimmers to follow, he had not specified to them the weight at which they were supposed to report back in the fall. Neither he nor his team had a firm set of expectations about the actual physical condition they were trying to maintain. The existing contract was too authoritarian in tone and was producing negative feelings, but little else.

Finally, support for the swimmers' role-identities was weak and needed to be strengthened. The implementation of a Theory Y style of management requires, as has been noted, an individual's full commitment to the objectives. Given the relatively low ranking of the sport identity, it seemed doubtful that the identity of swimmer would automatically be maintained during the summer. Without some external role-support, some of the swimmers may simply not have defined themselves as swimmers during the summer and returned to that role only in the fall. Given the relatively high ranking of the peer identity, it seems likely that involvement with one's peers was what kept most of the swimmers motivated to do well on the team. Perhaps the peer identity could be used to buttress the sport identity, since swimmers' peers are other swimmers, for the most part.

Moving in the Direction of Theory Y: Proposed Changes

After I gathered this initial data, I suggested to the coach a number of revisions to his off-season conditioning program. My first report to him was brief. I stressed the idea of developing a norm for the swim team "to return to practice in the autumn in the same shape or better than they left in the spring." My hope was that if the team were to develop this norm, peer pressure would be exerted on those swimmers whose personal commitment to maintaining condition was weak.

In order to help establish this norm, I urged the coach to move away from an autocratic contractual relationship with his swimmers to one of encouragement, support, and mutual goal setting. Although I did not explain theories X and Y to him at this time, I did suggest that he needed to work individually with each swimmer concerning strategies he could use in maintaining condition, rather than impose a set of specific exercise routines for the whole team to follow. I encouraged him to be more trusting of his swimmers, and in any event not to give orders that could not be followed. I urged the coach to develop specific minimum expectations for each swimmer regarding the shape in which to report in the autumn, and to reward those swimmers who met or exceeded the objectives.

I also said the photography sessions should be continued because the swimmers and their families liked having these records, but that we needed to rethink how to make the photographs more useful. I showed the coach an article that included a photograph with a set of measurements used in a study of Danish swimmers (Vervaecke & Persyn, 1981). I suggested that he have his assistant coach keep similar records; I would provide the photographs of the swimmers. It was not clear to me exactly how to proceed from here, and I asked the coach for feedback.

My report made an impact on the coach, and he revised his procedures to reflect several of the suggestions I had made. He gave each swimmer a specific "goal weight" of 5 pounds over their "taper weight" (their peak condition weight). They were supposed to report back to practice in the autumn at this weight. If they did so, the coach would eliminate one practice session each week. He scuttled the old contract program and encouraged each swimmer to devise whatever conditioning program best fit his schedule and situation. He discussed possible methods of training with each swimmer individually at the end of the season. He also gathered height, weight, chest, hips, waist, and thigh measurements at the end of the swimming season, just prior to summer vacation. He and his assistant coach designed a Body Firm Form for this data. The form included space for a photograph, along with the date and swimmer's name and measurements. It also included a table of normative weights by frame size and heights, obtained from the "Metropolitan Height and Weight Tables for Men and Women According to Frame, Ages 25–29," which appeared in the 1983 *Statistical Bulletin* (Jan/June, p. 2). The figures reflected a general population quite different from college swimmers. Nonetheless, they were convenient to use. These forms were mailed to each swimmer during the summer, approximately a month after the end of practice.

Results of the New Program

It is difficult to make exact comparisons between the old and new off-season training program for this Big Ten swimming team because of changes in team membership that occurred simultaneously with the change in program. The coach and assistant coach recruited heavily during the same spring and summer the program was being revised. This recruitment was very successful; 26 new freshmen swimmers arrived in the autumn of 1986. Some of these freshmen swimmers

THE BODY FIRM FORM

Fitness Progress Check

Goal weight = _____

Name _____ Date _____

Chest _____ Hips _____ (7 in. below waist, largest measurement)

Waist _____ Thigh _____ (largest measurement)

To use the Metropolitan Height and Weight Tables (based on lowest mortality at ages 25 to 29) complete the following:

Frame _____ (see chart below)

Height _____ (add 1 in. to barefoot height) _____

Weight _____ (men add 5 lbs) _____

Height		Desired weight (lb)		
Feet	Inches	Small frame	Medium frame	Large frame
5	2	128-134	131-141	138-150
5	3	130-136	133-143	140-153
5	4	132-138	135-145	142-156
5	5	134-140	137-148	144-160
5	6	136-142	139-151	146-164
5	7	138-145	142-154	149-168
5	8	140-148	145-157	152-172
5	9	142-151	148-160	155-176
5	10	144-154	151-163	158-180
5	11	146-157	154-166	161-184
6	0	149-160	157-170	164-188
6	1	152-164	160-174	168-192
6	2	155-168	164-178	172-197
6	3	158-172	167-182	176-202
6	4	162-176	171-187	181-207

Place photo here

Note. These were obtained from the "Metropolitan Height and Weight Tables for Men and Women According to Frame, Ages 25-59," that appeared in the *1983 Statistical Bulletin* (Jan/June:2).

were good enough to displace some of the upperclassmen, and some of those upperclassmen left the team.

Nonetheless, I was able to track the changes in physical measurements of 10 of the swimmers from the spring of 1986 to the autumn of that same year. These measurements are presented in Table 11.4. The summer off-season that lay between these two sets of measurements was the first where the new program was attempted.

Table 11.4   Physical Comparisons, Spring and Autumn, for 10 Swimmers in Revised Off-Season Program

Time of measurement	% Body fat	Weight	Chest	Waist	Hips	Thighs
Spring 1986	–	185.80	40.13	33.41	39.45	23.25
Autumn 1986	10.21	185.65	40.55	33.90	38.80	22.73
Differences		–0.15	+.0.42	+0.49	–0.65	–0.52

Note. Measurements are in pounds and inches; body fat measured by skinfold calipers.

As Table 11.4 indicates, the "goal weights" worked reasonably well. In fact, on average, these 10 swimmers reported back to practice lighter than they had been in the spring. It should be noted that this statistic is a bit misleading, as 7 of the 10 swimmers returned slightly over their goal weights and two were under them. The two underweight swimmers had lost enough weight between them (14 lb) to draw the average into negative figures. Even so, the situation was clearly better than the previous year, when the team had reported to practice heavier than in the spring (Table 11.1).

The specific chest, waist, hips, and thigh measurements reported in Table 11.4 are also of interest. The 10 swimmers gained on the average nearly 1/2 inch in the chest and waist, while losing nearly 1/2 inch in the hips and thighs. These average figures more closely represent the individual swimmers—7 of the 10 experienced a decrease in the size of their thighs and hips, while 6 of the 10 increased the size of their waist and 5 increased their chest size. While it is not surprising to see an increase in waist size in the off-season, the loss of muscle in hips and thighs was less expected and probably was due to insufficient exercise in those muscle groups. The increase in chest size was probably due to a more concentrated effort to work on those more impressive muscle groups.

In a follow-up survey of these 10 swimmers, only 2 reported that they did very little or no training during the summer. The others, while they varied in how much swimming or lifting they did, reported an effort to maintain condition by one schedule or another. When asked their reaction to receiving the goal-weight photo reminder in the mail during the summer, 7 of the 10 swimmers said it motivated them to start their off-season training. When asked if this was the right program for maintaining condition in the off-season, 6 of the 10 said it was, and the other 4 indicated more was needed. Most significantly, only one of the swimmers seemed cynical about the idea of trying to maintain conditioning. This was quite a departure from the evaluation of the previous Theory X contract program, where a majority of swimmers indicated that they did not comply with the terms of the contract, and several were pointedly defiant in their refusal to meet the authoritarian demands of the coach.

Some typical responses received to the question whether this was the right program for maintaining condition in the off-season indicate the positive tone of remarks generated by the Theory Y goal-weight photo program:

> It reminds and shows what you have done and what you have to do. It makes you see how you look and what you want to look like. It's the right idea and is supportive of the right program, but more is needed.

The new off-season training program produced equal or better results than the old program, while eliciting more positive feedback. There were smaller weight gains and more reported attempts at maintaining condition under the new program. The new program also provided an explicit goal for each swimmer and an objective set of measurements for assessment. The inclusion of the photograph enhanced the swimmers' image and identity and gave them a positive reason for self-motivation.

Refinements

Where might the swimming coach take his summer program from here? Further improvements lie in the direction of giving the swimmers specific goal measurements and body-fat percentages to aim for in addition to the goal weights. Perhaps most important, the coach must decide how best to educate each swimmer about how to avoid losing muscle and gaining fat, and then let each swimmer find a means to conduct his own off-season training problems.

Regarding the social-psychological problem of swimmer identity loss during the summer, the Body Firm Form can be refined still further to help. The university logo could be placed on the form to help reinforce identity with the school swim team. The team co-captains could write a letter to accompany the form or co-sign the letter written by the coach to indicate a team effort rather than an authoritarian decision by the coach. The form could be sent out twice during the summer: first a month after practice has ended to remind the swimmers to start their conditioning programs, and again a month before the start of fall practice as a progress check. The second time, the swimmers could be asked to record their weights and measurements and report those to the coach.

There is some evidence from the experimental psychology literature that suggests the Body Firm Form will yield fairly accurate self-reporting data if used in this way. Wicklund (1975, 1982) summarizes a number of studies that have researched the "theory of objective self-awareness" and finds that when respondents are confronted with an image of themselves, they are more likely to report accurately on personality traits and other types of behavior. They are also more likely to attempt to bring their behavior in line with previously existing standards of behavior. Duval and Wicklund (1972) theorized that this occurs because the respondent is stimulated by the self-image to direct attention inward and think more critically about himself. Because the Body Firm Form contains both a set of measurements and an image of the swimmer, it should produce a critical self-assessment and an increased motivation to live up to the agreed-on expectations for maintaining condition during the summer.

Lessons to Be Drawn

This applied research has been successful because certain strategies were followed. For example, it was a good idea to gather data on swim team members before attempting any changes or recommendations, because the data helped to convince the coach that the old program was not working. It also was not necessary to work out every detail before presenting a plan for a new program to the coach, because the coach has good ideas, too, and was able to turn a series of recommendations into his own practical program.

It was more important to work on clarifying expectations and demonstrating results than it was to explain in detail Theory X or Theory Y; too much jargon or theoretical talk loses the attention of the nonsociologist. Once you get the attention of a coach through demonstrating results, he or she may well be more likely to want to know about the theory.

In moving the coaching staff toward a Theory Y approach to the off-season, I believe I was humanizing the program and I believe this to be an important value for college athletics. Even so, it was important to work within the existing body of norms and the limitations of the system while trying to change elements of that system. Doing so made it more likely that outside advice could and would be used. Consequently, this program, while tending toward Theory Y, included more controls and monitoring than might be desired by Theory Y purists.

There was an important side benefit to doing this applied research. It is often difficult and time-consuming for sociologists to gather information on the reliability and validity of their research instruments. However, since the coach was interested in the outcome of the study, he used part of practice time to allow me to distribute and collect questionnaires, and he urged all of his swimmers to complete and return them. His assistance in these matters allowed me to collect a 100% sample of the team each time the *Sport Identity Index* was distributed. In addition, the coach encouraged and reminded his swimmers to participate in the interview sessions. Consequently, I was able to gather data on the test-retest reliability of the questionnaire over a 10-month period and probe the validity of the various scales. This data later became part of a student's thesis that compared the SII to the Twenty Statements Test (Hall, 1986). In other words, applied research can not only benefit the clients of that research, it can also benefit theoretical and methodological development of basic research instruments. Copies of the latest version of the SII are available from me for persons wishing to conduct their own research on sport identities.

References

Curry, T.J. (1986). A visual method of studying sports: The photo-elicitation interview. *Sociology of Sport Journal*, **3**, 204–216.

Curry, T.J., & Jiobu, R.M. (1984). Coaching and social organizations: How to win. In *Sports: A social perspective* (pp. 115–135). Englewood Cliffs, NJ: Prentice-Hall.

Curry, T.J., & Parr, R.M. (1988). Comparing commitment to sport and religion at a Christian college. *Sociology of Sport Journal*, **5**, 369–377.

Curry, T.J., & Weaner, J. (1987). Sport identity salience, commitment, and the involvement of self in role: Hypotheses and measurement issues. *Sociology of Sport Journal*, **4**, 280–288.

Duval, S., & Wicklund, R.A. (1972). *A theory of objective self awareness*. New York: Academic Press.

Hall, D.L. (1986). *A comparison of two measures of role identities: The 20 statements test and the sport identity index*. Unpublished master's thesis, Ohio State University, Columbus.

Maslow, A.H. (1954). *Motivation and personality*. New York: Harper.

McCall, G.J., & Simmons, J.L. (1978). *Identities and interactions*. New York: Free Press.

McGregor, D. (1960). *The human side of enterprise*. New York: McGraw-Hill.

Parr, R. (1987). *The sport and religious identities: Comparisons of self involvement using the SII*. Unpublished doctoral dissertation, Ohio State University, Columbus.

Stryker, S. (1980). *Symbolic interactionism: A social structural version*. Menlo Park, CA: Benjamin/Cummings.

Vervaecke, H., & Persyn, U. (1981). Some differences between men and women in various factors which determine swimming performance. *Medicine Sport*, **15**, 150–156.

Wicklund, R.A. (1982). How society uses self-awareness. In J. Suels (Ed.), *Psychological perspectives on the self* (pp. 209–230). Hillsdale, NJ: Lawrence Erlbaum, Associates.

Wicklund, R.A. (1975). Objective self-awareness. In L. Berkowitz (Ed.) *Advances in experimental social psychology* (Vol. 8, pp. 233–275). New York: Academic Press.

Chapter 12
Physical Challenge as a Treatment for Delinquency

Francis J. Kelly and Daniel J. Baer
Boston College

Kelly and Baer find recidivism to be considerably less than expected among delinquents in a physically challenging Outward Bound program compared with that of delinquents in a training school program. This study is included because it is an excellent example of action-oriented research. Not only do the researchers compare the effects of two different programs, they also critically examine additional factors that may have contributed to their findings. After considering such factors as type of offense, age of first court appearance, race, urban versus rural residence, presence of parents, and so forth, they suggest ways of reducing recidivism (by supplementing aspects of physically challenging programs) among adolescent delinquents.

The First Outward Bound school was established in 1941 in Aberdovey, Wales, to train merchant seamen for survival during the battle of the Atlantic. An assumption underlying the program is that rather than merely telling a young man he is capable of more than he thinks he can do, one must devise a set of circumstances whereby the youth can demonstrate this competence to himself. To accomplish this goal, Outward Bound exposes adolescents to severe physical challenge and pushes individuals to their physical limit.

At the time of this study there were three Outward Bound schools in the United States. Each school adapts a 26-day program according to its own physical

This study was funded in part by the Office of Juvenile Delinquency, Children's Bureau, U.S. Office of Health, Education and Welfare, Grant No. 66013; the Massachusetts Division of Youth Service; and the Committee of the Permanent Charity Fund, Boston, Mass. The authors gratefully acknowledge the contributions of John D. Coughlan, former director of the Division of Youth Service, and his staff; Joshua Miner III, President, Outward Bound, Inc.; and the directors and staff of the Outward Bound Schools, whose cooperation and support enabled the successful completion of the project. *Note.* From "Physical Challenges as a Treatment for Delinquency," *Crime and Delinquency*, vol. 17, no. 1 (October 1971), pp. 437–445. Copyright © 1971 by National Council on Crime and Delinquency. Reprinted by permission of Sage Publications, Inc.

environment—mountains, sea, or forest. All stress (1) physical conditioning, such as running, hiking, swimming; (2) technical training such as the use of specialized tools and equipment, camping, cooking, map reading, navigation, lifesaving, drown-proofing, and solo survival; (3) safety training; and (4) team training, such as rescue techniques, evacuation exercises, and fire fighting. The participants in each course are divided into eight patrols of twelve boys each. Each patrol is supervised by one or more trained instructors.

Since 1964 the Massachusetts Division of Youth Service and Outward Bound Schools, Inc., have collaborated in an effort to reduce recidivism in adjudicated adolescent delinquents. In the summers of 1964 and 1965, delinquent boys from the Division of Youth Service attended Outward Bound schools in Colorado, Minnesota, and Maine. Since these boys had a relatively low recidivism rate after returning from the program, further research seemed appropriate. A demonstration project was designed to systematically examine the effect of Outward Bound on adolescent delinquents. Its purpose was to determine whether Outward Bound was more effective in reducing recidivism in adjudicated delinquent adolescent boys than current correctional practice. Also, the study examined the relative effectiveness of the different Outward Bound schools to observe which elements in Outward Bound are the most useful change agents. Effectiveness was measured by comparing recidivism rates in two matched groups of adolescent delinquent boys. One group attended Outward Bound, while the other was handled in a routine matter by juvenile correctional authorities. Recidivism, here defined as a return to a juvenile institution or commitment to an adult institution for a new offense within one year after parole, was determined from a review of the Division of Youth Service files and those of the Massachusetts Commission on Probation, where all juvenile and adult court appearances in Massachusetts are recorded.

Participating Agencies

The Colorado Outward Bound School is located on the western slopes of the Rocky Mountains at an altitude of 8,800 feet. The course involves mountain walking, high-altitude camping, rock climbing, and rappelling (descending a sheer cliff by means of two ropes wrapped around the body). Each patrol climbs at least one of the 14,000-foot peaks in the area. As a climax, unsupervised groups of three or four boys cover sixty to ninety miles of unfamiliar terrain in three days.

The Minnesota Outward Bound School is located in the Superior National Forest near Ely, Minn., on the edge of the Superior-Quetico Wilderness. Participants are trained at the main camp for twelve days and then leave on a two-week, 200-mile canoe expedition. Selected readings, films, and discussions related to the students' experiences are presented upon their return from the expedition.

The Hurricane Island Outward Bound School is located ten miles off the coast of Maine at the entrance of Penobscot Bay. More than half the program involves training in seamanship and navigation. The course climax is a five-day cruise in thirty-foot whaleboats. Each group of twelve boys must live together in these small open boats without an instructor.

The three participating institutions of the Division of Youth Services were the Reception Center for Boys, which is the receiving and diagnostic unit; the Lyman School for Boys; and the Industrial School for Boys. Lyman and ISB are the training school facilities in Massachusetts to which adolescent male delinquents are assigned.

Subjects

The subjects for this study were 120 adolescent delinquents. Only boys who were 15-1/2 to 17 years of age, in good health and without any severe physical disability or severe psychopathology, and who had a minimum IQ of 75 and no history of violent assaultive or sexual offenses were eligible for selection. Eligibility also depended on a willingness to participate if selected.

Sixty subjects from the Reception Center and sixty from the Lyman School for Boys and the Industrial School for Boys were selected. The experimental group, consisting of thirty boys from the Reception Center and thirty boys from the two institutions, attended Outward Bound. The remaining sixty subjects, identified as the comparison group, were handled in a routine manner, some being institutionalized and some immediately paroled.

The experimental and comparison groups were matched on the basis of the following variables: age at time of selection for the study, IQ, race, religion, offense for which committed, area of residence, and number of prior commitments to the Division of Youth Service. With respect to these variables, the two groups corresponded not only to each other but also to the contemporaneous population of adolescent males in the custody of the Division of Youth Service.[1]

Procedure

Experimental group subjects from the reception center were sent directly to Outward Bound and were paroled immediately upon completion of the course. Subjects selected from the training schools included boys who were institutionalized for the first time, as well as recidivists.

The complete social histories for all subjects were reviewed and developmental, medical, familial, educational, and delinquent background data were recorded. The information served as the basis for the initial matching of the experimental and comparison groups.

Three psychologists served as participant observers.[2] One observer attended at least one course at each of the three Outward Bound schools. The observer's function was to participate in and observe the program and to record his impressions of the course and its impact on the participants.

Recidivism

Table 12.1 summarizes the incidence of recidivism in the experimental and comparison groups. The 20 percent recidivism rate of the experimental group is half that of the expected rate (40 percent) for boys of this age committed to the Division of Youth Service. On the other hand, the 42 percent recidivism found in the comparison group is consistent with the base expectancy rate. On a chi-square test of independence, the significant result ($\chi^2 = 5.80$, $p < .01$, one-tail hypothesis) supports the expectation that Outward Bound is more effective in reducing recidivism in adolescent delinquent boys than routine management in public institutions.

Table 12.1   Recidivism Rates for Experimental and Comparison Groups

Category	Experimental		Comparison	
Recidivists	12	(20%)	25	(42%)
Nonrecidivists	48	(80%)	35	(58%)
Total	60	(100%)	60	(100%)

Note. Chi-square = 5.80, $df = 1$ ($p < .01$, one-tail hypothesis).

To explain this outcome it is necessary to examine the program at Outward Bound. The participant observers report that Outward Bound encourages change in the adolescent delinquent.[3] The opportunities for concrete impressive accomplishment, as well as for excitement and challenge, promote personal growth. The need to pace oneself challenges the delinquent's impulsivity, while the requirement of persistence challenges his endurance. The necessity of obeying safety laws and camp regulations causes him to question his concept that laws and regulations are to be ignored, and his dependence upon his patrol leader for success and well-being causes him to re-examine his attitude toward authority figures.

Recidivism and Outward Bound

The participant observers report that the programs at the three Outward Bound schools differ in many respects. The Colorado and Hurricane Island schools emphasize severe physical challenge, felt danger, and high excitement. On the other hand, these programs do not attempt to meet the needs of individual participants but require all boys to adapt to the standards of these schools. Another important characteristic of these schools is that they make little effort to interpret verbally the meaning of the experience to the participants. However, the Minnesota school, while stressing physical challenge, has a relatively low objective danger and excitement level. This program emphasizes concern for interpersonal relationships and stresses reflection and development of a spiritual attitude.

The recidivism rates for the subjects attending the three Outward Bound schools is summarized in Table 12.2. It may be seen that the Minnesota School had a higher recidivism rate (42 percent) than the Colorado (0 percent) or Hurricane Island (11 percent) school. These results appear to support the belief that delinquent adolescents are action-oriented and respond to programs which challenge them in the sphere of physical activity.[4] Programs such as Colorado and Hurricane Island, which have a high degree of physical challenge and excitement—e.g., rappelling a sheer cliff—followed by period of relative quiet when the participants can realize, absorb, and accept their accomplishments, may account for the relative success of these programs. On the other hand, programs which call for consistent physical activity and endurance but without periods of high excitement or real danger are not successful in reducing recidivism. Perhaps if training schools incorporated these elements of severe physical challenge with high excitement into their programs, they would more realistically meet the needs of the adolescent delinquent.

Table 12.2   Recidivism Rates by Outward Bound School Attended

School	Recidivists		Nonrecidivists		Total
Colorado	0	(0%)	18	(38%)	18
Minnesota	10	(84%)	14	(29%)	24
Hurricane Island	2	(16%)	16	(33%)	18
Total	12	(100%)	48	(100%)	60

Note. Chi-square = 12.43, $df = 2$ ($p < .002$, one-tail hypothesis).

Background Variables

Although Outward Bound seemed to have an important effect, one must also consider several background variables when evaluating the recidivism rate of the experimental and comparison groups. The following five variables were most closely related to recidivism: number of commitments to the Division of Youth Service, type of offense, presence of both parents in the home, age of first court appearance, and age of first commitment. On the other hand, such variables as IQ, race, urban-rural residence, religion, and whether subjects were selected from a training school or the reception center were not important predictors.

In Table 12.3 it may be seen that the mean age at first court appearance for the recidivists was significantly younger ($t = 3.88$, $p < .01$) than for the nonrecidivists. Also, the mean age for first commitment for the recidivists was significantly younger ($t = 5.20$, $p < .001$) than for the nonrecidivists. However, no such difference was found within the comparison group. This suggests that Outward Bound may have a greater impact on the delinquent whose first court appearance occurs following the onset of adolescence. Many writers[5] have commented on the employment of delinquency as a masculine protest and as a device to assert independence. Perhaps the severe physical challenge of Outward Bound provides an opportunity to resolve this identity crisis.

Table 12.3   Age at First Court Appearance and at First Commitment for Experimental and Comparison Group Recidivists and Nonrecidivists

| | Experimental group | | | | | Comparison group | | | | |
| | Recidivists (N = 12) | | Non-recidivists (N = 48) | | | Recidivists (N = 25) | | Non-recidivists (N = 35) | | |
Variable	Mean	SD	Mean	SD	t	Mean	SD	Mean	SD	t
Age of first court apperance	12.8	2.3	14.6	1.6	–3.88[a]	14.3	1.8	14.0	1.9	0.58
Age of first commitment	13.9	2.2	16.0	0.9	–5.20[b]	15.4	1.7	15.2	1.8	–0.43

[a] $p < .01$.
[b] $p < .001$.

Those delinquents whose first court appearance occurred before the onset of adolescence may represent more characterologically deficient boys who do not respond either to currently employed correctional practices or to Outward Bound. The insignificant differences in age at first commitment and age at first offense for recidivists and nonrecidivists in the comparison group, when compared with the experimental group, suggest that existing training school programs do not realize positive change for some boys who have this potential.

Number of Commitments

Table 12.4 summarizes the incidence of recidivism and the number of commitments for the experimental and the comparison groups. It may be seen that, in the experimental group, four of thirty-eight (11 percent) of the first commitment boys recidivated, while eight of twenty-two (36 percent) of the subjects who had two or more commitments were returned. This significant outcome ($x^2 = 5.81$,

$p < .01$) indicates that Outward Bound was more successful for those who had at least one prior commitment. On the other hand, for the comparison group the number of commitments was not a significant predictor of recidivism. Further support for this finding may be seen from a comparison of recidivism for the first commitment boys in the experimental and comparison groups. While four of thirty-eight (11 percent) of the first commitments in the experimental group recidivated, thirteen of thirty-six (36 percent) of the first commitments in the comparison group were returned ($\chi^2 = 6.84$, $p < .01$). From these data alone it is difficult to discern whether it was the positive effect of Outward Bound or the negative effect of the training school which contributed to this finding. However, for the first commitment boys, at least, the data suggest that many have a potential for rehabilitation which is not realized by present training school programs. They also indicate that severe physical challenge does not meet the needs of delinquents with two or more commitments.

Table 12.4   Recidivism and Number of Commitments of Experimental and Comparison Groups

Group	Number of commitments				χ^g
	One		Two or more		
Experimental					
Recidivists	4	(11%)	8	(36%)	
Nonrecidivists	34	(89%)	14	(64%)	5.81[a]
Total	38	(100%)	22	(100%)	
Comparison					
Recidivists	13	(36%)	12	(50%)	
Nonrecidivists	23	(64%)	12	(50%)	1.14
Total	36	(100%)	24	(100%)	
χ^g	6.84[a]		0.87		

[a]$p < .01$, $df = 1$ (one-tail hypothesis).

Type of Offense

The offenses for which the subjects were committed were grouped into two categories: stubborn-runaway and other. The first group was composed of boys committed for being either stubborn or runaway children. These offenses have no adult counterpart and usually reflect intrafamilial conflicts expressed in disobedience, incorrigibility, or running away from home. The second group included the remaining delinquents, whose offenses were against persons or property, acts which, if committed by an adult, would constitute misdemeanors or felonies.

The incidence of recidivism and type of offense for experimental and comparison groups is summarized in Table 12.5. The most dramatic contrast between the experimental and comparison groups is found in the stubborn-runaway category. Whereas six of the fifteen (40 percent) experimental group subjects recidivated, ten of twelve (83 percent) in the comparison group were returned. This significant difference ($\chi^2 = 5.19, p < .01$) suggests that Outward Bound may have a greater influence on those subjects whose delinquency is a direct response to home conflict than does the traditional training school.

Table 12.5   Recidivism and Type of Offense for Experimental and Comparison Groups

| Group | Type of offense | | | | χ^g |
	Stubborn-runaway		Other		
Experimental					
Recidivists	6	(40%)	6	(13%)	
Nonrecidivists	9	(60%)	39	(87%)	5.00[a]
Total	15	(100%)	45	(100%)	
Comparison					
Recidivists	10	(83%)	15	(31%)	
Nonrecidivists	2	(17%)	33	(69%)	10.71[c]
Total	12	(100%)	48	(100%)	
χ^g	5.19[b]		4.25[a]		

[a]$p < .05$.
[b]$p < .01$.
[c]$p < .001$.
$df = 1$ (one-tailed hypothesis).

However, when comparing the recidivism rate for the stubborn-runaway category, we should note that in both the experimental group (40 percent vs. 13 percent) and the comparison group (83 percent vs. 31 percent) the stubborn-runaways were three times as likely as other types of delinquents to recidivate. Perhaps action-oriented programs by themselves fail to meet the needs of the stubborn-runaway offenders, who often return to the same home environment. It would seem that these offenders, who are perhaps more immature or emotionally disturbed or who may be responding to some family pathology, may require a more intensive and psychotherapeutic care than either Outward Bound or the training schools provide.

On the other hand, when subjects who committed offenses other than stubborn-runaway are compared (Table 12.6), it may be seen that the boys who attended Outward Bound had a significantly lower ($\chi^2 = 4.25$, $p < .05$) rate of recidivism (13 percent) than comparison group boys placed in training schools (31 percent). It may be that severe physical challenge, as represented by the Outward Bound program, is more effective with delinquents who act out in the community than it is with boys who act out directly against the home.

Presence of Parents in the Home

An important finding of the present study was the relationship between recidivism and the presence of both parents in the home. From Table 12.6 it may be seen that subjects in the experimental group who returned to homes in which both parents were present had a significantly lower ($\chi^2 = 6.67$, $p < .01$) rate of recidivism (7 percent) than the rate (33 percent) for boys who returned to other types of home conditions. On the other hand, there was no significant difference in the incidence of recidivism in the comparison group for individuals returning to either intact or broken homes. Since it is generally accepted[6] that the presence of both parents in the home is a favorable condition for growth, it may be that the boys from intact homes were initially less likely to become confirmed delinquents. The severe physical challenge of Outward bound may provide them a means of resolving some adolescent crisis.

Table 12.6   Recidivism and Presence of Both Parents in the Home

Category	Experimental Group				Comparison Group			
	Live with both parents		Other		Live with both parents		Other	
Recidivists	2	(7%)	10	(33%)	10	(39%)	15	(44%)
Nonrecidivists	28	(93%)	20	(67%)	16	(61%)	19	(56%)
Total	30	(100%)	30	(100%)	26	(100%)	34	(100%)
Chi-squares		6.67[a]				0.19		

[a]$p < .01$, $df = 1$ (one-tailed hypothesis).

Implications

The results of this study suggest that severe physical challenge may be an effective method of reducing recidivism in adolescent delinquents. Although the study involved sending delinquents to Outward Bound schools, it seems that training schools might profit from incorporating many features of the Outward Bound approach into their own programs. Action-oriented adolescents may respond more to action programs than to cognitively oriented counseling approaches. However, it should be recognized that although not effective with all delinquents, this approach could be of sufficient value to recommend it as a supplement, if not an alternative, to institutionalization.

Notes

[1]"Annual Report of the Division of Youth Service," Massachusetts Division of Youth Service, Boston, 1965.

[2]The Detailed reports of these observers are included in Francis J. Kelly and Daniel J. Baer, *Outward Bound: An Alternative to Institutionalization* (Boston, Mass.: Fandel Press, 1968), pp. 95-174.

[3]Kelly and Baer, *op. cit. supra* note 2.

[4]See, for example, William C. Kvaraceus and Walter B. Miller, *Delinquent Behavior, Culture and the Individual* (Washington, D.C.: National Education Association, 1995), pp. 62-68.

[5]See, for example, Erik Erikson, *New Perspectives for Research on Juvenile Delinquency* (Washington, D.C.: U.S. Government Printing Office, 1956); Louis Sontag, "Problems of Dependency and Masculinity as Factors in Delinquency," *American Journal of Orthopsychiatry*, October 1958; or Helen Witmer, *Delinquency and the Adolescent Crisis* (Washington, D.C.: U.S. Government Printing Office, 1960).

[6]See, for example, Paul Glasser and Elizabeth Navarre, "Structural Problems of the One-Parent Family," *Journal of Social Issues*, January 1965, pp. 98-109.

PART III

The Knowledge Transfer Phase

Part III has but a single article, for we encountered considerable difficulty identifying studies in sport sociology that appropriately reflected application designed to translate research findings. Although several studies could be modified or supplemented by editorial commentary to reflect this phase, we wanted to find an existing publication that included all aspects of knowledge transfer: synthesis of what is known about a problem, a review or assessment of solutions or suggested courses of action, and specific recommendations for implementation. After being unable to find such a sport sociology article, we turned to related subdisciplines and found an article in sport psychology that represented each aspect of knowledge transfer. We do hope that sport sociologists will be more concerned with translation and transfer of knowledge in the next few years and that future editions of this anthology will contain more examples of this particular level of application.

Chapter 13

Children in Competition: A Theoretical Perspective and Recommendations for Practice

Glyn C. Roberts
University of Illinois at Urbana-Champaign

We feel that Roberts's analysis of the competitive process best reflects knowledge transfer because it goes beyond review and synthesis. This article effectively organizes information pertaining to several aspects of the social comparison process: children's cognitive development, the attributions children make about winning and losing, and their evaluation of sport performance. The strength of this chapter lies in its insights: It cogently translates research in a way that practitioners can readily understand, it extends that research by discussing implications and solutions, and it makes specific recommendations for implementation. This article not only captures the knowledge transfer phase in spirit, it also offers concrete ways of meaningfully putting sport science research into practice.

Within sports, there is probably no area of greater concern to parents than the topic of the appropriateness of competition for their children. Should children be exposed to competition in organized sports such as Pee Wee Football, Little League, and so on? These arguments sometimes revolve around the potential for injury or physical harm for the children, but the concern is primarily with the social psychological effects of sports on the developing personality of children. It is this topic that creates the greatest controversy and the most heated debate. Some individuals regard competition as natural, healthy, exposing children to team discipline and win/loss experiences which are essential for building a sound personality and preparing the child to live in American society. To others, competition is regarded as harmful, psychologically injurious and having negative effects on the moral and social development of the child.

Note. From *Motor Skills: Theory Into Practice*, 1980, **4**(1), pp. 37–50. Copyright 1980 by *Motor Skills*. Reprinted by permission.

Anyone who is seriously concerned about the effects of the competitive process upon children should not force themselves into such polar positions. Bias either for or against competition blinds individuals to the true effects of competition on children. This issue is far too important for us to let our biases affect our judgment. Therefore, we need to suspend prejudgment and take a long, hard look at competition for children. More importantly, we need to consider competition from the point of view of the child within the experience. Adults tend to view competition from their own perspective and assume the same perspective applies to children. Therefore, the purpose of this paper is to put the issue of organized competition for children into the psychological perspective of the child. First, the competitive process is briefly defined and then the implications of the cognitive evaluations made by children in competitive environments is discussed. Second, this paper also recommends some practices to make the competitive experience more sensitive to the needs of children.

The Competitive Process

The competitive process consists of an individual, or team, attempting to achieve a goal or meet some standard of excellence. The process is considered to be evaluative in that the performance of the individual or team is favorably or unfavorably evaluated as achieving the goal or standard of excellence by others present—peers, teachers, parents, coaches, etc. (Martens, 1975). Recognizing that competition is an evaluative social process from the point of view of the child is an important point to remember.

It must also be remembered that competing is learned behavior! When children are very young they cannot and do not compete. This does not mean that little children do not play, run, throw balls, and swim or enjoy interacting with parents or peers in such games. The crucial element for children under about age five is that they gain enjoyment from a mastery of certain skills (Sherif, 1976; Veroff, 1969). However, when children are about five or six years of age, they begin to learn to compete and to compare their skills with peers. But children are 10 or 12 years of age before they develop a mature understanding of the competitive process and are able to accurately determine their competence (Nicholls, 1978). Therefore, it is important to take the age of the child into consideration within the competitive process.

Children in the age range of approximately five years of age through adolescence are going through a stage in their cognitive development in which they utilize social comparison processes almost exclusively in order to judge their own capabilities and self-worth (Veroff, 1969). This is the period of time when children's most important source of reference of their own abilities and competence is their peer group. Children socially judge their own competence and self-worth for all types of activities, not just sports. Adults also use social comparison processes (keeping up with the Joneses), but adults use objective criteria, too. Adults can and do use absolute standards. Children use relative standards. Rather than being satisfied with objective standards, or in contexts such as sports where objective standards are difficult to establish, children compare themselves to others. To children from about age five through adolescence, the social comparison process is *the* process by which they judge their own competence and their own self-worth (Veroff, 1969).

Of particular relevance to the social comparison process that children are going through within this age range is the importance of being competent in physical activities. Being favorably evaluated by their peers in sporting activities is very important to young boys in particular. Indeed, it has been suggested that competence in physical skills is the major are in which young boys in our society socially compare themselves (Roberts, 1977a, 1977b; Veroff, 1969; Scanlan[1]). Comparing themselves in sports is a most important source of information to children about their own relative competence and, by inference, their own self-worth. In our society, it is difficult to underestimate the importance of competence in physical skills for boys.

Parents, teachers, siblings, and peers are important in determining the emphasis that children will place upon competition during the crucial stages of the child's development. The development of the understanding of competition occurs in a particular social context. The child grows up with the family in a particular culture, and it depends upon the emphases that significant others and the culture put on the competitive process as to the emphasis the children place on competition and the social contexts in which competition is found (Nelson & Kagan, 1972). For example, we find that boys are steered toward competitive sports in our society. Sports competition is greatly valued and we steer boys in that direction. Girls, as a rule, are not steered into competition to the same extent. Therefore, the emphases we as parents, teachers, coaches, and siblings place upon the competitive process and the appropriate contexts of such competition are directly learned by our children.

It has been argued above that the social comparison process is important to children because of the normative information that is given to children when they win or lose in competitive sports. However, both Gerson (1977) and Sherif (1976) argue that the presence of others is not necessary for competition to occur, and state that the individual may compete with the self. Since adults can and do use absolute standards of social comparison, it is both possible and probable for adults to utilize intraindividual competitive processes. However, as discussed above, children adopt relative standards of competence for normative social comparison almost exclusively in the age range of five through early adolescence. Therefore, for children, the presence of others is essential for competition to occur.

The Attribution of Children in Competition

Having determined that the normative social comparison process is important for children in competitive environments, it is now necessary to discuss the evaluations made by children and the effect of these decisions upon their subsequent motivation and self-esteem. When we succeed or fail, all of us, and children are no exception, go through a process by which we judge why we succeeded or failed. We all make judgments or attributions to the causes. If we win, we usually attribute winning to our ability at that game. However, we could also say we won because of effort—we really tried hard today, and we beat our opponent because of this effort. We could also say we won because of luck. Our opponent may have had some bad luck or we may have had some good luck. Finally, our opponent could have been playing badly and was easy to beat. When we win or lose, all of us make such judgments about why we won or lost and these judgments generally incorporate ability, effort, luck, and the difficulty or ease of the task. There are other reasons used to explain the causes of winning and losing, but research has shown that the ones indicated above are used most of the time (Roberts[2]).

These four elements have been placed into a theoretical framework by Weiner and associates (1971, 1974). Weiner and associates propose a taxonomic model which focuses upon the beliefs individuals have relative to succeeding or failing at an achievement oriented activity. The individual is regarded as a naive scientist who is trying to answer questions about the environment such as why this or that event occurred, or why this particular match was won or lost. This approach considers man as an active, information processing organism with the inclusion of higher mental processes as determinants of human action. The attributions one makes following a win or loss are seen as having both emotional and behavioral consequences. The attributions one makes affect one's choice of activities, the pride or shame one feels, actual performance levels, the expectancy of future performance levels, and the amount of motivation exhibited (Weiner, 1974; Weiner et al., 1971).

When evaluating performance, the child processes the contribution of each of the elements as to the cause of the outcome. These elements have been placed into a two dimensional model illustrated in Figure 13.1.

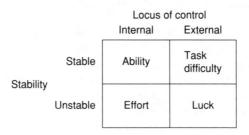

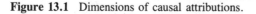

Figure 13.1   Dimensions of causal attributions.

The first dimension is termed locus of control and refers to whether the elements are internal or external to the person. Two of the elements, ability and effort, are considered to be internal and under the personal control of the individual to some extent. The other two elements, luck and task difficulty, are external and considered to be outside of the personal control of the individual. The degree to which the child attributes the success or failure to internal or external causes affects the degree of pride or shame experienced. Attributing winning or losing to an internal element maximizes the degree of pride or shame felt, while attributing the win or loss to an external cause minimizes the degree of pride or shame. For example, if winning is attributed to high ability, then pride in winning is maximized.

The second dimension is termed stability and pertains to the stability over time of the elements. Two of the elements, ability and task difficulty, are considered to be relatively stable and do not change much over time. The other two factors, luck and effort, are considered to be unstable and do change from moment to moment. Weiner and associates argue that the stability of the factors determine the changes in expectancies of future performance following a win or a loss. Attributing winning or losing to a stable element usually means that the same outcome is to be expected in the future. Attributing winning or losing to an unstable element means that the outcome may change in the future. For example, if losing is attributed to effort, then an increase in effort may lead to a win.

Figure 13.2 illustrates how this process operates in a sports context (Roberts, 1977a). Following a win or a loss, the children are assumed to use the information about the game to make their attributions about the causes of winning and losing. Within sports, many bits of information may be used. For example, the win/loss history of the team (Roberts, 1975), the pattern of wins/losses (Gould & Roberts[3]), the influence of the coach (Iso-Ahola, 1975), and the referee (Spink, 1978) have all been investigated and found to influence attributions to a greater or lesser extent.

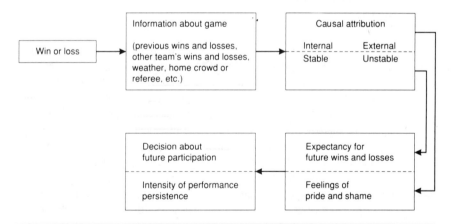

Figure 13.2 The attribution process.

The attributions children make in sporting situations fall within the locus of control and stability dimensions. Attributions along the locus of control dimension affect the feelings of pride or shame, while attributions along the stability dimension affect the expectancy of future wins or losses. It is assumed that these attributions affect the child's subsequent achievement behavior. For example, if the child believes that losing is attributable to his or her own lack of ability (a stable, internal attribute), then that child expects failure in the future and feels shame in losing. Therefore, it is not surprising that the child may not be very motivated to perform in the same situation in the future and, indeed, may seek to drop out of the activity if given the choice. Conversely, if the child believes that winning is attributable to his or her high ability, then that child expects success in the future and feels pride in winning. Therefore, the child enjoys the activity, is motivated to perform, and seeks every opportunity to repeat the experience. In this way, the attributions the child makes affect the decisions about whether he or she is going to drop out of the activity, the motivation exhibited, the amount of enjoyment and satisfaction perceived, and so on.

The data currently available generally support the attributional approach. Children, when asked to causally attribute winning and losing in sports, do make attributions consistent with the above dimensional predictions. When children win in organized sport competition, they do use the internal attributions of effort and ability to explain why they won and use the external attributions of luck and task difficulty to explain why they lost (Iso-Ahola, 1975; Roberts, 1975, 1978; Gould & Roberts[3]). Factors such as team versus self attributions, the previous win/loss record of the team, and the sequencing of winning and losing are sytematically taken into account by the children (Iso-Ahola, 1975; Roberts, 1975, 1978; Gould & Roberts[3]). Therefore, children can and do process the environmental evidence available to them and make rational decisions about the causes of events.

Age Considerations

The attributions children make are also a function of their age. There is evidence that shows that children emphasize different elements in making their attributions depending upon their age. In an important recent study, Nicholls (1978) looked at the cognitive reasoning capabilities of children aged 5 through 13 years of age. Nicholls was particularly concerned with the attributions to effort and ability and found that children go through four stages of cognitive reasoning in the age range under study. When children were five or six years of age, they could not distinguish between cause and effect of outcomes. Children tended to focus upon outcome in their evaluative judgments and ignore effort and ability cues. Children who were seven through nine years of age did begin to distinguish cause and effect but focused upon both outcome and effort. These children believed that equal effort leads to equal outcomes. The third level of reasoning occurs at about ages nine through eleven when effort is recognized as being necessary for success, but ability attributions are also made. However, ability is only used to explain success when children did not exert effort. It was only when children were aged 13 and 13 years of age that they began to systematically utilize the concepts of ability and effort and recognize that outcomes are determined jointly by effort and ability. Therefore, the level of cognitive reasoning of the child affects how the child views the experience of being placed into organized competitive sports.

When children are young, or at least under the age of about 10, they fail to recognize that the outcome of a game is determined by both ability and effort. Therefore, winning and losing in sports is not particularly informative to children in relation to their abilities. These children believe that effort is the prime determinant of outcomes and they try hard. Children do not recognize when their ability is low and they continue to pursue the activity with enthusiasm. We have all observed young children who continue to be enthusiastic about an activity despite apparent strong evidence which suggests that they are not good at the activity. However, when children become older, they do recognize that effort and ability are necessary for success and behave accordingly. As children mature and begin to more accurately attribute the causes of events, their perception of attainment more closely parallels what is their actual attainment. The shift in cognitive reasoning allows children to accurately perceive their own abilities.

There is other evidence that children have these shifts in cognitive reasoning abilities. In studies where children were asked to award stars to other children who either succeeded or failed and who exhibited ability or effort, children utilized different cues at different ages (Salili, Maehr, & Gillmore, 1976; Weiner & Peter, 1973). When children were less than 10 years of age they based their awards on outcome alone, ignoring whether effort or ability was present. However, when children were 10 through 12 years of age approximately, then the amount of effort expended at the task became the most important criterion for awards. If children tried hard, even if they failed, then they were still rewarded for trying. Interestingly, when American children were aged 13 and over, outcome again became the most important source of evaluation. This was not true of other cultures which still continued to reward effort (Salili et al., 1976). These data support Nicholls (1978) in that children did have shifts in cognitive reasoning which affected their behavior.

The interesting datum here is that American children apparently experience a "moral regression" (Salili et al., 1976) by reverting to emphasizing outcome after age 13. The important question is, why? It is argued here that it is due to the emphasis upon winning which exists in our culture. As we all know, most adults are very outcome oriented and the folklore of coaching is replete with anecdotes such as "coming in second is like kissing your sister," or "winning isn't everything, it's the only thing," and so on. The prevailing attitude is that it is not how you play the game, it is whether you win or lose that is important. The emphasis we place on competition and being first is such that our children learn these beliefs and behave accordingly.

Implications

It is when you consider the above information with the assumptions made earlier that the implications become clear. Competition in sports is an evaluative system of normative social comparison in which being competent is important to children and to young boys in particular. Therefore, when we formalize the competitive experience as we do when we organize children's sports, we place the children in a very intensive evaluation process. For children who are able to accurately attribute cause and effect relationships, this evaluation gives them important normative information relative to their own sport competence. Organized sports, then, elevate the importance and the effect of this information on the children.

The implications of this are profound. If older children do perceive their attainment more accurately and analyze the causes of success and failure in the logical fashion predicted by attribution theory, then their motivation in sport and the effort they will apply should be quite closely related to their perceived attainment in sports. Children who believe themselves to be good in sports should be more achievement oriented in behavior than children who believe themselves to be poor in sports. The differences in sport attainment would therefore be maintained or increased (Roberts[4]).

In young children, effort might be *less* closely related to actual attainment if they perceive attainment less accurately and analyze the causes of success and failure less logically than older children. There are data that show that academic effort and attainment are related (Bloom, 1976). If children are, in fact, accurate in self perception and are logical in explaining outcomes as the data suggest, this inequality of achievement behavior becomes inevitable in a competitive environment (Nicholls, 1978). If the amount of effort that is applied does become increasingly dependent on attainment in sports with age, this could help explain why children do have their shifts of interest and motivation at about 10 through 13 years of age.

When children begin to accurately process the information available to them relative to their own sport competence, then their behavior becomes grounded in this information. (It must be remembered that information relative to their sports competence is not given solely by the win/loss record of themselves or of the team. Children also get sports competence information from the coach and from their peers. This is particularly true within team games). If the information suggests low competence, the children may begin to lose motivation and interest in the activity. They develop what has been termed "sports learned helplessness" (Roberts, 1977a). These children have the belief that they are not very good in sports and their behavior has little effect on the outcome, so why try hard anyway? These children develop what we often call an "attitude problem." The child is not motivated to perform and is often disruptive to others. The extreme case of sports-learned helplessness is the dropout. This child perceives low sports competence and sees little opportunity to improve or to effect any change so he or she drops out of the activity completely. This decision may be traumatic to the child and generate low confidence and low self-concept. Even for the child who receives information that he or she is good at sports we sometimes still have dropouts. When children are older, they begin to realize that every time they compete their abilities are exposed, and continual intensive competition with the consequent normative social comparison becomes too much for them. These children drop out despite receiving the usual favorable information relative to their own competence. These children drop out because of the intensity of competition in organized sports. We term this phenomenon "psychological burnout."

Developing the argument of Nicholls (1978), if we are committed to the fullest possible development of children, then we must attempt to maintain the motivation of all children, not just those who are the high achievers. Something is wrong if we systematically encourage some at the expense of others. Yet, this inequality becomes inevitable in a competitive system of organized sports in which children experience intensive normative social comparison. This is particularly unfortunate in children's sports where ability is often a function of the physiological maturity or experiences of the child. The physiologically mature and experienced children are the ones who are most likely to enjoy success and who probably benefit most from the competitive experience. But, if we assume that social interaction in games is important for social and moral development, we should attempt to keep all children within the competitive experience.

When children are left to their own devices in organizing their games, children recognize inequity and restore equity by exchanging players from one side to another. Children's unorganized competition is not an intensive social comparison experience and all children benefit. Adult intervention, on the other hand, formalizes teams and structures success and failure for the children if inequities exist between teams initially. Therefore, it is recommended that we encourage non-competitive sports environments for children which will encourage attributions which produce higher effort and more motivation on the part of all participants (Ames, Ames, & Felker, 1977). In this way we reduce the negative impact of the competitive environment. It is strongly recommended that we organize children less and deemphasize competition and recognize that our task with young children is to maintain interest, motivation, and participation and not to create dropouts or psychologically injure children (Roberts[4]).

It would appear that if we are concerned for the welfare of the children who participate, then a massive reorganization of children's sport is warranted. The ideal solution is to abolish organized competitive sports for children under approximately age 13, but let us be realistic. Organized sports for children are with us to stay. Indeed, the number of participants is increasing with each succeeding year. Therefore, we must rethink the procedures by which we handle children in competitive environments. The practical solution is to attempt to make the organized competitive experience more sensitive to the needs of the child.

Recommendations for Practice

The following recommendations are not meant to be exhaustive, they are merely an attempt to get us pointed in the right direction.

Sensitize Parents, Teachers, and Coaches to the Competitive Process

The first and probably the most important recommendations to make is that we must sensitize parents, teachers, and coaches to the psychological processes and stresses experienced by the child who is involved in competitive sports. Understanding how the child perceives the competitive experience is very important and is an aspect that should be understood by all adults who have direct dealings with children in competitive environments. At the very least, each coach should have some knowledge of child development in order to develop some sensitivity for children. Since the bulk of this paper has been directed at the psychological processes and stresses experienced by the child, the remainder of the paper will be devoted to procedures through which a coach can be more effective both as a coach and as a teacher of children.

Children Are Not Miniature Adults

Coaches would become much more effective in helping children to cope with the competitive experience if they remembered that children are not miniature adults. The perceptions and psychological reactions of children to competition are not the same as an adult's. Children increase in their accuracy of self perception as a function of cognitive maturity and, probably, performance history (Bloom, 1976; Nicholls, 1978). Children have shifts in the importance of various elements in attributing why they won or lost. Young children do not recognize that effort and ability are necessary for success, and it is only when children are approximately 13 years of age do they develop a mature understanding of the attributions underlying winning and losing. Since coaches are outcome oriented, the coach may be making attributions based upon the outcome of the game and making postgame comments to the children that are in conflict with the attributions of the children. This will depend upon the age of the children; but, particularly when children are under age 13, the children may be making attributions to effort and be feeling reasonably satisfied with their own performance even though they may have lost. When the coach begins to harangue the team based upon his/her own attributional schema, the comments may be in conflict with the conclusions the children have drawn based upon their own attributional schema. As a result, the children become unsure of themselves, feel ill at ease, and fail to understand the comments of the coach. More importantly, the coach may lose the confidence of the players. Therefore, understanding the attributional bases of children is an important facet of coaching children.

An example of the conflict which may occur between adults and children is illustrated in the following incident. For a recent project, both sandlot and Little League Baseball games were observed by the writer. After one sandlot game, the experimenter was talking to two boys as they walked home from the game, asking them about their feelings and trying to tease out their attributions about the game. When they got closer to their home, one of the boys suddenly turned to the other and asked who had won. The other boy wasn't sure and the two boys began to argue. The experimenter intervened and asked why they are arguing: if they couldn't remember who had won, he suggested to the boys, then it was not really important. One boy turned to the experimenter and said, "But my father always asks me who won!" It is well to remember that children may not be making the same attributions as adults when they win or lose in competitive activities. Therefore, it is up to the coach or parent to try to make post-game statements that are in concert with the cognitive maturity of the child.

Maintain High Expectancies of Performance

Another area in which we must guard against deflating children is in the area of expectancies. As we have seen, the judgments children make affect their expectancies for future performance which in turn affects their motivation and their enjoyment of the activity. An important source of information to children relative to their expectancies is the coach or the parent. When children are unsure of their abilities and potential, the coach becomes an important source of reference for the child. Therefore, the expectancies the coach conveys, either verbally or non-verbally (some coaches are superb actors!), are very important to the child. Other research has demonstrated that the expectancies of performance are often matched by children (see Rosenthal, 1973). For example, the child sent into the game may be expected to perform poorly. The coach tells him/her to get in there and do his/her best, but the coach's attitude reflects that he/she does not expect the child to do very well. The coach may have given the child a low expectancy. The child often feels uncomfortable because he/she has been given the impression that his/her abilities are low. Further, he/she doesn't want to let his/her teammates down because their social approval is important. To make matters worse, when this child does perform well on occasion, the coach often conveys the impression that it was luck. Obviously, the coach is not doing much for the child if the coach holds those beliefs and those expectations.

This effect is sometimes called the self-fulfilling prophecy or the "pygmalion effect" (Rosenthal, 1973). The expectancies one has of a child are often matched by the child. Therefore, coaches should always expect the best from players, encourage the players, and give them ability and effort encouragement if they want to maximize the performance of players. In this way, the motivation and beliefs of players in themselves is increased. Whether these players actually do perform better is another issue, but psychologically the coach has done his/her best for the child. This is particularly true of players with low self-confidence and low self-esteem. Having high expectations for these children encourages their performance because they do not believe that they have these abilities and lack confidence to really try to perform well. This is where a sensitive coach can really help a ball player.

Children are particularly sensitive to the comment that other children make about their performance. As a coach, try to control and countermand any negative comments children make to each other. It is well to remember that children are going through a social comparison stage in which the comments other children make about their performance are particularly important. Therefore, if other children are "down" on a particular child, and the coach perceives the child is undergoing some anguish, then the coach should try to control the comments of the other children. The comments can shatter the confidence of a low performing, but potentially good ball player. The coach cannot control what children say to each other when they are out of his/her presence, but the coach, or parent, can reflect a positive attitude toward all players which the other children will observe. The coach's attitudes and comments are important sources of reference for players about their own and other children's performance and potential.

Deal With Each Child Individually

Coaches often use the outcome of the game to make comments to the team about their effort, their ability, and so on. It is recommended that coaches do not use the *team* outcome as the basis of talking to individual players. Talk to each individual player about his/her contribution to the game. Find a positive statement to make. Do not use the team outcome to reflect disappointment or elation in talking to the children on a group basis. The judgments children are making relative to their contribution to the game are very different. Therefore, the coach should treat the children accordingly and talk to each child about the game and, particularly following a loss, help the children overcome their negative feelings about the loss. The low self-confidence player, in particular, may be taking the loss very hard. When talking to the players, the coach must take into account their individual attributions. It is even suggested that the comments of the coach to individual players should be the same regardless of the outcome of the team! Coaches should not talk to the players as a team or blame them as a team, but talk to them about their performance within the game situation regardless of the outcome. This is very difficult to do, but it is very important that the coach try. Indeed, coaches would be well advised to *listen* to what the children are saying and listen to the attributions they are making before inflicting their own opinions upon the children. Sometimes coaches are more concerned for giving the players their own analysis instead of just sitting back and listening. The coach may learn a lot about the children that way and it will help the coach to deal with each child individually.

One means of differentiating between players is to remind them on occasion of the physiological differences between them. Some children develop earlier and at a faster rate than others. Often, the children who are physiologically more mature are the superstars of junior leagues. The puny little child who feels out of it today may be as big as superstar Johnny or Mary and just as good a player next year. The coach should not let youngsters or less developed players drop out of the game because of inappropriate judgments that they are making about their own abilities. Remind ball players of the differences between individuals in terms of age, maturation, and motivation. For example, a child may perform poorly and make attributions that he/she is ''not good'' and that he/she cannot play decent baseball (basketball, whatever). The coach may say to the players such things as, ''Now wait a minute, you are younger, smaller, and have been playing less time than those other ball players. You have the ability and the potential, and as soon as you grow a little and have some more experience, you will be a very good ball payer.'' The coach can do a great deal to prevent children from making ego deflating attributions that are no in accord with the child's actual abilities.

The above analysis of the competitive experience, and the comments proffered relative to making the competitive experience more humane for children, were drawn from the extant literature and educated opinion. But, the major point to stress is that to understand the child within the competitive experience, we must view the experience from the point of view of the child. When we make decisions for children in the competitive experience, we must consider the cognitive maturity of the child and make our decisions and comments with the perceptions of the child uppermost in our mind.

Most coaches are sensitive to children and are more concerned about the child than the game. This is as it should be. But too many coaches are not. Sometimes, when I observe these less sensitive coaches wildly gesticulating during a game, instructing players about positions, tactics, and the like, and shouting comments to children such as, "Hey Johnny, watch the ball," I am very tempted to shout at the coach, "Hey coach, watch the child."

References

Ames, C., Ames, R., & Felker, D.W. Effects of competitive reward structure and valence of outcomes on children's achievement attributions. *Journal of Educational Psychology*, 1977, **69**, 1-8.

Bloom, B.S. *Human characteristics and school learning*. New York: McGraw-Hill, 1976.

Gerson, R. Redesigning athletic competition for children. *Motor Skills: Theory into Practice*, 1977, **2**, 3-14.

Iso-Ahola, S.E. A test of attribution theory of success and failure with Little League baseball players. *Mouvement*, 1975, **7**, 323-340.

Martens, R. *Social psychology in physical activity*. New York: Harper and Row, 1975.

McHugh, M.C., Duquin, M.E., & Frieze, I.H. Beliefs about success and failure: Attribution and the female athlete. In C.A. Oglesby (Ed.) *Women and sport*. Philadelphia: Lea & Febiger, 1978, 173-191.

Nelson, L.L., & Kagan, S. Competition: The star spangled scramble. *Psychology Today*, 1972, **5**, 53-56; 90-91.

Nicholls, J.G. The development of the concepts of effort and ability, perception of academic attainment and the understanding that difficult tasks require more ability. *Child Development*, 1978, **49**, 800-814.

Roberts, G.C. Win-loss causal attributions of Little League players. *Mouvement*, 1975, **7**, 315-322. (Proceedings of the 7th Annual Canadian Psycho-Motor Learning and Sports Psychology Symposium).

Roberts, G.C. Children's assignment of responsibility for winning and losing. In R. Smith & S. Smoll (Eds.), *Psychological perspectives of youth sports*. New York: Hemisphere Publishing Corporation, 1978.

Roberts, G.C. Children in competition: Assignment of responsibility for winning and losing. Proceedings of the NCPEAM, 1977a, pp. 328-340.

Roberts, G.C., & Russell, D.G. The forgotten factor: Psychological processes of competition. *Australian Journal of Sports Medicine*, 1977b, **9**, 38-43.

Rosenthal, R. The pygmalion effect lives. *Psychology Today*, 1973, **7**, 56-60; 62-63.

Salili, F., Maehr, M.L., & Gillmore, G. Achievement and morality: A cross-cultural analysis of causal attribution and evaluation. *Journal of Personality and Social Psychology*, 1976, **33**, 327-337.

Sherif, C. The social context of competition. In D. Landers (Ed.), *Social problems in athletics*. Urbana, IL: University of Illinois Press, 1976.

Spink, K.S. Win-loss causal attributions of high school basketball players. *Canadian Journal of Applied Sport Sciences*, 1978, **3**, 195-201.

Veroff, J. Social comparison and the development of achievement motivation. In C.P. Smith (Ed.), *Achievement related motives in children*. New York: Russell Sage, 1969.

Weiner, B., & Peter, N. A cognitive-developmental analysis of achievement and moral judgements. *Developmental Psychology*, 1973, **9**, 290-309.

Weiner, B., Frieze, I., Kukla, A., Reed, L., Rest, & Rosenbaum, R.M. *Perceiving the causes of success and failure*. Morristown, NJ: General Learning Press, 1971.

Weiner, B. *Achievement motivation and attribution theory*. Morristown, NY: General Learning Press, 1974.

Notes

[1] Scanlan, T.K. Children in competition: Examination or anxiety in social comparison responses in the laboratory and the field. Paper presented at the joint NCPEAM/NAPECW Conference, Orlando, FL. 1977.

[2] Roberts, G.C. Causal attributions to explain winning and losing. Paper presented at the Psychomotor Learning and Sport Psychology Symposium. Calgary, Canada, 1977.

[3] Gould, D., & Roberts, G.C. Task enjoyment and task attributions following outcome gain and loss. Paper presented at the joint NCPEAM/NAPECW Conference, Orlando, FL, 1977.

[4] Roberts, G.C. Organized sport for children: Social psychological dimensions. Paper read at the joint NCPEAM/NAPECW Conference, Denver, Co, 1978.

SECTION 4

Implementation

In keeping with the conceptual model described by Yiannakis in chapter 1, the articles in this section illustrate various ways in which applied sport sociology contributes to implementation. The section is divided into two parts: Part I contains four articles that reflect the contents of application, while Part II contains one chapter that discusses promotion of services, an aspect of implementation not clearly delineated or described in the model. The articles in Part I consider the vast potential for implementation; they cover a range of topics within diverse contexts or settings, demonstrating the variety of forms that an applied sociology of sport can take. In contrast, the article in Part II represents a totally different perspective of implementation through its suggestion that sociologists apply marketing principles to promote their profession.

The implementation phase of applied sociology of sport represents more than specific prescribed practices or simple cookbook answers. This section in particular defines applied sport sociology as a multifaceted enterprise that promotes the formation of interpretive connections by demonstrating how various types of research, social issues, and personal perspectives may bring about social change. Whether sport sociologists are engaging in explanatory or operational research; disseminating information to specific audiences; serving as consultants, assistants, or advisors; translating research findings; or becoming active agents working for the amelioration and solution of problems and for change in sporting practices, the prospects for implementation are extensive and seemingly without limit.

PART I

Contexts of Application

Each article in Part I represents a pioneer effort because each addresses in some way how program or policy recommendations can be converted into plans of action, installed in specific contexts or settings, or actually implemented. These articles demonstrate the variety of topics that can be considered within contexts that range from physical education and sport to management, administrative, and corporate settings.

Chapter 14

Applications of Sport Sociology to Sport Management

Allen L. Sack
University of New Haven

In this article Sack applies sociological principles to sport management and identifies areas of conceptual knowledge that could be included in curriculum content. Discussing the links between sociology, sport, and sport marketing, Sack suggests that knowledge of social factors influencing sport consumers (and sport consumption), application of marketing principles to the sporting goods industry, a general understanding of the role of sport in the lives of individuals, and principles from organizational theory are only a few domains that link sociology of sport to the context of sport management.

The late 20th century has witnessed a sport and leisure boom of substantial proportions (Eitzen & Sage, 1982). The public's seemingly insatiable appetite for mass-spectator sports, coupled with a narcissistic preoccupation with physical fitness, has produced a multibillion-dollar industry. Included in this industry are professional sport franchises, health and fitness centers, country clubs, ski resorts, marinas, pari-mutuel industries, college athletic departments, sporting goods retailers, athletic clubs, coliseums, sports media, and recreation departments. According to Parkhouse (1984, p. 12), "This multibillion dollar sports industry requires a new breed of executives who meet job requirements in a number of increasingly complex and varied sports related fields."

In the 1960s, college and universities began to develop programs in sport administration and management to train these new sport executives. The first program was established in 1966 at Ohio State University. The University of Massachusetts began its program in 1971 and was followed in the next few years by St. John's University, Biscayne College (now St. Thomas University in Miami), and Western Illinois University (Yovovich, 1984). By 1980, over 40 colleges and universities offered some kind of degree in sport management and administration. The number has now risen to 100 or more (Hardy, 1986). As Hardy (1985) points out, this proliferation of programs has not occurred without problems.

Paper presented at AAHPERD Convention, Cincinnati, OH, 1986. Printed by permission of Allen L. Sack.

Many schools and departments entered sport management to offset declining enrollments in other areas. In their rush to take advantage of a new market, schools often developed programs with little regard for whether they had adequate staffing and resources to deliver a quality education. According to Hardy (1985, p. 2), "many of these programs offer little more than window dressing, with few faculty devoting full time to the area, few courses related to knowledge needed for careers, few connections with the industry itself." Often, curriculum development has been dictated more by a need to fit already existing courses and subspecialities into a thriving new area than by a concern for student needs.

Given the role that political expediency has sometimes played in curriculum development, it is important to examine exactly what contributions various courses make to the understanding of sport management. Parkhouse (1984, p. 13) warns prospective students to "exercise caution when choosing a program where the curriculum includes an overabundance of required courses in areas not related to sports management." Her point is well taken. But it is not always clear which courses are relevant and which are merely window dressing.

With this in mind, an attempt will be made to build a case for including sport sociology in the sport management curriculum. Sport sociology is not only useful to the sport manager, but it should be a foundation course in any program in this subject area.

Defining Sport and Its Environment

One of the major contributions sport sociology makes to sport management is in defining sport and its environment. Students who enroll in their first sport studies course seldom have a clear conception of what they are about to study. Not only does sport sociology offer precise definitions of the sport institution, but it helps students to understand better the complex relationship between sport and other major social institutions. Such knowledge is invaluable for sport managers. Peter Ueberroth's success in managing the Los Angeles Olympics was undoubtedly related to his ability to grasp the intimate connection of sport to both economic and political institutions. College athletic directors, as well as those who manage a wide variety of youth programs, have to understand the role of sport in relation to institutions like the family and education. Sport sociology courses help the sport manager to make sense of this complex and constantly changing institutional environment.

Management textbooks (e.g., Stoner, 1982) often divide an organization's external environment into economic, legal, political, technical, and socio-cultural segments. Again, sociology is a powerful tool for the sport manager who must respond to developments in these areas. Sport sociology examines cultural values, gender roles, race relations, social attitudes toward violence, and many other aspects of an organization's external environment. Such knowledge can be crucial to the day-to-day operations of a sport organization. For example, demographic trends and social values affect marketing decisions. Social attitudes toward race and sex are often translated into legislation that in turn can have a dramatic impact on the organization's personnel policies. And a better understanding of the role of violence and aggression in society can help a sport manager plan strategies for dealing with disruptive crowd behavior, or shape legislation to ensure the safety of fans and players alike.

Sociology and Sport Marketing

Mullin (1985) points out that sport organizations have often neglected marketing. Given the intimate connection between sport and the media, sport managers have generally assumed that a sport will market itself. However, increased competition for the sport consumer's dollar, even in professional and intercollegiate sports, has forced sport managers to use sophisticated marketing techniques not unlike those common to other businesses. Not only does Mullin's work contain an excellent discussion of these techniques, but it allows one to see the obvious links between sport marketing and sport sociology.

One of the major contributions of sport sociology to sport marketing lies in the identification of the demographic and social factors that influence the sport consumer. Studies of social stratification, for instance, are an important source of data for a marketing information system. Sport sociologists have shown that sport spectatorship and participation are often a function of social class. Sport, as Veblen (1953) pointed out, can act as an important status symbol. The market for polo and Ivy League football, for example, is different from the market for what sport sociologists call "proletarian" sport. The product extensions sold at these events and the corporate sponsors associated with these diverse sport products would also be expected to vary. A careful examination of the products advertised during various televised sporting events reveals that sponsors have a good grasp of social stratification.

The sporting goods industry also must be extremely sensitive to the subtleties of class and status. The clientele that frequents a skiing and climbing shop, for example, is likely to be very different from that which shops for snowmobiles and bowling equipment. Sailboats are preferred by people of established wealth, power boats by the *nouveaux riches*. For certain consumers, there is much more to bicycling than riding a bike. One must also be wearing the appropriate high-tech clothing and riding a $1,200 Bianchi. And skiing is not really skiing unless it is on Rossignols. Sport sociology studies these status symbols and relates sport consumption to the entire way of life of a specific class or status group. Such knowledge is invaluable to the sport marketer.

Understanding the role that sport plays in the lives of individuals and in the larger social system is as important to sport marketing as it is to sport sociology. Few products generate the emotional intensity and evoke the strong feeling of collective identification that sport does. High school and college sport can unite entire regions, and the Olympics generate strong loyalties nationally. The Los Angeles Olympic Committee's ability to successfully market the Olympic spectacle, as well as a wide variety of products bearing the Olympic seal, is simply one expression of this phenomenon. The sale of T-shirts, beer mugs, jackets, and other product extensions has become a million-dollar business at the college and professional sport level as sport fans support their teams with almost religious fervor. This quality of sport has been one of the major contributions to its commercialization.

The study of sport subcultures is another important area for sport marketing. Members of sport subcultures such as runners, bicycle racers, rock climbers, skiers, and aerobic dancers are members of consumer subcultures as well. Each subculture has its own magazines, mail-order catalogs, and other mechanisms for keeping up with the latest innovations in equipment and fashions. Knowledge of the subcultural and other characteristics of consumers, in addition to demographic factors like age, sex, income, occupation, and geographical area, are important in determining market segmentation. Hence sociology courses such as the study of sport subcultures or population and demography can be extremely helpful to sport management.

The role of social research methods in marketing management also deserves special attention. According to Mullin (1985, p. 210), "the most important factor in marketing success is the ability to collect accurate and timely information about consumers and potential consumers, and to use these data in the formulation of marketing plans." Needless to say, a knowledge of research methodology and statistics is crucial for sport marketing. A good sport sociology course should familiarize students with the methods of social science research; while upper-level social research courses introduce students to the logic of sampling, questionnaire construction, and the wide variety of other skills required to carry out their own survey research. Social research methods courses also introduce students to computer software packages that are often used in marketing research.

Sport Management and Organizational Theory

Any sociologist who takes the time to read a sport management textbook will find that management draws heavily on the basic concepts and theories of sociology. It is to be expected that chapters on management theory would contain copious references to sociologists such as Max Weber, Elton Mayo, Chester Barnard, and Kurt Lewin. Perhaps more important, however, is the subject matter: Much discussion of key management functions like organizing and leading also tends to read like textbook sociology. Standard sociological concepts a student is bound to encounter in these texts include bureaucracy, informal structure, formalization, complexity, power and authority, rationalization, human relations, centralization, professionalization, social conflict, and division of labor. In fact, it may not be an exaggeration to say that business management is a type of applied sociology. The sociology of sport, however, is different in that it applies these concepts to a very distinctive subject matter.

The sport sociologist makes extensive use of organizational theory when surveying the types of organizations that make up the world of sport. A course that surveys the organizational structures found in amateur and professional sport is a necessary part of any sport management curriculum. How do sport organizations interact with each other and with their environments? What kinds of leadership styles predominate in sport organizations? How is power distributed, and who makes decisions? What is the nature of organizational conflict and change? These questions, routinely raised by sociologists studying sport, have obvious relevance for the sport manager.

Summary and Conclusions

The major purpose of this chapter was to discuss the contributions that sociology and sport sociology can make to applied areas like sport management. Academic sociologists are often reluctant to associate themselves with applied areas. However, the distance between theory and practice is not as great as many sociologists might think. Even if sport sociologists never work for clients outside of a university, the knowledge they generate is of practical value to others who do.

The contributions of sport sociology to sport management are significant enough that sport sociology should be a core course in every sport management program. Not only do such courses provide a valuable knowledge base, but they help to recruit nonmajors to the program. Sport sociology courses tend to be very popular. The subject matter is fascinating. Every effort should be made to let students know that their interest in sport can lead to a fulfilling career in management. Likewise, students pursuing graduate degrees in sport management could greatly benefit from courses in research methods, sport subcultures, sport and complex organizations, and sport and social inequality.

There is one other significant way that sport sociology contributes to all professionally oriented sport programs. By requiring that students think critically about the world in which they live rather than passively memorize a body of technical knowledge, sport sociology, as a liberal discipline, encourages the independent thought and self-direction necessary for positions of leadership. For similar reasons, one might also recommend courses in sport history, sport psychology, and the philosophy of sport. Although sport sociologists must do a much better job of selling the applied dimensions of their discipline, the major contribution of sociology will always be its ability to make people more aware of themselves and the complex social forces that shape all human behavior.

References

Eitzen, D.S., and Sage, G.H. (1982). *Sociology of American sport*. Dubuque, IA: Brown.

Hardy, S. (1985). *Department of Sports Management Handbook.* (Available from Robert Morris College, Pittsburgh, PA).

Hardy, S. (1986, April). *Sport management curriculums: The need for a business orientation.* Paper presented at the National Symposium on Graduate Study in Physical Education, Cincinnati, OH.

Mullin, B. (1985). Information based approaches to marketing sport. In G. Lewis & H. Appenzeller (Eds.), *Successful sports management* (pp. 101–123). Charlottesville, VA: Michie.

Parkhouse, B. (1984). Sport management. *Journal of Physical Education, 55,* 12–13.

Stoner, J.A. (1982). *Management.* Englewood Cliffs, NJ: Prentice-Hall.

Veblen, T. (1953). *The theory of the leisure class.* New York: Mentor Books.

Yovovich, B.G. (1984, August). Colleges teaching a management game plan. *Advertising Age,* pp. 22, 24.

Chapter 15

Sociology of Sport Organizations: Management and Marketing

Eldon E. Snyder
Bowling Green State University

> Similarly to Sack, Snyder identifies concepts and principles from sport sociology that could be incorporated into sport management courses (organizational theory, management, and marketing). However, he moves a step closer to implementation in describing alterations to his own course content. Snyder discusses the distinction between administrators and managers, ethical considerations and role conflict, and managerial responsibilities. He also applies principles from stratification, subcultures, race, gender, and social values to the marketing of sport products and services.

A couple of years ago I became aware of the increasing proportion of students enrolled in my sociology of sport classes who were majoring in sport management. Paralleling the emergence of sport management was the increased emphasis in sociology on a more applied perspective. Both sport management and applied sociology are reflections of changes in the employment opportunity structure and the need to adjust academic programs based on these changes. That is, there are more opportunities for employment in sport management than in physical education; similarly, there are more jobs in the applied, nonacademic settings of sociology as teaching positions diminish.

The growing interest in sport management and applied sociology converges with arguments made by Melnick (1980), who suggested that sociologists of sport should consider professional opportunities in areas such as

- developing recreational sport facilities;
- providing consultant services to community sport organizations;
- formulating and implementing policy as members of local, regional, national, and international sport commissions and agencies;
- planning and developing recreational sport programs for retirement communities;

Paper presented at the meeting of the North American Society for the Sociology of Sport, Las Vegas, NV, 1986. Printed by permission of Eldon E. Snyder.

- advising state and national governmental agencies on policy-related sport issues; and
- serving as consultants to amateur and professional sport groups and organizations. (pp. 7-8)

Similarly, Sack (1986) has pointed out the contributions that sociological theory and methods can make to the sport and recreation industry. It was in the context of these changing needs of students and the greater emphasis on the applied perspective that I started to include some of the following material on aspects of organizations, management, and marketing in my sociology of sport classes.

Typologies of Organizations

Sport management majors are currently finding positions with professional teams; collegiate and high school athletic conferences; health clubs and spas; industrial and corporate fitness centers; racquet clubs; aquatic facilities; sport arenas; soccer, tennis, and other sport federations; YMCAs and YWCAs; retail sporting goods stores; community recreation departments; collegiate athletic departments; hospital health promotion programs; Olympic training facilities; and sport media industries. Many students have had recreational or work experiences with these organizations, yet they may not understand some important differences among them. To assist students in this respect, I have them list the organizations and try to explain the differences among them. Some differences are obvious; students can readily identify professional sport organizations versus nonprofit recreational organizations. When they have completed this exercise, I suggest to them that organizations can be classified by using the following typologies available from organizational studies.

A Typology: The Primary Beneficiary

Blau and Scott (1962) have classified organizations based on the primary beneficiary into the following types:

- Mutual-benefit associations—the rank-and-file members benefit.
- Business concerns—owners and managers benefit.
- Service organizations—clients or outsiders are the beneficiaries.
- Commonweal organizations—the public at-large benefits. (pp. 45-58)

The significance of this typology for students is that it highlights the differences in beneficiaries and objectives of organizations as disparate as community recreation programs, corporate fitness centers, health spas, and hospital health promotion programs. These typological differences will have consequences in a number of areas, including recruitment of members, sources of legal and financial control, and allocation of resources.

Typology: Inducements and Involvement

Somewhat more complex distinctions are reflected in a modification of Etzioni's (1961) typology, which uses a twofold classification. First, there are three ways organizations may induce members to participate: *coercive* (using force), *remunerative* (using monetary or other extrinsic rewards), and *normative* (offering moral and educational development of the participants). The second dimension of the typology is based on three types of involvement by the members: *negative* (participants have negative feelings toward the organization), *extrinsic/social* (participation is based on extrinsic or social rewards), and *intrinsic/social* (participation is based on intrinsic and social pleasures). These distinctions produce three major types of organizations (see Table 15.1).

Table 15.1   Organizational Inducements and Types of Involvement by Members

| | Primary inducement for members to participate | | |
Type of involvement by members	Coercive	Remunerative	Normative
Negative	Type I		
Extrinsic/social		Type II	
Intrinsic/social			Type III

Examples of Type I organizations are institutions such as prisons or mental hospitals where individuals are not voluntary members. I suggested to my sport management majors that sport and recreation programs in these organizations often reflected the coercive nature of the organization and were likely to promote a negative attitude in the participants. Other organizations that may approximate Type I set-ups include compulsory physical education programs in military organizations and schools. In these situations, the programming and leadership should consider the probable lack of motivation by some participants. Moreover, sport in these contexts is not sold or marketed. Revenues for the organization come from another source—i.e., the public sector and tax money. Hence the organization is a "protected species."

Type II organizations are business concerns designed to make a profit. Managers must assure survival and success by attracting participants through marketing and sales. In doing so, the managers consider both the costs of the internal operations and factors external to the organization that are necessary to maximize profits and produce a return on investment (Mullin, 1980). One might say these organizations are "wild"; they must struggle for survival. Their existence is not guaranteed, and they require a steady flow of customers. Analogous to biological organisms, they must be adaptable and innovative when the external environment changes

(Corwin, 1967). Students must understand the contrasts between and financial implications of Type I and II organizations.

Involvement in Type II sport organizations by participants (customers) is based primarily on extrinsic and social payoffs. These rewards might be monetary return, social recognition, trophies, prestige, or other such valuables. An exchange theory is in evidence as the individual considers the cost and benefits of participation. Many racquet, golf, and swim clubs, as well as professional sport organizations and collegiate revenue sports, would be classified as Type II organizations.

Organizations classified as Type III are designed to offer personal, physical, social, and educational development (skills, fitness, coordination, social graces, attitudes, and values); they are not oriented toward making a profit. Individuals are attracted to this type of sport organization because they enjoy the social interaction, the fun, and the autotelic rewards of participation. City recreation programs, church leagues, high school sports, and nonprofit leisure sport associations would qualify as Type III organizations. In these contexts, the extrinsic rewards are subordinate to other rewards. However, the overall mix of intrinsic, social, and extrinsic rewards will vary with the individual participants.

These dimensions of participant involvement are incorporated in a model of commitment that I have discussed elsewhere (Snyder, 1985; Snyder & Spreitzer, 1989). The typology may be flawed because organizations have multiple goals and because individuals have mixed reasons for participating. Yet it is a helpful tool for making students aware of the similarities and differences among sport organizations and how these variations are reflected in goals, strategies, decision making, autonomy, innovation, financing, and leadership, as well as in their interaction with the external environment. Additional analysis might focus in-depth not only on the formal structure of organizations but on the negotiations, including conflicting interests, among members, which form a complex shifting network of social relationships. This interactionist perspective is suggested by Denzin (1977), who notes that

> the sum total of these relationships—whether real or only symbolized, whether assumed and taken for granted or problematic and troublesome— constitute the organization as it is sensed, experienced, and acted upon by the individual or relational member. Power, control, coercion and deception become central commodities of negotiation in these arenas that make up the organization. (pp. 905-906)

Sport Administration and Sport Management

Drawing on the work of Mullin (1980), it is useful to distinguish between the terms "administrator" and "manager" (see also Duncan, 1978). An administrator usually holds a position in a public organization where revenue is generated by taxes, student fees, or grants; in short, the administrator rarely sells a product to generate revenue. Rather, the administrator monitors allocated resources that are budgeted toward the facilities, staff, equipment, and other expenses of the ongoing organization (Mullin, 1980). Hence, marketing and sales are not a primary concern; other goals, such as education, skill development, and fitness of the participants are paramount. In contrast, the manager deals not only with expenditures but also marketing and sales, As Mullin (1980) points out, the manager's performance is appraised by the organization's return on investment, market penetration, and growth.

Figure 15.1 illustrates the administration–management dichotomy and the corresponding goals, activities, and sport organizations (Snyder & Spreitzer, 1989; Spillard, 1985). In practice, the distinction between the administrative and managing roles is seldom clear-cut. For example, while administrators may be executives of nonprofit organizations, they are also likely to be involved in some fund-raising activities. This has become increasingly true where economic conditions have resulted in defeats of bond issues and public support of school and community sport programs has declined (Yiannakis, 1984). Likewise, managers of organizations that must generate revenues are usually also promoting some aspects of individual development and well-being. University athletic departments are hybrids—they are often divided into nonrevenue and revenue sports. The latter must be marketed and sold as in any other economic-type organization. I encourage students to study Figure 15.1 and identify the potential ways these organizations operate. Students enjoy brainstorming on the various marketing and promotional schemes that can be used by economic sport organizations. Ultimately, the marketing task is to focus on the potential customers' level of involvement and attempt to reverse, develop, revitalize, synchronize, or maintain a continuing demand for the sport product.

Role Conflict

In presenting this diagram to students I find it useful to inform them of the potential role conflicts that the administrator or manager may experience. For example, in public school sports or youth leagues where the primary goals are education and individual development, the community demands for a winning team may subvert these objectives. Thus, administrators of athletic organizations may support coaches who use unfair or illegal tactics or who encourage players to compete when they have injuries. At the university level, at least in the revenue sports, the importance of winning, gate receipts, television money, and postseason tournaments becomes even more evident. Hence, the Mertonian thesis of using "innovative" but ethically questionable means to achieve desirable goals is often manifest. In short, coaches and administrator-managers are often faced with the interrole conflict of trying to achieve both educational and winning or profit goals. While these are not always incongruent, student-athletes may be expected to neglect their academic role in favor of athletics, and coaches may "use" athletes in ways

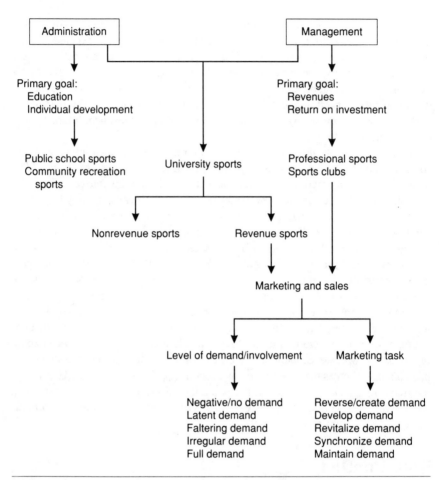

Figure 15.1 Sport administration and management dichotomy: goals and activities.

that are detrimental to their physical and mental well-being; thus, the educational goals of the institution may be violated.

I also urge students to consider the potential ethical issues that frequently arise for managers of sport clubs and those in staff positions of professional sport organizations. For example, in a family recreation facility, is it justifiable to sell profitable concession and snack bar items that are of questionable value to personal health? Is it ethical for a professional hockey team to promote violence to attract customers? Should the media be used to present sport in a deceptive way? Should "sex appeal" that is sexist in nature be used in commercials to attract customers? In short, I feel students should consider the profit motive as potentially inconsistent with the well-being of their customers and sport participants.

At this point, it also is appropriate to introduce students to the concept of "organizational deviance." This is committed by individuals who act for and in the name of the corporation; their actions, however, violate the norms and laws surrounding the organization (Ermann & Lundman, 1978; McCaghy, 1976). Organizational deviance would include the submission of fraudulent college admission scores or bogus grades, and illegal payments made to athletes by athletic department representatives, as well as the fraudulent business practices, price-fixing, providing illegal goods and services, political corruption, and racketeering that may occur in other areas of the business sector.

Additional Management Topics

The list of topics outlined in Table 15.2 might be expanded into a full-blown course on the sociology of sport management. Caplow (1983) defines an organization

> as a social system deliberately established to carry out some definite purpose. It consists of a number of people in a pattern of relationships. . . . The organization assigns a *position* to each of its members, and the incumbent of a position has a set part to play in the organization's collective program. [italics in the original] (p. 2)

The position of manager incorporates responsibility for the functioning and control of an organization so that the program can be achieved. In brief, the responsibilities of management incorporate

- The right to manage, or authority
- Maintaining communication to hold the organization together
- Achieving productivity
- Maintaining morale to sustain productivity
- Adapting to external changes

Topics that might be included under each of these headings are listed in Table 15.2 (Caplow, 1983). Each of these topics can provide opportunities for individual student or group projects as they relate to different types of sport organizations.

Marketing and Sales

A number of sociological concepts can be applied to marketing and sales in the field of sport and management. For example, studies in the sociology of sport on social stratification, sport subcultures, race, gender, social values, crowd behavior, and sport media are important background topics for marketing sport products and services. Additionally, marketing can be studied as a social activity, a point of view enunciated by Prus (1989). For example, how are customers/clients recruited? What dilemmas (role conflicts) do sellers encounter as they bargain with prospective customers? How do they deal with these conflicts? How do

Table 15.2   Management Topics

Authority
Managerial succession
Direct and indirect control of the purse strings
Hawthorne studies
Tables of organization methods:
    Taylor's "scientific management"
    Centralized-decentralized authority
    Authoritarian-democratic leadership styles"
    Dealing with subordinate managers: Hawthorne
        studies and "human relations research"
    Coalitions
    Crisis management: Murphy's law, Parkinson's law

Communication
Communication networks: formal and informal
Socializing the recruit (grapevine)
Rewards and sanctions
Grievance procedures: open and closed door policies
Justice
Security and maintenance of organization boundaries
Incongruence
Nonverbal communication
Microgeography of office space

Productivity
Supervision
Output restriction
Effective work management

Morale
Recruiting
Evaluation
Distributive status

Change and innovation
Adjusting to change: the market
Changing social values
Demographic shifts
Technological progress
Adjusting goals

salespeople maintain enthusiasm when the numbers of sport customers are declining? How is customer loyalty developed? These are paraphrases of questions raised by Prus in his research on the social activity of the marketplace.

Using symbolic interactionism, Prus considers seller and buyer behavior as a "socially constructed activity" that includes interactors' frames of reference, interpretations, exchanges, negotiations, and concessions. That is, marketing and sales are social activities that emerge—they are "constructed"—during the interaction process. With regard to sport marketing and sales, it is helpful to study similar behavior in a variety of other social settings. Buyer behavior does not require a separate theory from other forms of involvement, such as one's occupation, religion, church, marriage, or as a parent, thief, alcoholic, or tennis player. Each of these spheres of activity may be viewed as a career of involvement and entail varying degrees of attachment, commitment, and personal identity. Indeed, involvement in one activity may enhance or detract from involvement in another (Snyder, 1985). As Prus (1989) notes, the career involvement model in purchasing situations may include initial involvement (first-time purchase), continuity (buyer loyalty), disinvolvement (dropping products or services), and reinvolvement (revitalizing purchasing). These same degrees of involvement approximate the degrees of consumer demand for sport noted earlier in Figure 15.1. In summary, the central theme of marketing and selling sport behavior, products, and services draws on the generic concepts of other forms of involvement, attachment, and adherence behavior. Further, analysis of sport markets might be enhanced by a synthesis of symbolic interactionism and exchange theories that focus on the individual identities, meanings, levels of involvement, and satisfactions—extrinsic, intrinsic, self-esteem, and social prestige—that people receive from sport. In general, people will "buy into" sport if it "sells" these satisfactions. In marketing sports, we need to consider not only who benefits but how they benefit.

Summary

In sociology as well as in the fields of health, physical education, and recreation, there is a trend toward a more applied orientation. One aspect of this change is the emergence of sport management programs as an academic area of study. Sack (1986) alerted sociologists of sport to the contributions we can make to this emerging field. Consequently, I have worked out a corpus of material with a sociological perspective on organizational theory, management, and marketing. The current discussion is offered as a resource to others who are interested in presenting material on this topic.

References

Blau, P., & Scott, W.R. (1962). *Formal organization*. New York: Chandler.

Caplow, T. (1983). *Managing an organization*. New York: Holt, Rinehart & Winston.

Corwin, R. (1967). Education and the sociology of complex organizations. In D.A. Hansen & J.E. Gerstl, *On Education: Sociological Perspectives*, (pp. 156-223). New York: Wiley.

Denzin, N.K. (1977). Notes on the criminogenic hypothesis: A case study of the American liquor industry. *American Sociological Review, 42*, 905-920.

Duncan, J. (1978). *Essentials of management*. London: Pitman.

Ermann, D., & Lundman, R. (1978). Deviant acts by complex organizations: Deviance and social control at the organizational level of analysis. *Sociological Quarterly, 19*, 55-67.

Etzioni, A. (1961). *A comparative analysis of complex organizations*. New York: Free Press.

McCaghy, C. (1976). *Deviant behavior*. New York: Macmillan.

Melnick, M. (1980). Toward an applied sociology of sport. *Journal of Sport and Social Issues, 4*, 1-12.

Mullin, B. (1980). Sport management: The nature and utility of the concept. *Arena Review, 4*, 1-11.

Prus, R. (1989). *Pursuing customers*. Newbury Park, CA: Sage.

Sack, A.L. (1986, April). *Sport sociology in the sport management curriculum.* Paper presented at Annual Meeting of the American Association of Health, Physical Education, Recreation and Dance, Cincinnati, OH.

Snyder, E. (1985). A theoretical analysis of academic and athletic roles. *Sociology of Sport Journal, 2,* 210-217.

Snyder, E., & Spreitzer, E. (1989). *Social aspects of sport.* Englewood Cliffs; NJ: Prentice-Hall.

Spillard, P. (1985). *Organization and marketing.* New York: St. Martins.

Yiannakis, A. (1984). Sports marketing and fund raising. *Journal of Physical Education, Recreation, and Dance, 55,* 20-22.

Chapter 16

Applications of Sport Sociology to the Teaching Profession

John D. Massengale
University of Nevada, Las Vegas

In considering implementation within the context of physical education, Massengale suggests how sport sociologists can foster professional sensitivity and deal realistically with the social forces that impinge on the physical education environment. Describing how broad social influences such as power, tradition, and an acceptable value system influence physical education settings, he argues that the application of scientific knowledge from sport sociology to professional preparation of teachers encompasses broad social considerations instead of narrow vocational interests. His focus on a more sensitive analysis and a more realistic way of handling the complexities and consequences of social forces indicates that new thinking, new direction, and new leadership may be required. These notions illustrate the type or nature of policy recommendations that could be implemented in a program of action in teacher preparation.

Sport sociology has made significant contributions to the teaching profession. However, these applications and contributions usually receive very little attention because they lack a true market value and are not performance-based. Nonetheless, established applications and contributions should be featured and used as foundations for the discipline. The discussion that follows will consider how sport sociology promotes the erosion of unwanted tradition, aids in the accumulation of scientific knowledge that can be gathered no other way, enhances the broadest sense of social process rather than academic schooling, and identifies the influential social exchange and power that permeate nearly every aspect of the teaching profession.

Paper presented at the meeting of the North American Society for the Sociology of Sport, Boston, MA, 1985. Printed by permission of John D. Massengale.

Erosion of Unwanted Tradition

Any casual review of scholarly efforts in the field of sport sociology will reveal a trend toward topics that tend to be exciting and sensational—especially those topics that pertain to competitive athletics and the reform of the status quo. At the same time, traditional American education, particularly physical education, receives very little attention from sport sociologists; after all, there is no sociology of physical education. This may be because in too many cases and for too many sport sociologists, tradition has evolved to mean old-fashioned, conservative, out-of-date, inflexible, authoritarian, exploitative, negative, or dysfunctional. Such a perspective does tradition an injustice. Rather, it should be described as the transmission of culture, the passing-on of highly valued, worthwhile elements from one generation to the next, or the professional use of time-honored and well-established practices (Massengale, 1984). In particular, the field of sport sociology has enhanced the erosion of unwanted tradition in the American athletic system, while permitting highly valued traditions to flourish.

The practical application of sport sociology to the teaching profession is one area that continues to go unrecognized—because it is not sensational, not exciting, not disruptive, not performance-based, and it has no apparent market value. Yet applied sport sociology could become an important part of the teacher preparation curriculum if some of the basic applications were more universally understood and appreciated for their significance. For instance, sport sociology has influenced the erosion of unwanted tradition in the teaching profession through the following areas: school architecture, school curricula, grading concepts and policies, scheduling, government policy, private enterprise, the media, wellness movements, leisure studies, alternative educational policy, rehabilitation theories, organizational deviance, value clarification, identity loss, stigma formation, and equal opportunity.

Sport sociology has the potential to influence tradition in all of those areas, with or without the association of competitive athletics. Yet the teaching profession is mostly composed of people who have no idea what a sport sociologist does for a living. Moreover, a national survey (Southard, 1982) revealed that only 7% of the physical education teacher preparation programs required a course in the sociology of sport.

Gathering Scientific Knowledge

Applying the sociology of sport to the teaching profession will necessitate new thinking, new direction, and new leadership. Aspiring sport sociologists, and their mentors, must become much more concerned about doing things that have practical significance to someone. For example, gathering scientific knowledge by applying sport sociology to the teaching profession would require that less soft science research be conducted with hard science models. Social learning and applied behavioral science are not controlled by unalterable natural law, and they risk losing their natural characteristics when forced into an unnatural, restrictive, and tightly controlled research design. Collecting and categorizing social facts, then treating them with inferential statistics, does not necessarily increase scientific knowledge regarding the nature, meaning, or result of the sport experience (Hollands, 1984). But gathering knowledge about the nature, meaning, and result of the sport experience might be the very thing that could be produced by applying sport sociology to the teaching profession.

The nature of applied sociology of sport lends itself to scientific knowledge that concerns larger social issues. As an intellectual force, natural science is incomplete and inadequate (Gross, 1968). Applied sport sociology can make up for some of this inadequacy, especially in the teaching profession (Sage, 1985). Social consequences, social complexities, social awareness, and social consciousness can all be taught, measured, and applied throughout the American educational system and should not be restricted by practicing sport sociologists solely to competitive athletics. By applying sport sociology to the teaching profession, social facts, gathered during a normal social process, can greatly supplement previously established scientific knowledge.

Hence anyone in the American educational system, regardless of skills or interests, can benefit from sport sociology. Lessons in social consciousness can be placed in a sport curriculum, just as they can be placed in any other curriculum, if social consciousness is established as a serious outcome or objective.

Broad Social Process

Social process is a system of operations that produces values considered both necessary and significant in the socialization and education of a society (Ulrich, 1969). It is face-to-face social exchange that produces action and can bring about individual and collective changes in behavior. It is social exchange that requires continual adjustment, establishes power, remains observable, and carries the potential to produce mutual satisfaction. Most of all, social exchange lies easily within the realm of sport sociology.

The broadest form of social process makes available a basis of selective action and decision. It is highlighted by action and interaction, closed and open social systems, exchange bargaining and negotiation, conformity and deviance, reciprocal relations, feedback, and creative tension. The social process that surrounds the teaching profession is composed of elements that sport sociologists would normally find interesting.

By applying sport sociology to the teaching profession, then, one might produce the broadest possible sense of social process in an educational setting, rather than a limited version of academic schooling. Such a process could become entirely credible, would be easily observed, and could be subjected to scientific analysis. In our educational system, real social process could become everything that the teaching profession does that is related to learning.

On another level, an educational setting would supply sport sociologists with a variety of subjects who had some association with sport: members of the teaching profession, as well as assorted primary groups, secondary groups, peer groups, significant others, and other appropriate population units. Theoretically, one might reach nearly every student in America, instead of just the elite of any given sport.

Applying the sociology of sport to the teaching profession will require a rejection of the notion that knowledge generated by the sociology of sport is not useful to teachers of physical education (Hanson, 1982). At the same time, sociologists must accept that the sociology of sport is the most useful when it is applied to the entire population and not solely to elite athletes (Coakley, 1983). After all, organized sports are an important ingredient for good programs of physical education (Rees, 1984). Sports competition constitutes a major portion of what is taught in physical education classes and remains the medium through which the teaching profession purports to teach a sizable portion of its values. Sport sociology can best be applied within a curriculum that highlights beneficial social attitudes, with those attitudes being planned, examined, analyzed, and rewarded by teachers.

Social Influence and Power

One of the strongest possible applications of sport sociology to the teaching profession is currently realizing only a small portion of its potential. That application comes through the social influence and power that is associated with educational organizations. Like all organizations, educational ones are greatly influenced by forces that are external to them (Gross, 1968). The impact of these external forces, from a sociology of sport perspective, seems to emerge naturally as a focal point for scholarly study and application.

An educational institution, or a group of educational institutions, have major organizational objectives, with students, teachers, supervisors, and administrators directly linked to those goals. With their roles come certain privileges and obligations that seem to be necessary for successful relationships and interaction. However, there is seldom full agreement on organizational objectives or the privileges and obligations associated with the various roles.

Similarly, the formal organizational goals of educational institutions are usually vague and ambiguous (Gross, 1968). For instance, a goal might take the form of some statement such as "to educate young people." As school personnel seldom agree on organizational goals, or what rights and obligations accompany them, those goals will remain vague and ambiguous, with some of the most ambiguous being associated with organizational sport. Both literature and experience indicate that a major source of pressure applied to educational administrators at all levels is conflicting views concerning the goals and objectives of organizational programs. Often the most visible and explosive of those programs are sport-related. That may be the very reason why the corps of school administrators is so heavily occupied with former physical education teachers and coaches.

The ambiguity and vagueness seem to heighten when perceptions of a division of labor are considered along with privileges and obligations. Students, teachers, administrators, governing boards, and the public often fail to agree on who has the legitimate authority to do anything. In the realm of sport, such controversies might include who hires coaches, who determines varsity award letter qualifications, who determines varsity or intramural eligibility, who establishes priorities for athletic facilities use, and who gets to spend student body's money. The disagreements suggest that role conflict is built into the American educational system and that this is an excellent place to apply sport sociology. Role conflict as an area of applied sport sociology has flourished during the past decade. However, most of the effort has been aimed at one narrow area, namely, the teacher/coach role conflict (Massengale, 1981).

From a formal-organizations perspective, and from the perspective of work-and-occupations sociology, educational organizations represent a potentially rewarding arena that cannot be separated from the vagueness and complexity of American sport. Together, they offer the complexity of social reorganization, the mysteries of behavior analysis, and the problems of structural diversity.

For too many years, the influence of social power in sport has been passed over as merely a reflection or microcosm of American society (Coakley, 1983). Yet it is not a simple social context that provides a simple and singular explanation, but an excellent place to test hypotheses related to social organization and behavior. Moreover, it does not necessarily require a varsity team for a subject. Thus it is a perfect arena for the applied sport sociologist to make an appropriate contribution to the teaching profession.

Concluding Statement

There are pitfalls as well as benefits to a closer alignment with the applied side of any discipline. Sport sociology is no exception. But pitfalls should not discourage the application of sport sociology to the teaching profession; instead, they should guide and direct the practicing sport sociologist. Some useful pitfalls include the overgeneralization of single-situation sociological data, the blind acceptance of unverified sociological prepositions, the hunches and speculation that seem to accompany vague and ambiguous social situations, and the lack of accuracy in identifying multidimensional social forces. What applied sport sociology really has to offer the teaching profession is a more sensitive analysis and a more realistic way of handling the sources and consequences of multiple social forces.

References

Coakley, J.J. (1983). From elites to everybody: A changing agenda for sport sociological study. *Journal of Physical Education, Recreation and Dance*, **54**(3), 21–23.

Gross, N. (1968). Some contributions of sociology to the field of education. In R.M. Pavalko (Ed.), *Sociology of Education* (pp. 19–32). Itasca, IL: Peacock.

Hanson, D.L. (1982). Applications. In H.M. Eckert (Ed.), *The academy papers: Synthesizing and transmitting knowledge, research, and its applications* (pp. 67–70). Reston, VA: American Alliance for Health, Physical Education, Recreation and Dance.

Hollands, R.G. (1984). The role of cultural studies and social criticism in the sociological study of sport. *Quest, 36*(1), 66–79.

Massengale, J.D. (1984). Social process and traditional physical education. In N.L. Struna (Ed.), *Proceedings of the Annual Conference of the National Association For Physical Education in Higher Education* (pp. 69–74). Champaign, IL: Human Kinetics.

Massengale, J.D. (1981). Role conflict and the teacher/coach: Some occupational causes and considerations for the sport sociologist. In S.L. Greendorfer & A. Yiannakis (Eds.), *Sociology of sport: Diverse perspectives* (pp. 149–157). Berkeley, CA: Leisure Press.

Rees, C.R. (1984). Applying sociology to physical education: Who needs it? In N.L. Struna (Ed.), *Proceedings of the Annual Conference of the Association for Physical Education in Higher Education* (pp. 54–59). Champaign, IL: Human Kinetics.

Sage, G.H. (1985, August). *The role of sport studies in sport pedagogy.* Paper presented at the Annual Meeting of the International Association for Physical Education in Higher Education, Garden City, NY.

Southard, D. (1982). A national survey: Sociology of sport within American college and university physical education professional preparation programs. In A.O. Dunleavy, A. Miracle, & C.R. Rees (Eds.), *Studies in the sociology of sport* (pp. 365–732). Ft. Worth: Texas Christian University.

Ulrich, C. (1969). *The social matrix of physical education.* Englewood Cliffs, NJ: Prentice-Hall.

Chapter 17

Corporate-Sponsored Sport Research: A Holy or Unholy Marriage?

Don Sabo
D'Youville College

Merrill J. Melnick and Beth Vanfossen
SUNY at Brockport

Sabo, Melnick, and Vanfossen's article not only represents a totally different context for applied sport sociology, but it also contains a rather nontraditional approach to implementation. Their argument for more corporate-sponsored sport research suggests a plan of action that might be considered antithetical by sport sociologists in academia. However, they point out that since sport is one of "the most public of subjects," it can attract more broad-based interests with sufficient resources to carry out large-scale or national sport research projects.

In a recent analysis of the field, Coakley (1987, p. 76) observed, "The sociology of sport in the United States still lacks full legitimacy in both physical education and sociology, and growth since the late 1970s has not been significant." He predicted, "the achievement of full legitimacy and significant growth will continue to be slow in the future." While Coakley is to be commended for his accurate and comprehensive review of significant events in the historical evolution of sociology of sport, his ideas about legitimacy can be debated. He limits the sources of legitimacy for the subfield to the hallowed halls of academe, and thus overlooks the fact that academic endeavor, especially research, also receives legitimacy from nonacademic sectors.

Sport sociologists, in general, have chosen to deal with the most public of subjects—sport—in the most private of ways. Research and theory has issued in mainly academic publications and venues. This decision has doomed sociology

Paper presented at the meeting of the North American Society for the Sociology of Sport, Cincinnati, OH, 1988. Printed by permission of Merrill J. Melnick, Don Sabo, and Beth Vanfossen.

of sport to limited public acceptance and very limited national exposure—when in fact, the wellsprings of legitimacy do not solely reside with academia, particularly when the focus of research and discourse is sport. Rather, legitimacy also derives from the public-at-large and major social institutions such as the media, education, government, and the economy. Why, then, has sport sociology not gained visibility or respectability in the public mind and the private sector?

In the case of sociology of sport, "small" has not been "beautiful." The research literature, with a few notable exceptions, has been characterized by small, convenient investigations rather than large, national ones. The latter, of course, require considerable human and fiscal resources. To whom can sport sociologists turn to secure the necessary resources? Are there organizations interested in subsidizing large-scale sport research projects?

Foundations have been less-than-enthusiastic supporters of sport research. Eva Auchincloss, cofounder and former executive director of the Women's Sports Foundation (WSF), spent many years soliciting foundation funds, with meager success. She contends that traditional foundations generally fail to see the relevance of sport research (personal communication, February 19, 1988). Perhaps the taint of insignificance and intellectual inferiority that has historically plagued physical education and sport has also tinted perceptions of sport research projects. This stigma has no doubt also inhibited the funding of such projects within academia.

To date, there appear to be no major sport studies funded by U.S. government agencies. Yet state-sponsored sport research is common in Canada and Scandinavia, and even more so in Eastern European countries. In the Soviet Union, for example, the state clearly monopolizes funding of sport research and, in turn, establishes research priorities and policies. Hall (1987) reported that *Goskomsport* (the Soviet Sport Committee) has direct control over allocation of research funds and places a priority on research that can augment individual athlete or team performance. *Goskomsport* itself is funded through the state, sport lotteries, and gate receipts, although in the current atmosphere of reform, the head of the Scientific Department of *Goskomsport* has been charged to depend more on private-sector funding.

Fortunately, the American picture for funding of sport research is not so bleak with regard to voluntary organizations such as the U.S. Olympic Committee and the National Collegiate Athletic Association. For example, the latter has endowed a research foundation that may spur future large-scale sport research. In the private sector, some national corporations have recently emerged as willing supporters of sport research.

Corporate Sponsorship of Sport Research

An alliance between corporate America and sport has been growing since the late 1960s. Corporations now spend $6.2 billion annually to promote their products through sports, with television and newspaper advertising accounting for $4 billion, or 63% of the total ("6.2 Billion," 1987). One of the leading investments materializing today is "title sponsorship"—that is, a company buys the right from a sports promoter or organizer to name an event after itself. Examples are the Coors International Bicycle Classic, the Sunkist Fiesta Bowl, and the Kemper Open. In 1988, corporations spent an estimated $1.75 billion on event sponsorship (Gloede, 1988). Today, at least 400 corporations have event-marketing departments with their own separate budgets, compared with 10 in 1982 ("Nothing Sells Like Sports," 1987).

Another new investment direction with obvious implications for sport researchers is sports-related nonadvertising promotion and publicity, an area in which corporations spent $400 million in 1986 ("6.2 Billion," 1987). This area is a catchall for promotion of corporate goodwill, public relations, and research. It represents a growing base from which modern sport researchers may acquire funding.

The Corporation/Sport Nexus: A Holy or Unholy Marriage?

A review of sociological literature on the transformation of capitalism from its earlier forms to what is now sometimes referred to as "advanced monopoly capitalism" will no doubt raise some serious ethical issues for sport sociologists interested in tapping the coffers of corporate America. Preliminary analysis reveals that the relationship between advanced monopoly capitalism and sport research is neither unidirectional nor simple, but is better seen as historical, relational, and complex.

To sort through some of these complexities, we have identified two different perspectives of the corporation–sport nexus. We regard these perspectives as ideal types in the Weberian tradition, that is, as "technically constructed concepts, intended merely to serve as fixed points of reference for measuring the extent of the divergence" of particular intellectual standpoints (Salomon, 1934, p. 161). First, there is the *radical perspective*, with intellectual roots in Marxism, which sees ties between sport and corporations as an "unholy marriage" (Goodman, 1981). Adherents of this orthodox view warn against the "corporate colonization of sport research," through which researchers become co-opted servants of corporate interests, research becomes marketing, and promotion is given preference over truth. Once co-opted, research knowledge becomes grafted to the ideological sphere of capitalism, thus preventing participants and spectators from seeing the exploitation and inequities within the system. This position was articulated as early as 1971 by Hoch, who warned against the exploitation of sport by the power-elites of monopoly capitalism.

By contrast, adherents of the *liberal perspective*, while conceding that the corporate sponsor–sport relationship may be inherently flawed and, indeed, ideologically suspect, still maintain that there is a potential for a better marriage than the radicals would care to admit. They contend that a symbiotic relationship *is* possible, that a researcher's ethics are not automatically contaminated by corporate contact, and that *both* corporate sponsor and researchers harbor ideologies that may or may not be conflictual; in fact, they may even be mutually reinforcing. Which of these perspectives is correct?

Method

This chapter presents a discussion of the merits of the radical and liberal perspectives in light of the realities of doing corporate-sponsored research. Participant observation by one or more of the authors was used to explore the extent to which the research process and researcher autonomy were influenced or co-opted by factors related to corporate sponsorship.[1] A case-study approach was used to analyze three corporate-sponsored national surveys, which the authors helped to conceptualize, implement, and present to the public.

1. *The Miller Lite Report on Women in Sports (1985)*. This national study of a random sample of 7,000 members of the Women's Sports Foundation was sponsored by Miller Brewing Co. of Milwaukee, Wisconsin. It is believed to be the most comprehensive survey of athletic women ever undertaken in the United States. It addressed questions about sports and fitness activities, spectatorship, early childhood experiences, coed sport, sex discrimination, and attitudes toward race and gender.

2. *The Wilson Report: Moms, Dads, Daughters and Sport (1988)*. This national survey was sponsored by Wilson Sporting Goods Co. of River Grove, Illinois. Telephone interviews were conducted with a national, randomly chosen sample of 1,004 mothers and fathers, and 513 of their daughters, aged 7 years to 18 years. The chief research goal was to explore how family factors influence girls' involvement in sports and fitness activities.

3. *The Women's Sports Foundation Report: Minorities in Sport* (Sabo, 1989). This national study was sponsored by Miller Brewing Co. and involved a secondary analysis of the High School & Beyond data base, generated by the Center for Educational Statistics, Washington, DC. A panel design allowed us to analyze subsamples of more than 14,000 black, Hispanic, and white youths from their sophomore year in high school (1980) through the senior year (1982), and 2 and 4 years beyond that (1984 and 1986, respectively). The researchers were interested in learning (1) whether minority athletes derived the same academic, social, and psychological benefits from athletic participation as whites; (2) whether minority athletes experienced more or less upward educational or occupational mobility than minority nonathletes; and (3) whether whites derived more mobility benefits from athletic participation than blacks and Hispanics.

All three studies were done in cooperation with the Women's Sports Foundation (WSF), established in 1974, a non-profit educational organization dedicated to enhancing the sport experience for all girls and women.

Initiating a Corporate-Sponsored Study

Space does not permit detailed examination of how funding for each study was secured. However, the process underpinning the Women's Sports Foundation minority report was typical.

The idea for this study evolved from discussions with women of color, who expressed their anger and frustration with the failure of sport researchers to deal with minority issues. In addition, the foundation had expressed a commitment to improving the sports experience for women of color. It was assumed by all interested parties that ignorance was part of the problem; that is, basic research on women of color was scant, and hence there was little understanding regarding the position and experiences of minority female athletes. How could sport researchers change this situation?

A three-page proposal was formulated, pointing out that a comprehensive national survey on this topic had never been undertaken. It argued that the time was ripe for both scientific and public discussion of minority issues in sport and itemized several major lines of inquiry. The researchers also specified *who* would be interested in the results of such a study—for example, minorities, educators, parents, leaders within the black and Hispanic communities, women's organizations, and government policy-makers. Deborah Anderson, executive director of the foundation, collaborated on working out the vision and substance of the proposal. In the same manner in which academics specify the target audience (or market) in a publishing prospectus, the authors briefly identified the potential media impact of such a study.

The researchers then contacted the San Francisco-based sports promotion firm of Auchincloss & Turner, Inc., which also served as the public relations arm of WSF. After considerable written correspondence, numerous telephone conversations, and a meeting in New York City, the firm agreed to search out a corporate sponsor. They contacted the public relations manager for Miller Brewing Co. Discussions and negotiations between the researchers and the public relations manager followed for approximately 6 months. Finally, more than 2 years from the day the idea was conceived, the researchers were awarded $24,000 to execute the study.

Holy or Unholy Marriage?

In exploring research autonomy in the three studies, the central line of inquiry was to determine the extent to which this autonomy was maintained during four key stages of the research process: (1) planning the study, (2) design and operation, (3) data analysis and interpretation of findings, and (4) writing the final report and holding a news conference. Researcher autonomy was conceptualized along several dimensions, including extent of researcher involvement in planning and design, control of the data analysis, and the researchers' influence on outcomes.

Planning the Studies

All three projects were planned via a "committee process," that is, researchers joined colleagues, foundation officers, and corporate officials in creating the overall plan for the study. In the case of the 1985 Miller report on women athletes, a sociologist, John Pollock, spearheaded project design and development in close consultation with WSF officials and members of an advisory panel (all were researchers within academic institutions). Likewise, social scientists were mainly responsible for planning *The Wilson Report*, but with input from foundation officials. Planning was done either directly by researchers or in cooperation with an advisory board that was composed of nationally recognized experts in the field. In the third study, researchers exerted nearly complete control over the planning of the WSF minority report. The researchers analyzed an already existing data set and presented their intentions to the corporate sponsor and WSF officials.

Design and Operationalization

The details of the three research designs were worked out solely by researchers. While funding constraints influenced the number of subjects surveyed or number of hypotheses tested, matters pertaining to overall design, sampling procedures, identification of theoretically relevant or demographically pertinent variables, definition and measurement of concepts, and construction of questionnaire or interview protocols were the province of researchers.

It was recognized that certain variables had marketing relevance for the sponsors: for example, information regarding spectatorship habits and patterns of sport involvement. However, there was no direct lobbying or pressure by corporate officials to include these items. The relevance of potential findings for social science theory and minority advocacy remained uppermost in the minds of the researchers. For example, it was assumed that the data might cast valuable light on longstanding scholarly debates, such as whether females derive the same social and academic benefits from sports as males do, or whether the social mobility of blacks is spurred by athletic participation, as it is for many whites.

It should also be noted that input from nonacademic sources often proved valuable. Sometimes, academics can become so immersed within a research literature that they are held prisoner by theoretical convention. The curious mixture of corporate, foundation, athletic, and social scientific backgrounds and minds associated with these studies did not serve to contaminate or commandeer the research process but rather, injected creativity and innovation. For example, Willye White (a member of the WSF board of directors, a coach, and a five-time Olympian) cornered one of the researchers and argued, "If you are going to do a study of minority athletes, you had better pay attention to the differences between athletes from city, suburban, and rural schools!" We discovered that the mainline sport research literature on minority athletes had not considered this important variable, and we decided to explore its theoretical utility. Interestingly, the "school location" variable turned out to be one of the significant predictors in the study, one that future sport researchers will need to consider.

Data Analysis and Interpretation of Findings

Data analyses for the Miller report on women and *The Wilson Report* were done by professional research companies (New World Decisions and Diagnostic Research, respectively.) In both instances, data analyses were supervised by an in-house social scientist in cooperation with the researchers. Advisory panel members lobbied for analyses that reflected their particular theoretical interests and priorities. With regard to the foundation minority study, the authors were in complete control of the data analysis and, upon completion, consulted with members of the advisory panel for additional input and suggestions for further analysis.

There were variations in the rigor of the data analysis. The 1986 Miller Report on women athletes used descriptive statistics and cross-tabular analysis. No controls were introduced. The other two studies employed multiple regression analyses with appropriate controls. In the minority study, the longitudinal design increased statistical reliability.

With respect to the interpretation of the research findings, corporate officials remained in the background while the researchers were at the helm of the process. Though there was a tendency for researchers to listen to "their own kind" first, input from others proved very useful.

The Final Report and Press Conference

In each case, the project director and/or senior researchers were responsible for writing the first draft of the final report. Drafts of the report were then circulated to members of the advisory panel for reaction and input. Telephone discussions were lively and lengthy; written correspondence traveled via overnight mailings. Revisions were made, but primary authorship remained with the senior researcher(s).

It must be noted that these final reports were written for both the American public and the research community. Though elaborate theory was avoided and language was adapted to suit the public palate, methods and data analysis procedures were reported in detail and efforts were made to keep interpretations well within empirical and statistical boundaries. The basic guideline followed in the minority report, for example, was to take as conservative an interpretive tack as possible. Marginally significant findings were cautiously reported, and every effort was made to highlight just those findings for which there was significant statistical support.

Then there were the news conferences. What typically happens at a news conference is that an extremely abbreviated version of the study is reported to the media. It was at this stage of the research process that public relations professionals became involved. As is their function, they were primarily interested in maximizing the media impact of the study. For example, it was calculated that more Americans heard or read something about the 1986 Miller report on women than watched the Super Bowl that year, for a total of almost 145 million media impressions (Ketchum Public Relations, 1986). The minority report generated more than 40 million media impressions during the 3 months following its August 16, 1989, national news conference.

The public relations professionals also helped the researchers formulate their presentation to the news media. They pressured researchers to highlight findings that, in their opinion, would have the greatest public relations impact. They also attempted to inject more exciting language into the report to "tease" and "grab" the media. Researchers had to struggle at times to choose language that, while highlighting significant findings, did not transcend or run contrary to the data analysis. For example, at *The Wilson Report* news conference, the phrase "sports are now sexy" was used to communicate the idea that young female athletes are no longer inhibited by concerns that athletic participation will mar their femininity. While the term "sexy" had popular appeal, some of the researchers felt it confused the issue by interjecting sexual connotations.

At the national news conferences, television, newspaper, radio, and magazine media were actively involved. There was no way for researchers to control or effectively predict what findings would capture the media's attention or whether controversy and misunderstanding would occur. Researchers were among an array of individuals who, in effect, became spokespersons for the study. These included celebrity athletes, WSF officials, corporate figures, and public relations professionals. The researchers tried to educate everyone with whom they interacted on the purposes, methods, findings, strengths, and weaknesses of the study. In some instances the educational or briefing process was quite extensive. For example, Olympian Nancy Hogshead served as spokesperson during a post–news conference national media tour for the 1986 Miller Report on women. She was made intimately familiar with the contours of the study.

The Major Findings

Seven findings pertaining to researcher autonomy were culled from the participant observations made during the execution of these three national corporate-sponsored research projects:

1. The researchers were able to ask substantive questions and test critical hypotheses that had definite implications for sociological theory.
2. Corporate officials did little to influence the formulation of research questions, selection and testing of hypotheses, and interpretation of results.
3. Public relations professionals urged researchers to highlight what they considered "more salient" and "controversial" findings that were assumed would attract media and public attention. Researchers had to struggle some-

times to keep interpretations of data and the language of news releases consistent with statistical findings.

4. Corporate officials wanted to market their image and products. Jobs, promotions, and profit depended, in part, on successful public relations outcomes. Yet, like the researchers, the officials accepted an ethic of social responsibility in these studies that sought to better the lives of athletes and equalize the opportunities among women, blacks, Hispanics, and youth. It was also recognized that researchers, like their corporate counterparts, gained professionally from the successful completion of each project—in prestige and notoriety, promotion, job mobility, salary increments, and merit pay.

5. Researchers lost much of their influence and control over the studies when the media became involved. For example, public relations professionals pushed hard to report findings in provocative ways, and journalists often structured interviews and stories to fit their editorial priorities. Few or no opportunities existed for the researchers to clarify misinterpretations on the part of the public.

6. Corporate promotion of results enabled the researchers to engage in mass education via television, radio, newspaper, and magazine media. The researchers were able to speak out on issues concerning sport, inequality, family dynamics, racism and sexism, race relations, discrimination, and social change.

7. The synergy between researchers, women's sports activists, athletes, and corporate officials often resulted in innovative theory and hypothesis testing.

Interpretation of Findings

These observations suggest that neither the liberal nor the radical perspective adequately accounts for the political or methodological complexities involved in doing corporate-sponsored research. As researchers, we view the liberal/radical debate within a larger historical context. At this juncture of the 20th century, it remains uncertain whether a humane social order can be constructed within western capitalist political economies. One critical question is whether the progressively larger concentrations of economic power within the hands of corporate elites will erode our quasi-democratic political institutions and create greater inequality and oppression. Or will forces *within* modern corporations, government, education, the American polity, and sociology of sport press toward a more democratic and humane future for all citizens?

This larger issue is already being debated within academic circles. For example, Milton Friedman (1988, p. 189), professor of economics at the University of Chicago, takes the position that "business has no social conscience" and that "it should only be concerned with making as much money as possible while conforming to the basic rules of society, both those embodied in law and those embodied in ethical custom." According to his argument, there can be no "doctrine of social responsibility" when discussing the role and function of business in a free society. The pursuit of profit is all that matters. By implication, corporate-sponsored sport research can only be justified if it directly contributes to profit maximization.

The opposing school of thought argues for a humane capitalism, one that is socially responsible and meets people's and society's needs. Philosopher Robert Almeder (1988) takes the pragmatic position that the doctrine of social responsibility is necessary if capitalism is to survive at all.

Sport researchers are faced with a similar decision between research for profit and socially responsible research. Are we going to sell our methodological skills in the corporate marketplace without any concern for the social scientific import or social implications of our work? Or are we going to seek corporate dollars to design and implement studies that genuinely expand knowledge of sport in society and further some aspect of the public good? The political and ethical issues remain the same, whether we are talking about "socialism with a human face," "capitalism with a human face," or "sport research with a human face."

Conclusions and Speculations

The three case studies discussed in this chapter show how a useful approach for understanding the potentials and pitfalls of corporate-sponsored sport research can be chiseled from a critical analysis of the changing, dialectical relationships among the corporation, institutions of higher learning, and social science (Gruneau, 1983; Messner & Sabo, 1990). The power and influence of the corporation in modern life is expanding. This trend has been especially evident in the developing relationship between the corporate-industrial complex and the university. Nineteenth-century education grew more responsive to the burgeoning needs of industrial society, and "the men who ran the schools differed little in their attitudes and outlook from the men who ran the businesses" (Katz, 1973, p. 124). With satirical vengeance, Veblen (1918) was one of the first to explore the multipronged infusion of business functionaries and entrepreneurial practices into American higher education. During the 19th century, the administrative helm was passed from stiff-collared and spiritually minded clergy to starch-shirted and efficiency-minded businessmen (Gella, Jansen, & Sabo, 1978). On this point, Spring (1971, p. 149) observes that since 1900 the power of schooling has tended to be in the hands of businessmen, political leaders, and professional educators who have been instrumental in the development of the corporate state."

Whether they like it or not, university presidents, physics professors, and sport sociologists are not insulated from these larger politico-economic trends. The modern ivory tower is ultimately permeated by outside influences. Liberal sport researchers have been partially blind to this porosity and are apt to overestimate the "objective" aspects of their relationship to corporate sponsors while underestimating the dangers of ethical compromise and political co-optation.[2] By contrast, radicals, while highlighting the potential for co-optation, have underplayed the possibility that corporations, at certain times and in some ways, may be enlisted as coagents of social reform.

It is ironic that both liberals and radicals seem to have failed to comprehend fully the extent to which human agency reshapes culture and reconstructs institutions. As Crosset (1988) points out, while most academic sociologists (Marxists and structural functionalists alike) have busily analyzed the relationship between sport and society, their heads have been buried in the proverbial sands of one grand theory or another. They have not endeavored to *change* society in fundamental, applied ways. In the end, theory has precluded rather than facilitated professional agency! Hence, we find it useful to make a distinction between "establishment-oriented applied researchers" and "social-activist applied researchers": The former claim to be value-free, while the latter openly admit that research is undertaken to bring about social change.

The emerging cultural-studies perspective within sport sociology offers an alternative appraisal of the potential influence of corporate-sponsored sport research in reconstructing the institution of sport. Cultural-studies practitioners recognize the political role that sport media play in proliferating ideologies that, at once, reflect and reproduce oppressive social relations (Hall, 1990). As Hargreaves (1982, p. 115) argues, sport and sport media are "resources out of which a class fashions its hegemony." Yet as Jhally (1989, p. 74) points out, hegemony is not simply imposed on unsuspecting subordinates (or sport researchers). Instead, "the hegemonic process is one of negotiation, compromise, and struggle in which the ruling class, or more precisely the ruling bloc, gives concessions in one area so that it may receive them in another." By actively entering into the convoluted dialogue among corporations, the media, the public, and the academy, sport researchers have an opportunity to influence the processes through which knowledge is constructed and the institution of sport is constituted.[3]

In conclusion, we recommend that, for better rather than worse, sport sociologists enter the emerging marriage between sport research and corporate America with open eyes. They must be free of illusions of apoliticality, have social scientific goals clearly in mind, and carry well-formulated, socially responsible agendas to help guide them through the political, academic, and ethical intricacies of corporate-sponsored research. To paraphrase Nietzsche, marriage is a long conversation. As such, the dialogue between the corporate sector and sport researchers is apt to have a protracted and intricate future.

References

Almeder, R. (1988). Morality in the marketplace. In J.E. White (Ed.), *Contemporary moral problems* (pp. 197–205). New York: West.

Coakley, J. (1987). Sociology of sport in the United States. *International Review for Sociology of Sport*, **22**(1), 63–79.

Crosset, T. (November, 1989). *Toward a new paradigm*. Paper presented at the North American Society for the Sociology of Sport, Cincinnati.

Friedman, M. (1988). The social responsibility of business is to increase its profits. In J.E. White (Ed.), *Contemporary moral problems* (pp. 187–192). New York: West.

Gella, A., Jansen, S., & Sabo, D. (1978). *Humanism in sociology: Its historical roots and contemporary problems*. Washington, DC: University Press of America.

Gloede, B. (1988, February 8). The future of sports marketing *Sports, Inc.*, pp. 19–25.

Goodman, C. (1981). Corporate colonization of sport. *Arena Review*, **5**: 1, 2.

Gruneau, R. (1983). *Class, sports, and social development*. Amherst: University of Massachusetts Press.

Hall, M.A. (1990). How should we theorize gender in the context of sport? In M. Messner & D. Sabo (Eds.), *Sport, men and the gender order: Critical feminist perspectives*. Champaign, IL: Human Kinetics.

Hoch, P. (1972). *Rip off the big game*. New York: Anchor Press.

Jansen, S.J. (1989). *Censorship: The knot that binds power and knowledge*. New York: Oxford University.

Jhally, S. (1989). Cultural studies and the sports/media complex. In L. Wenner (Ed.), *Media, sports, and society* (pp. 70–93). Newbury Park, CA: Sage.

Katz, M. (1973). *Class, bureaucracy and schools: The illusion of educational change in America*. New York: Praeger.

Ketchum Public Relations (1986). *Publicity report on the Miller Lite Report on women in sports*. (Available from Ketchum Public Relations, Chicago.)

Messner, M. & Sabo, D. (Eds.) (1990). *Sport, men, and the gender order: Critical feminist perspectives*. Champaign, IL: Human Kinetics.

Miller Lite Report on Women in Sports. (1985). (Available from Miller Brewing Company, Milwaukee.)

Nothing sells like sports. (1987, August 31). *Business Week*, pp. 48–53.

Sabo, D.F., with the Women's Sports Foundation (1989). *The Women's Sports Foundation Report: Minorities in Sport*. (Available from Women's Sports Foundation, New York.)

Salomon, A. (1934). Max Weber's methodology. *Social Research*, **1**(2) 156–167.

6.2 billion for sports marketing. (1987, September). *USA Today*, p. 2C.

Spring, J. (1972). *Education and the rise of the corporate state*. Boston: Beacon.

The Wilson Report: Moms, Dads, Daughters and Sport. (1988). (Available from River Grove, IL: Wilson Sporting Goods Co.)

Veblen, T. (1918). *The higher learning in America: A memorandum on the conduct of universities by business men*. New York: B.W. Auebsch.

Notes

[1]All three authors collaborated on the WSF minority report. Don Sabo consulted for WSF on the 1986 Miller Lite Report on American Women in Sport and as an advisory panel member. As ongoing consultant for WSF, he coauthored the research proposal for the Wilson Report with Deborah Anderson and saw the project through to completion.

[2]For an erudite critique of liberal philosophy and mainline sociology's commitment to the objectivity ethos, see Sue Curry Jansen's *Censorship: The Knot that Binds Power and Knowledge*. (1989; New York: Oxford University Press).

[3]An additional complexity of doing applied sport research within the evolving political economy is worth noting. Though many radical sociologists are quick to critique corporate-sponsored sport research, they have not expressed marked political reservations about government-sponsored sport research. Government funds are somehow regarded as "cleaner" than corporate funds, less tainted by ethical compromise and ideology. Yet, even a cursory knowledge of 20th-century political history shows that the state can act as a politically restrictive influence on researcher autonomy, academic freedom, and the research process itself.

PART II

Promotion of Services

The suggestion that sport sociologists actively engage in promotion of services is a relatively novel one, which in itself might be the source of considerable debate. Although the implementation phase of Yiannakis's model does not explicitly deal with the issue of promotion, we feel the suggestion that promotion is an implicit aspect of implementation warrants further discussion. For this reason, we have included an article by Santomier, who takes a more entrepreneurial orientation to implementation. His action program is specifically aimed at the promotion of services offered by sport sociologists. Santomier suggests that if sport sociologists are going to successfully solve problems in physical education and sport, or if they are going to be successful consultants and entrepreneurs, they will need to effectively utilize marketing principles.

Chapter 18

Marketing and Promoting the Sport Sociologist

James Santomier
New York University

Santomier takes a more entrepreneurial orientation to implementation, and his action program is specifically aimed at the promotion of services offered by sport sociologists. Applying principles of marketing, Santomier suggests that if sport sociologists are going to solve problems in physical education or sport or be successful consultants and entrepreneurs, they need to effectively market their services.

Opportunities for consultancies and entrepreneurship are presenting themselves with increasing frequency to faculty at universities, presumably because the U.S. economy continues to move in the direction of entrepreneurship and technical development (Bird & Allen, 1989). A recent study of the faculty at two large research universities found that slightly more than 70% had a personal paying consultancy within the previous two years. A smaller percentage of faculty (7.6%) was involved in other business activities such as developing, testing, or producing a product, service, process, or technique for the market (Bird & Allen, 1989). Faculty consulting is increasingly accepted because it

- provides a direct avenue for personal contact between industry and academe, which helps to reduce organizational rigidity for both parties;
- often leads to or results in a more formal research arrangement between industrial partners and faculty; and
- may gradually lead the faculty member into a business venture.

Faculty involvement with business and industry may be controversial, however, due to potential conflict-of-interest issues.

At the same time, complementary and alternative professional opportunities for university-based sport sociologists have prompted an interest on their part in marketing. This chapter will discuss the nature of service marketing and present guidelines to assist sport sociologists in marketing and promoting their services.

Paper presented at the meeting of the North American Society for the Sociology of Sport, Cincinnati, OH, 1988. Printed by permission of James Santomier.

Marketing Services

As competition for clients continues to increase, more and more professionals and professional service organizations are embracing the marketing concept (Stanton, 1981). This focuses on all activities of the organization that emphasize satisfying customer needs, integrating these activities with marketing to accomplish the organization's long-range goals. The marketing concept does not suggest that other business functions should be given a secondary priority, but suggests that such activities as product development, pricing, sales forecasting, and market research be integrated with other functional areas (Guiltinan & Paul, 1982).

Marketing is a comprehensive, dynamic, and integrated business process. It results in the interaction of numerous activities that are market- or client-oriented. Strategic marketing is a hierarchical process that involves developing a concise statement of objective; selecting an optimal strategy to achieve the objective; and developing a tactical plan to realize the strategy (Guiltinan & Paul, 1982). The actual marketing effort involves three phases:

1. analysis;
2. planning; and
3. control.

Analysis Phase

Within the analysis phase, there are five concepts that are important in developing an overall marketing plan:

- the generic product (or service) definition, which emphasizes very broadly the basic client system needs that are being served;
- the target market definition, which, usually because of limited resources, narrows or limits the product offering to certain clearly defined groups within the overall market;
- differentiated marketing, which, when more than one target group is being served, differentiates between service offerings and communications;
- customer behavior analysis, which usually involves formal research and analysis in determining who, why, how, and so on; and
- differential advantages, which include those elements in the organization's reputation or resources that can be exploited to create a special value in the minds of potential clients.

Planning Phase

Within the planning phase, two concepts should be considered:

- the identification of multiple marketing tools such as the service offering, participants, promotion, physical evidence, place, process, and price; and
- integrated marketing planning, which involves the overall coordination of the various marketing activities that have been identified.

Control Phase

The third phase, control, involves

- continuous marketing feedback concerning changes in the external environment as they affect service performance; and
- a marketing audit, which involves evaluating elements such as objectives, resources, and opportunities, target groups, and communication channels.

Building Client Trust

Conceptually, marketing products and marketing services are essentially the same. In each situation, a comprehensive marketing plan is structured focusing on the elements of the marketing mix. Although there are similarities in the process, significant differences exist between product marketing and service marketing. The strategies and activities involved in marketing products are, in most cases, inappropriate for marketing services (Stanton, 1981).

When marketing services, the individual doing the selling, in this case the sport sociologist, determines to a significant degree the satisfaction the client will receive from that service. Clients' perceptions and behaviors differ from those associated with products when services are purchased because services are perceived to involve less quality and a less-enjoyable buying experience. Services are unique in that they are intangible, often simultaneously produced and consumed, require greater client participation, are nonstandardized, and carry a greater provider-importance for the consumer.

Intangibility, which prevents the customer or client from actually sampling the service before purchase, is perhaps most important when marketing services. In addition, buying services is considered to be more expensive and carries greater risk than buying products (George & Kelly, 1983). Therefore, sport sociologists, as service providers, must educate prospective clients about the opportunities and the limitations of their services. When doing this, the provider becomes involved in the process of "risk-reduction" to overcome client uncertainty.

When selecting professional services, clients generally feel more comfortable with a provider who has experience. Using an experienced professional helps reduce perceptions of risk and anxiety. However, the client's preference for experience often causes professionals to limit their services to special markets. To overcome this need for experience and help differentiate their services, sport sociologists may

- merge with other professionals or consulting firms that have had experience;
- reduce fees, although this could lead to an image problem; or
- emphasize special attributes such as credibility, contacts, improved methods and procedures, personal involvement in projects, and state-of-the-art support such as computers and communications systems.

Just as important, it should be understood that the sport sociologist's statements regarding the benefits or results of his or her services (whether they appear in advertising or are discussed with prospective clients) serve indirectly as a basis for a guarantee and should be identified and delivered while the service is being provided. Moreover, because the provider not only sells the service but delivers it, the impressions made by the sport sociologist are critical to the overall satisfaction of the client. Communication skills, qualifications, and abilities all help reduce uncertainty. Thus, in addition to emphasizing the benefits and quality of the service during the prepurchase phase, sport sociologists should reemphasize them during the actual delivery of the service.

The Marketing Plan

In developing a marketing plan, sport sociologists should first carefully define their skills and services and package this definition for presentation. How the promise of service is packaged in brochure, letter, design, appearance and by whom become central to the service itself because these are elements that the customer finally decides to buy or reject (Levitt, 1981).

Second, sport sociologists should target their prospective client systems. A client system may be a person, a small group (e.g., a team, committee, or staff unit); a total organization system (e.g., a company, agency, bureau, or association); or an interorganizational system (e.g., community, state, national, or international) (Lippitt & Lippitt, 1978).

Some sport sociologists may prefer to specialize and provide services to certain types of client systems, while others may prefer to generalize with respect to the type of client system but specialize with respect to the nature of the problems and the methods used. Targeting is the conscious and deliberate process of studying the entire market to determine which groups offer the best potential to the provider. This represents a serious step for the sport sociologist; because the entire marketing effort is devoted to those customers selected as targets.

Market Research

Market research is important in the initial stages of the marketing process because it enables the provider to understand the problems of the client, to determine what specific benefits are desired by the client, and to provide appropriate information needed to instill confidence in the client. Market research should help the sport sociologist answer the following questions:

- Who is the target audience?
- What do the clients want?
- What does the competition offer them?
- What can I offer them?
- What do they think I offer them? (Luther, 1982).

If the answers to these questions are already known, market research may not be necessary. However, it will be very difficult for sport sociologists to direct and position their marketing strategies without this information. Once the sport sociologist's services have been defined, potential markets identified, and market research completed, the next step involves developing an effective marketing mix.

Marketing Mix

Marketing mix describes the four components that constitute the marketing system. They include the product (i.e., the service), the price structure, the promotional activities, and the distribution system. Due to the inseparability of the service from the person of the seller, direct sale is usually the only channel of distribution for services. And the price of services is usually determined by market demand and competition. Because of the special characteristics of services, the marketing mix should focus on promotional activities.

The Marketing Mix Worksheet presented here lets the service provider identify and list those variables over which he or she may exercise some control, and develop a comprehensive marketing plan. After the target market or markets have been identified, sport sociologists should

1. identify those services that have the best potential to satisfy client needs (e.g., statistical analyses and feasibility studies);
2. identify the most appropriate ways in which potential clients can be persuaded to use their services (e.g., through brochures, personal selling, or advertising);
3. determine the best way, time, and location to distribute their services;
4. place a monetary value on their services;
5. identify all individuals who may be involved in facilitating the delivery of their services (e.g., employees and other related personnel who may have an influence on potential clients' perceptions);
6. create or select an environment that is conducive to interacting with clients; and
7. develop and implement operating procedures to facilitate the delivery of services (e.g., with personnel policies manuals or organizational charts).

Marketing Mix Worksheet

Marketing Mix: Those variables over which you have control

A. Service Offering (creation): Potential client satisfactions or benefits—you will be offering a "bundle of benefits"

_____

_____

B. Promotion (stimulation): The process of assisting and/or persuading a prospective client to support or participate in the services of your organization
   Identify most effective methods of promotion (= promotion mix)

_____

_____

C. Distribution (facilitation): Major factor is location with respect to present and potential clients

_____

_____

D. Price (valuation): Placing a value on the services you offer—includes money costs, opportunity costs, energy costs, etc.

_____

_____

E. Participants (contact): All human actors who play a part in service delivery and thus influence the client's perceptions—i.e., you and organization's personnel (concerns include training, commitment, incentives, appearance, interpersonal behavior, and degree of involvement)

_____

_____

F. Physical Evidence (design): The environment in which the service is assembled and where the organization and clients interact; plus any tangibles that facilitate performance and communication of service (Concerns include furnishings, colors, noise, stationery, technology, etc.)

_____

_____

G. Process (operationalization): The actual procedures, mechanisms, and flow of activities by which the service is delivered (Concerns include policies, procedures, employee discretion, client involvement, etc.)

_____

_____

Promotional Mix

While promotion carries the greatest relative importance in the marketing mix, personal selling has the greatest relative importance in the promotional mix.

Promotion is used to inform, persuade, and comfort the client and may involve a combination of personal selling, advertising, and sales promotion. The overall goals of a promotional campaign should be to

- help build and maintain a favorable image of the service in the minds of clients who have been targeted;
- inform clients of new services being offered;
- remind clients of existing services and of the organization itself; and
- convince potential clients that the organization's services are superior to those of competitors.

Regardless of the promotional mix, however, the emphasis should be on the benefits derived from the service rather than the service itself.

Advertising, personal selling, sales promotion, and publicity or public relations are the most appropriate elements to include within the promotional mix. Depending on the nature of the services, client characteristics, and other factors, the importance placed on each element in the promotional mix will vary. Even very similar organizations in the same professional field will have different promotional mixes, depending on the size of the organization, its competitive strengths and weaknesses, and its managerial strengths and weaknesses, style, and philosophy.

The promotion of services should involve extensive communication, verbal interaction between the provider and the client, and continuity in the promotion campaign. Seminars, newsletters, and informative advertising are important and appropriate risk-reduction techniques that may be used by sport sociologists. When advertising their services, sport sociologists should communicate their clients' satisfaction to others and make sure the nature of the services they provide is clearly understood (George & Berry, 1981). Advertising is efficient because it reaches large numbers of potential clients at a relatively low cost. However, advertising is limited because it does not allow for situationally specific adjustments.

Personal Selling.   Sport sociologists interested in marketing their services will be involved necessarily in personal selling (Kurtz, Dodge, & Klompmaker, 1979), which emphasizes the importance of personal contact and client input. The client is actually buying the provider's time, and the relationship established between the two is critical to reducing client uncertainty and giving reassurance that the client made the right decision. In personal selling, the salesperson focuses on understanding the client's personal and professional characteristics. In other words, sales professionals need to think both humanistically and strategically about their clients (MacKay, 1988).

The contemporary concept of personal selling emphasizes benefits rather than persuasion. The purpose of selling is to provide benefits to various customers and clients. The sales professional first attempts to identify the client's needs and then directs the entire sales effort toward satisfying these needs. The outcome of this process is the provision of benefits to the client.

One significant advantage of personal selling is that sales professionals can tailor the promotional message specifically to the characteristics and needs of individual prospective clients. In this way, they act as problem solvers for each target client. They can present a generic message, observe the effect of the message on the target client, than adjust the presentation based on the observed effect. Thus, personal selling can be an extremely intense promotional method. Clients can easily ignore, dismiss, or forget advertising and other promotional methods; however, it is much more difficult to ignore, dismiss, or forget personal selling presentations (George, 1984).

The question of ethics also arises with personal selling. How far one may go to please clients is a question professionals are likely to face more often as competition intensifies. Although there may be temptations to make ethical compromises, such compromises should be avoided. Even so, personal selling and its accompanying ethical problems may have a demoralizing effect on some professionals. A sales training program and discussions with other sport sociologists with experience in personal selling may help to resolve some of the philosophical and psychological issues related to sales.

Word-of-Mouth.   Another important but sometimes overlooked element of the promotional mix is word-of-mouth. One of the most important sources of information for the consumer, particularly in the later stages of the buying decision, word-of-mouth is important because (a) consumers rely on it for trustworthy information and for assistance in making better buying decisions; (b) personal contacts offer social support for those buying decisions; and (c) the information provided by word-of-mouth is often backed up by social pressure and surveillance. Thus, a question that should be asked by the seller/provider is ''How do you encourage and direct positive word-of-mouth communications about your services?'' Sport sociologists can do this by first providing high-quality professional services and then capitalizing on positive word-of-mouth statements—through development of communication materials that customers may make available to noncustomers, targeting of advertising to opinion leaders, or guiding prospective customers in soliciting word-of-mouth information (George & Berry, 1981).

Questions to Ask.   The following questions may give sport sociologists some guidance in developing an effective promotional campaign for their services:

- What are the viable client systems or system segments for your services?
- What are the specific benefits of your services that will cause clients to buy?
- What specific combination of services do the client systems prefer?
- How much do you expect them to pay?
- What should your sales presentation emphasize?
- What advertising appeals are effective for the specific client systems?

Concluding Remarks

A successful marketing effort requires a strong commitment on the part of the sport sociologist. A marketing program can be developed only after relevant market research and the selection of target groups, an analysis of the immediate business environment, and the identification of appropriate, specific, and measurable objectives. Following these initial analytical steps, sport sociologists should then evaluate and select the most appropriate marketing mix and integrate and coordinate their various marketing activities. Finally, sport sociologists must continuously monitor the progress of the marketing activities, keep up-to-date on changes in the business environment, and evaluate feedback on the quality of the services delivered.

Marketing professional services can involve problems and challenges that are not associated with marketing products, and addressing these issues may be difficult for some sport sociologists. However, if they hope to help solve some of the practical problems confronting physical education and sport and be successful consultants and entrepreneurs, they must make a serious commitment of time and resources to effectively market their services.

References

Bird, B.J., & Allen, D.N. (1989). Faculty entrepreneurship in research university environments. *Journal of Higher Education*, **60**, 583–596.

George, W.R. (1984). *Marketing for nonprofits*. Unpublished manuscript.

George, W.R., & Berry, L.L. (1981, July/August). Guidelines for the advertising of services. *Business Horizons*, pp. 52–56.

George, W.R., & Kelly, J.P. (1983, July-September). The promotion and selling of services. *Business*, pp. 14–20.

Guiltinan, J.P., & Paul, G.W. (1982). *Marketing management: Strategies and programs*. New York: McGraw-Hill.

Kurtz, D.L., Dodge, H.R., & Klompmaker, J.E. (1979). *Professional selling*. Dallas: Business Publications.

Levitt, T. (1981). Marketing intangible products and product intangibles. *Harvard Business Review*, **59**, 94–102.

Lippitt, G., & Lippitt, R. (1978). *The consulting process in action*. LaJolla, CA.: University Associates.

Luther, W.M. (1982). *The marketing plan: How to prepare and implement it*. New York: AMACOM.

MacKay, H. (1988). Humanize your selling strategy. *Harvard Business Review*, March-April, pp. 34–46.

Stanton, W.J. (1981). *Fundamentals of marketing*. New York: McGraw-Hill.

SECTION 5

Future Directions
and the Emerging Debate

Whereas the three articles in Section 2 discussed general issues, problems, and controversies that surrounded application within the previous 20 years, the three articles in this section include some of the most recent thinking on the "emerging debate." Two of the articles are reactions to Yiannakis's model; however, they focus on separate issues. Both offer new and divergent perspectives on the future development of applied sociology of sport.

Each contribution in this section not only extends debate but also challenges and suggests potential modification and expansion of the theoretical model we have advocated. Rather than bringing closure to the issue of application, these articles create a setting that suggests ferment, ongoing debate, growth, and future inspiration.

One article represents a criticism and debate over whose knowledge is important, while the other seems to accept application by arguing that a more vigorous pursuit of application will further theoretical, substantive, and methodological advances in sport sociology. The third article (by Yiannakis) is partly a rebuttal to the first and partly an elaboration of ideas raised in chapter 1, "Toward an Applied Sociology of Sport: The Next Generation."

Regardless of the positions taken in any of these three articles, we trust you have recognized a clear shift in the debate—from outright rejection of an applied sociology of sport in 1965 to a position that now accepts application but debates knowledge of what, from whom, and for whom. In its own way each article contributes to breadth as well as a heightened consciousness with respect to application. Although it may be unrealistic for you to take an active role in this debate, we hope you carefully reflect on the issues raised in these three articles and come to appreciate the fact that sport sociology has expanded the nature and type of knowledge it will bequeath to the next generation by offering insight into the usefulness, effectiveness, and potential for change that an applied sociology of sport may hold.

Chapter 19

Whose Knowledge Counts? The Production of Knowledge and Issues of Application in the Sociology of Sport

Alan G. Ingham
Miami University

Peter Donnelly
McMaster University

This chapter represents a recent article by Ingham and Donnelly that takes issue with Yiannakis's approach to applied sociology of sport. Although they agree that intervention into social process is necessary, they disagree with the orientation and underlying assumptions of his model. Essentially, Ingham and Donnelly feel that Yiannakis takes a programmatic and mechanical approach to application that not only professionalizes academics but politicizes science. Arguing that his orientation is biased toward a positivistic and functionalistic perspective that conceals ideological conflicts, they criticize Yiannakis for failing to contextualize the political and philosophical implications of his model. Ingham and Donnelly maintain there are implicit connections between knowledge production, knowledge application, and the political formulation of social policy. Moreover, they feel that the choice of the term *applied* has limited the sport sociologist to the roles of operator, technical advisor, and knowledge broker. They make a distinction between applied and practical research and advocate the latter as a style of research and intervention.

It is timely to re-address the problematics of knowledge production and knowledge dissemination in the sociology of sport: knowledge *from* whom and *for*

Note. From *Sociology of Sport Journal*, 1990, **7**, pp. 58–65. Reprinted by permission.

whom? knowledge for what ends? whose interests influence the perception of what is really useful knowledge? and to inquire if the marketplace is to determine knowledge hierarchies in the university. This essay was prompted by and is a response to Yiannakis's (1989) article, "Toward an Applied Sociology of Sport: The Next Generation." Because Yiannakis considers the "next" generation with *selective* reference to the "past" generation of the 1960s and 1970s, we are obliged in our rejoinder to consider the past in a different light. And we will make connections between the prestige hierarchy in the university and the marketplace of physical culture precisely because Yiannakis has not contextualized his arguments in this regard.

Our articulation of the connections between academics, professionals, and the public will obviously be very different from that of Yiannakis. He does not share our orientation to the way that sociology, as a source of *practical*[2] knowledge, can be of importance to the public in assisting political understanding (Mills, 1959). And he greatly underestimates the sociological knowledge of many scholars involved in the sociology of sport.[3] We question Yiannakis's sociological imagination because the connections between the intramural politics of the university, the political economy of culture, and the physical educator's quest for authority are not explored critically. Rather than simply reviewing the (predominantly American) literature on applied sociology, we consider it to be imperative to situate any discussion of practical/applied sport sociology in the much larger debates about the professionalization of the academic, the scientization of politics, and the politicization of science. These are discussed here in terms of categories and connections in academe; and we follow with a consideration of practical versus applied sociology in an attempt to present a practical alternative to Yiannakis's programmatic call for an applied sociology of sport.

Categories in Academe

To follow Gouldner (1979), we suggest that discourse in the university has become, despite the lip service paid to the liberal education curriculum of the arts and sciences, a contested terrain. In the contest for prestige and remuneration, the humanistic intellectual must compete with the technical intelligentsia and, in some cases, with technicist pedagogues. Depending on the missions of the university, the knowledge prestige hierarchy varies as does the epistemological prestige hierarchy.

It is useful to compare Gouldner's categories with McCain and Segal's (1969) positivistic attempt to portray the intellectual value-differences between "players, operators, and bystanders." According to McCain and Segal, the players are motivated to compete in the game of science in which the stars of the field are those who formulate the paradigm.[4] The operators are motivated by a desire for public recognition and its resulting rewards—prestige, power, and other remunerations, inside and outside the academy, as determined by those who realistically are the brokers of "really useful knowledge." The bystanders were trained as scientists but they do not engage in the intellectual craft of the player and are more interested in disseminating knowledge than adding to it.

Juxtaposing the categories developed by a Marxian (Gouldner) with those developed by two positivists (McCain and Segal) produces anomalies, but the anomalies are worth pursuing because they are inherent in Yiannakis's arguments and are central to our critique. The anomalies involve the Weberian concepts of value references and value preferences and are manifested in our craft in the awarding of prestige to those who produce and disseminate knowledge. Yiannakis wants sport sociologists to make deliberate interventions into social process, a position that we endorse. But whose interventions will count? The humanistic intellectual or the technical intelligentsia? The academic or the professional? The academy or the market? The practical heterodox or the practical orthodox?

It appears that Yiannakis has, wittingly or unwittingly, limited his mission to that of the operator or the technical intelligentsia; but there is some ambivalence concerning involvement and detachment in his role as a change agent. In connecting his cultural capital to market capital he has linked *one* paradigm in sociology (*one* version of practicality) to the marketplace in physical culture. And because his version of "applied" knowledge is both positivistic and functionalist, he finds himself in a quandary—how to deliberately intervene in social process while remaining value-neutral in the intervention. In the neopositivistic rules of the game the player deliberately disengaged herself from the conjunctural issues of the day and, in this sense, deliberately alienates her work from the immediate problems of the rest of the population (cf. Corrigan, 1979, p. 6), while the operator selectively uses the projects of this deliberate alienation[5] to authorize interventions on the grounds that facts speak for themselves and that the facts were produced by individuals who were not value-referenced or value-preferenced.

Yiannakis defines problems (which we agree are problematical) that need a sociological reading. But he appears to have adopted an orthodox liberal democratic position in posing the problems and an orthodox orientation to the social amelioration of the human condition. Since the orthodox political reading of events has produced consistent failures in social policy, why would we wish to adopt such an agenda for the sociology of sport? There is no indication here that Yiannakis wishes to bring us out from behind the aegis of "normal science" and, in a political way, make our (sport) sociological knowledge really useful for those who are subordinate in the capital/labor relation and/or who cannot pay the consultants' fees.

The commercialization of "applied" sport sociological knowledge is hinted at throughout Yiannakis's article in references to the "private sector," "consulting," "management and marketing," and "knowledge broker." We have little sympathy with individuals who use the time and opportunity afforded by their privileged and frequently taxpayer-supported positions in academia to establish private business ventures and to disseminate knowledge that is not submitted to knowledgeable peer review (i.e., a review conducted by a scholar of note, cf. Singer, 1989). This serious ethical concern is endemic in schools of business administration where widgets anchored in empiricist methods take precedence over wisdom (Subotnik,

1988). This moral and ethical issue concerns empowerment—whose knowledges count and for whom? If Yiannakis is seeking to empower the already powerful, then we object to his stance.

Yiannakis's knowledge flowchart is, in terms of a power flow, one that imposes knowledge from above to below. We believe that "social scientific research is much too important to be left to the sociologists and makers of social policy. It must start being something which is open to people and to all forms of organization in helping them to make sense of their world" (Corrigan, 1979, p. 7). Similarly, in the culture of critical discourse, "claims and assertions may *not* be justified by reference to the speaker's social status" and this has "the profound consequence of making all authority-referring claims potentially problematic" (Gouldner, 1979, p. 3). Thus, our starting points in the "practical research act reverse Yiannakis's flow."

Connections in Academe

There are coherent and strategic connections between knowledge production, knowledge application, and the political formulation of social policy. Where the prestige hierarchies in the academy, the state, and the private sector appear to intersect best is in the recently developed rapport between those academics who produce "quantitatively unassailable" data[6] (Subotnik, 1988), the technobureaucrats who seek to manage the affairs of either the state or civil society, and the politicians who seek ideological mileage in date produced by the previously noted politically acceptable academics. In Britain these connections are evident in Hayek's (1973, 1976) intellectualism, research performed by Seldon's Institute of Economic Affairs, and Thatcherite social policy. In the United States the connections existed between Friedman (1962), Gilder (1973, 1978, 1981), and Reaganite policymakers.

Marx, Weber, Mannheim, members of the Frankfurt School, and Gouldner have all been troubled by such connections in which the technobureaucrats belong to a mercenary army that follows the directives of the ruling class (Dahrendorf, 1959). It appears that the technical intelligentsia follow similar directives, and in an instrumental and formally rationalized society their version of rationality will prevail. As Butler (1975) recognized, with respect to the growing strength of the technical intelligentsia in an increasingly technocratic society,

> technocratic society leads to the alienation of the person because it imposes the absolute prestige of the scientific viewpoint of detached observation. This viewpoint is not restricted to the scientific laboratory where it belongs. It insinuates itself into ordinary human activities and relationships. The result is a general spread of non-involvement and emotional non-commitment. (pp. 199-200)

The symptoms of malaise resulting from just such alienation are evident everywhere in North American society today.

Given these well-established connections, it is important for Yiannakis to declare his ideological position as a knowledge broker. For example, applied sociology could support the current "politics of greed" (Loney, 1986) even if it is disguised in the rhetoric of "a kinder, gentler nation." It could support the politics of professionalization as expressed by those who authorize and distribute credentials (e.g., Bennett's formulas for the improvement of education and the implementation of technocratic evaluations of teacher preparation programs and teacher competency). Or it could support or contribute to the amelioration and political empowerment of oppressed and suppressed groups. The failure to declare one's ideological position is more characteristic of those engaged in the former than in the latter.

Practical Versus Applied

We do not use the notion of "applied" sociology. We believe that sociological knowledge can be practical and that sociologists of whatever subdisciplinary affiliation are capable of making the interpretive connections between personal troubles, social issues, and large-scale historical transformations in social structures. The real question is whether or not they want to. And if they do, in a practical sense, whose knowledges will be found to be acceptable in the marketplace of physical culture? In this regard, Yiannakis's proposals are flawed because he fails to connect the academic's and the professional's differential quests for prestige, or to note how the professional may (as a consequence of seeking prestige) privilege one epistemological position over another (Dewar & Ingham, 1987; Gouldner, 1979; Ingham & Lawson, 1985; Szelenyi, 1982).

Applied research poses a dilemma for positivists because it brings *opinions* to the fore much more overtly, especially in the articulation of a style of research and a style of intervention. We agree with Yiannakis that sociology should contribute to the "amelioration of the human condition"; but we are concerned about which aspects of the human condition are to be selected for special consideration and about who is establishing the priorities. These are intensely political acts deeply rooted in the opinions/ideologies of the researchers. If we take it as given that sport sociologists are not neutral about racism (one is either racist, to a greater or lesser extent, or not), if we accept that opinions about homosexuality and feminism expressed in the locker room may be quite different from those expressed in the classroom or conference room, and if we acknowledge that there are many sociologists who still believe that the poor are responsible for their own condition, then the advocacy of an applied sociology of sport is by no means a straightforward proposition.

Unlike Yiannakis, we are prepared to acknowledge that in the problem identification, problem prioritization, and problem solution process, the value-referenced position of the scientist connects with the definition of a problem and its solution. Yiannakis is concerned that "becoming a change agent sometimes poses problems for the sport sociologist. . . . There is inevitably some loss of scientific objectivity" (p. 11). But in the application process, the idea of an objective, value-neutral sociology is passé.

Even in the natural sciences some researchers are coming to realize that the scientific process is socially embedded and that the influence of the sociocultural milieu is pervasive. Social psychological and sociocultural conditions tend to lead research in predetermined directions, rendering the view of science as an objective enterprise somewhat mythical. While we do not support the radical extreme of this view (i.e., that scientific facts, or truth, are just what a specific scientific community endorses at a particular time, that facts are created to fit into predetermined categories, and that truth is the truth of those in power), it does follow that the interpretation of "facts" is extremely vulnerable to influence and that the truth is necessarily problematic. This is particularly so with respect to applied social science. To revive only debates about objective/subjective, value laden/value free, normative/nonnormative sociology is to miss the point. Practical sociologists recognize that application is an act of political involvement that cannot be performed by either objectivistic or sardonic observers of the human condition.

The notion of time is another element that differentiates practical from applied sociology. Like Yiannakis, we would like to propose practical solutions to practical problems, but we know that immediate opinions are not necessarily the best. Problems develop and fluctuate in political intensity, and the intensity of an identified, prioritized problem is a social construction of politicians who seek strategic power or of media representatives who engage in the "bad news theory of good news" agenda (Hall, 1978), or of certain sectors of the professoriat who enjoy going public/going commercial. Applied scientists are ruled by mechanical time, practical scientists are not. The former meet deadlines, the latter disseminate knowledge in the expectation that their work will eventually influence social politics and policy (cf. John Kennedy, Kenneth Galbraith, and Michael Harrington concerning poverty in the USA).

But the principal difference between applied sociology and practical sociology is a political difference. Following Weber, we ask what can be done to preserve a remnant of human dignity and freedom in a world that is suffering from the effects of growing rationalization and the increasing hegemony of technical instrumental rationality. Should we enhance this movement with our expertist knowledge or should we use our knowledge to deconstruct the movement? Given Yiannakis's functionalist and positivist position, we suspect that monolithic solutions are likely to be proposed in the knowledge-transfer phase for politically diverse and divisive social problems. Whose expertise counts in the political process? Who is the authorized expert in the authority-referral process? The self-reflexivity of the practical sociologist inevitably results in suspicion about the role of the "expert" and trepidation about going public/going commercial. Nothing in Yiannakis's program for an applied sociology of sport hints at such caution.

Conclusions

Why do we need to be concerned with programmatic calls for an applied sociology of sport if, given our vantage point, sociological knowledge is practical knowledge?

We endorse Yiannakis's position, albeit with the reservations previously noted. But our reservations remain resolute not because we wish to consolidate our status within the extant relations but, in the spirit of amelioration, because we wish to deconstruct the principles on which they are based (cf. Baron, 1985). A great deal of research in the sociology of sport already falls into what Yiannakis terms the explanatory phase or exploratory research, and we believe it can have practical value if it is not epistemologically or linguistically alienated from the public. For example, research on children, drugs, delinquency, the "isms" (class, race, sex, age, handicap, etc.), community/stadia, labor relations/human rights, educational and health concerns, and violence is essentially practical research on practical problems. Direct application, what Yiannakis terms implementation, tends to be a much more personal act for practical sociologists. Rather than submitting a consultant's set of recommendations it might involve counseling (e.g., the Adlers and university athletes or Roscoe Brown and professional athletes), working for the rights of high performance athletes (e.g., the Queen's University group), or establishing an agency to work against apartheid or for degree completion by professional athletes (e.g., Lapchik's Center for the Study of Sport and Society). There are many sport sociologists in many countries who, as a direct continuation of their academic work, are engaged in advocacy, policy, and community and political work in order to bring about the "amelioration of the human condition."

If Yiannakis is calling for more concentrated efforts, the formation of more action-oriented groups of researchers, and greater involvement of the sociology of sport organizations, then we would wholeheartedly endorse those efforts. The collective selection of targets/topics by organizations could be problematic (e.g., the ICSS is unlikely to endorse a project to improve the lot of student-athletes because the scholarship system is a uniquely North American phenomenon), but this should not detract from the attempt to develop more applied strategies to ameliorate the human condition in sports (and elsewhere).

Adopting an applied agenda, rather than a practical social science, is likely to confirm our ties to the extant system as a whole. Indeed, if the technical intelligentsia is connected to technobureaucratic imperatives and to the dominant politics, then the public loses its ability to participate critically and reflectively in the process (cf. Gouldner, 1976, p. 40). Knowledge produced by scientists can never ultimately validate the goal after which a political leader strives (Giddens, 1972, p. 13). But this does not mean that a politician cannot choose his/her scientist or that scientists cannot chose a politician.

In conclusion, applied sociology and practical sociology are not the same. The former can be linked to managerialism while the latter may lead to emancipation. In the former, science can be used to conceal ideological conflicts anchored in class, gender, and race relationships; in the latter the connection of science to politics is seriously questioned. Yiannakis encourages us to read sociology. We urge him to read sociology, especially Gouldner and others who have been concerned with the way in which intellectuals and politicians make their connections during conjunctural moments in social/historical time.

In the final analysis, the continuation and further development of a practical sociology of sport should be encouraged but the development of applied sport sociology consultants should be given very careful consideration.

References

Baron, S. (1985). The study of culture: Cultural studies and British sociology compared. *Acta Sociologica*, **28**(2): 71-85.

Butler, (1975). Technological society and its counter-culture: An Hegelian analysis. *Inquiry*, **18**, 195-212.

Corrigan, P. (1979). *Schooling the Smash Street kids*. London and Basingstoke: Macmillan.

Dahrendorf, R. (1959). *Class and class conflict in industrial society*. Stanford: Stanford University Press.

Dewar, A., & Ingham, A.G. (1987). *Really useful knowledge: Professionalist interests, critical discourse, student responses*. Presented at the Conference on Movement and Sport in Women's Lives, Jyväskylä, Finland.

Friedman, M. (1962). *Capitalism and freedom*. Chicago: University of Chicago Press.

Giddens, A. (1972). *Politics and sociology in the thought of Max Weber*. London: Macmillan.

Gilder, G.F. (1973). *Sexual suicide*. London: Millington.

Gilder, G.F. (1978). *Visible man: A true story of post-racist America*. New York: Basic Books.

Gilder, G.F. (1981). *Wealth and poverty*. New York: Basic Books.

Gouldner, A.W. (1976). *The dialectic of ideology and technology*. New York: Seabury.

Gouldner, A.W. (1979). *The future of intellectuals and the rise of the new class*. New York: Seabury.

Gruneau, R. (1978). Conflicting standards and problems of personal action in the sociology of sport. *Quest*, **30**, 80-90.

Hall, S. (1978). The treatment of "football hooliganism" in the press. In R. Ingham (Ed.), *Football hooliganism* (pp. 15-36). London: Inter-Action Press.

Hayek, F.A. (1973). *Law legislation and liberty: Rules and order*. London: Routledge & Kegan Paul.

Hayek, F.A. (1976). *Law legislation and liberty: The mirage of social justice*. London: Routledge & Kegan Paul.

Ingham, A.G., & Lawson, H.A. (1985). Preparation of researchers in physical education: A biographic perspective. In *Proceedings, International Conference on Sports and Physical Education, Yokohama, Japan* (pp. 641-682).

Loney, M. (1986). *The politics of greed: The new right and the welfare state*. London: Pluto Press.

McCain, G., & Segal, E.M. (1969). *The game of science*. Belmont: Brooks/Cole.

Mills, C.W. (1959). *The sociological imagination*. New York: Oxford University Press.

Singer, B.D. (1989). The criterial crisis of the academic world. *Sociological Inquiry*, **59**(2) 127-143.

Subotnik, D. (1988). Wisdom or widgets: Whither the academic enterprise? *NEA Higher Education Journal*, **4**(1): 67-80.

Szelenyi, I. (1982). Gouldner's theory of intellectuals as a flawed universal class. *Theory and Society*, **11**, 779-798.

Willis, P. (1980). Notes on method. In S. Hall et al. (Eds.), *Culture, media, language* (pp. 88-95). London: Hutchinson.

Yiannakis, A. (1989). Toward an applied sociology of sport: The next generation. *Sociology of Sport Journal*, **6**, 1-16.

Notes

[1]While we were preparing this response to Yiannakis, we learned that Peter Donnelly had been appointed as new editor of this journal. In order to avoid conflict of interest in the review process, this article was submitted to Jay Coakley in his capacity as retiring editor.

[2]While Yiannakis follows established tradition and practice in his use of the term "applied," we prefer the term "practical." Applied suggests a positivistic dualism—the opposite being basic or pure—that we cannot endorse because it suggests that the scientific process is devoid of values.

[3]Throughout Yiannakis's article it is asserted that we need to read sociology, learn the lessons from sociology, or consult what sociologists have to say. This is a position sometimes characteristic of physical educators engaged in the sociology of sport. It is unlikely that those engaged in the sociology of religion in religious studies departments or rural sociology in geography departments would make similar statements. If we call ourselves sociologists of sport, regardless of our departmental affiliation, shouldn't we have read and be reading sociology?

[4]Even among the players the majority will not be stars. Most players are engaged in the mopping-up process—what the paradigmatic star suggested but did not actually pursue; what gaps need to be explored and how the principles of the paradigm can be established.

[5]This deliberate alienation of neopositivists (objectivist fantasy) should be distinguished from the structurally prescribed alienation/marginalization of those who, while engaged in objective and critically incisive thinking (cf. Gruneau, 1978), are unwilling to conform to the dominant political standpoint.

[6]Such academics have succumbed to the hegemonic tendencies (Willis, 1980, p. 94) and to the conservative definition of liberalism in their notion of liberal democracy.

Chapter 20
Rethinking the Applied Social Sciences of Sport: Observations on the Emerging Debate

Laurence Chalip
University of Maryland

Whereas Ingham and Donnelly challenge Yiannakis's model of application through criticism, Chalip explores its potential development by discussing how to make social knowledge more accessible, usable, and readable. His discussion begins with a consideration of the nature, character, and impetus of social knowledge, and he attempts to relate social theory and research to the practical utilization of knowledge. His focus is on the link between the advancement of social knowledge and knowledge utilization. Although Chalip feels that social knowledge per se is rarely adequate to use in determining action or policy, he nevertheless believes that assimilation of new data and alternative theories into the existing knowledge base does have an impact on decisions and policy. Because he views social knowledge as self-reflexive and multifaceted, he advocates the use of more collaborative and inclusive research efforts to generate knowledge. He envisions an applied sociology of sport that empowers because social knowledge impacts the world it describes. To Chalip, social knowledge is an outgrowth of the creative, transformative impact of human action.

Early generations of American sociologists consisted predominantly of reformists concerned that their research have impact beyond the academy (Fuhrman, 1980; Hinkle & Hinkle, 1959; Page, 1969). However, subdisciplinary specialization, emergent jargon, the ascent of esoteric theories, and increasingly inbred communities of academic discourse have detached modern sociology from its activist origins. Indeed, some modern sociologists wonder whether social science

Note. From *Sociology of Sport Journal*, 1990, **7**, pp. 172–178. Reprinted by permission.

theories are fundamentally useless; Andreski (1972) contends that social research is inherently obfuscatory; Scott and Shore (1979) claim that the political nature of real-world decision processes makes these processes incapable of incorporating rational social scientific deliberation. Recent programmatic discussions about an "applied sociology of sport" (Ingham & Donnelly, 1990; Luschen, 1986; Yiannakis, 1989, 1990) are best understood in the context of social scientists' contemporary efforts to formulate an appropriate relationship between social research and theory on the one hand and practical utilization of research and theory on the other.

There is every reason to expect that lively concern with practical relevance will be useful to the sociology of sport. Rees (1986, p. 289) notes that "sociologists of sport should be very interested in application because the job market in academe is quite bleak." Even more important, concern with practical relevance can stimulate development of constructive insights, productive theories, and rewarding methods. Rossi (1981) describes four compelling examples from classic sociological research: Sewell's work on status attainment originated in the attempt to forecast demand for higher education in Wisconsin; studies of occupational prestige were generated from the military's desire to find ways to retain its scientists; Lazarsfeld's work on personal influence began with the efforts of *True Story* magazine's publishers to convince advertisers that the magazine was reaching opinion leaders among housewives; community studies were initiated to determine the impacts of social and techological change on American life. Furthermore, Rossi notes that 19 of the 31 presidents of the American Sociological Association between 1950 and 1981 did substantial quantities of applied social research. He explains the apparent contradiction between this fact and the prevalent notion that "applied" work is an intellectual dead end:

> Most interesting and revealing in light of the earlier discussion about the lower esteem accorded applied work is that so many of the presidents are not remembered generally as applied social researchers because over time some of their most important applied research has been redefined as basic work in what appears to be an Orwellian exercise in rewriting history. (Rossi, 1981, pp. 453-454)

The salubrious effect of practical concern on social knowledge seems to be general, since it extends throughout the social sciences. Miller (1983) observes that practical need provided the impetus behind psychological research into information processing, selective attention, and information overload. Foster (1969, pp. 144-150) points out that applied concerns gave rise to acculturation studies, cross-cultural psychology, and economic anthropology. Ferber and Hirsch (1978) show that experiments on income maintenance, supported work, health insurance, electricity rate variation, and housing allowances provide useful information about the conditions under which particular economic theories secure or forfeit their validity. Hansen (1983) finds that policy research is advancing theories of political economy and organizational decision making. Rogers and Leonard-Barton (1978) note that market researchers have made significant contributions to our understandings of attitude formation, innovation diffusion, and behavior change. Meanwhile, the need for practical knowledge has contributed to the development of such methods as sociometry, multidimensional scaling, group interviewing, field experimentation, qualitative research, and attitude surveys (Rogers & Leonard-Barton, 1978; Rossi, 1981).

The link between practical concern and the advancement of social knowledge is consistent with Deutsch, Platt, and Senghaas's (1971) finding that real-world demands or conflicts have generated most of the significant social scientific advances of this century. They analyze 62 social scientific advances from 1900 through 1965. The overwhelming majority are found to originate from innovative, interdisciplinary environments that are vigorously concerned with practical matters. They find that the percentage of advances originating from such settings has been increasing.

One implication of these findings is that applied sport sociologists need not be mere consumers and merchants of social research. Properly conceived, applied sport sociologists are sociologists *sui generis*. Indeed, the following analysis of the relationship between social knowledge and its utilization concludes that applied sociologists of sport not only *can* be sociologists sui generis, they *must* be. The paradigm of applied sport sociology that emerges from an examination of knowledge utilization requires applied sport sociology to be the enterprise of a disputatious, many-valued community of scholars who work in collaboration with the persons, groups, and communities they study. The consequent paradigm addresses Ingham and Donnelly's (1990) concern that applied sociology of sport not merely serve the power elite. Nevertheless, the paradigm remains faithful to Yiannakis's (1989) vision of vigorous intentional application.

Knowledge Utilization

Concern about social science's practical efficacy has inspired a substantial body of research into the nature and means by which social knowledge is used (e.g., Sunesson & Nilsson, 1988; Webber, 1986; Weiss, 1980). The consistent finding is that social research is almost never applied directly, even when that research has been executed expressly for purposes of application. However, social knowledge does obtain a distal impact on decisions and policies because social knowledge is gradually assimilated into decision-makers' knowledge base, causing their perspectives and frames of reference to accommodate. This finding about social knowledge utilization is consistent with Janowitz's (1970, pp. 243-259) contention that social knowledge serves to enlighten decisions and policies but is unlikely to direct them uniquely.

Knorr-Cetina (1981) seeks to explain why social research obtains merely an enlightenment impact. She observes that action, like theories, is underdetermined by the facts available. In each practical situation there are unique circumstances, myriad uncertainties, and competing interpretations. Consequently, practical action must be self-constituting and its ramifications are rarely fully predictable. While social knowledge can minimize uncertainty and reduce the number of viable interpretations, social knowledge is rarely adequate in and of itself to determine action. Hence the distal, rather than proximal, impact that social knowledge obtains.

Research into the ways that knowledge is accommodated by the decision-maker clarifies the route by which social science obtains its enlightenment value. Early research suggested that well-crystallized attitudes and opinions are resistant to change via new information (Lord, Ross, & Lepper, 1979). However, subsequent research shows that as the number of persuasive bits of evidence and the range of evidence sources increase, attitude and opinion changes become more likely (Harkins & Petty, 1981). This is apparently because the information recipient is compelled to contemplate extant understandings and their inadequacies (Petty & Cacioppo, 1979). A significant reason for belief perseverance is that the decision-maker's old beliefs are likely to seem sensible in terms of their underlying theory about the relationships among pertinent phenomena (Murphy & Medin, 1985). However, when an alternative theory is available to the decision-maker, and when the decision-maker has had an opportunity to ponder that theory, new data consistent with the alternative theory can be assimilated and used, even when those data are not consistent with previously held beliefs (Anderson, 1982; Anderson, New, & Speer, 1985; Anderson & Sechler, 1986). This is not to suggest that decision-makers never admit extrarational criteria. However, it does suggest that social knowledge is often used inadequately because decision-makers' naive social theories are unable to accommodate requisite social knowledge or because social knowledge has been assimilated to a naive theory that is inconsistent with the social scientist's own interpretation of the same knowledge.

A key implication is that applied social research should not be atheoretical. Rather, if it is to maximize its impact, applied social research must be *doubly* theoretical in the sense that it must elucidate a social scientific interpretation while simultaneously specifying the naive understandings of stakeholders. Further, it must probe the differences between social scientific explanations and the naive theories of stakeholders. This requires a closer collaboration between the researchers and those who are researched than that which typically obtains.

Collaborative Social Inquiry

Social scientists have no Archimedean point from which to construct or apply social knowledge. The social scientist is embedded in society, and society's self-understandings and consequent actions are affected by the knowledge that social scientists produce. It is epistemologically and methodologically contradictory to treat social phenomena as if they derive from fixed principles of social behavior while at the same time treating those phenomena as changeable. The very act of taking social action presupposes that phenomena addressed are changeable via human agency. The conundrum has long been understood. George Herbert Mead (1899) summarized it almost a century ago:

> In the physical world we regard ourselves as standing in some degree outside the forces at work, and thus avoid the difficulty of harmonizing the feeling of human initiative with the recognition of series which are necessarily determined. In society, we are the forces being investigated, and if we advance beyond the mere description of the phenomena of the social world to the attempt at reform we seem to involve the possibility of changing what at the same time we assume to be necessarily fixed. (pp. 370-371)

The critical point is that social knowledge is self-reflexive. Social knowledge has an impact on the world it describes. In order to grapple with self-reflexiveness, the social scientist must explore the creative, transformative impact of human self-understandings and consequent human actions while simultaneously locating the paths along which understandings and actions are ramified. Theories that incorporate their own self-reflexiveness require analysis of the interactions among beliefs, intentions, actions, values, and information. These are, after all, both cause and consequence of self-reflexiveness.

An ideal means by which to probe social theory reflexivity is to exploit the feedback between social scientific conceptions and their consequences. By attempting to maximize the effect of feedback, the social scientist is well placed to study the impacts of data and theory. This requires that theories and data be fed back to stakeholders and that their proximal and distal responses be incorporated into analyses and recommendations. Commenting on his experience of this process, Goodwin (1975) observes,

> This confrontation can have an emotional impact upon participants, affecting their views of the world and thereby their subsequent actions. The new actions can be used to test the old predictions made, while continuing historical analysis can trace the significance of events not considered by the scientific models, and so on. [This procedure] advances knowledge while potentially advancing the solution of social problems. (p. 58)

It is essential to think broadly about who the stakeholders are and to disseminate data and theories widely. Content analysis of social problem research over four decades (viz., Gregg, Preston, Geist, & Caplan, 1979) illustrates the reasons. Studies of rape, suicide, delinquency, job dissatisfaction, substance abuse, and race relations were coded for attributions about each problem's causes. In four of these six problem areas there is an overwhelming and continuing predominance of person blame (e.g., attributions to personality or strength of will). Rape and race relations are the only two topics in which explanations show increased attention to family, peer group, and societal factors. Significantly, these are the only two areas "in which there are organized social movements and organized, politicized constituency groups within the research community'' (Gregg et al., p. 51). The point is that headway was made toward balance explanations only after stakeholders contributed to the social science discourse.

Social science data are configured by the role relations and value commitments that social scientists adopt vis-à-vis the individuals, groups, and communities they study (Johnson, 1975). Distortions are minimized when social phenomena are investigated by social scientists who, among themselves, differ in the role relations and value commitments they choose (see Bredemeier, 1973, for an extended discussion). The objectivity of social science *as a community of discourse* should not be confused with the value-neutrality of *individual* social researchers. Robust social knowledge results from triangulation by a diverse community of individually fallible social scientists.

Conclusions

Sociology has a great deal to offer sport practitioners. Sociological tools potentially applicable to sport include sociodrama, sociometry, needs assessment, impact assessment, evaluation research, policy analysis, organization development, and consumer research. Nevertheless, it is constructive to bear in mind that social science disciplines (sociology, psychology, anthropology, economics, etc.) are merely the administrative conveniences of our academic institutions. In the real world, problems and needs are multifaceted and multidisciplinary. There are no uniquely sociological problems or needs. If sport sociologists seek to be useful, they will need to work in partnership with social scientists from kindred disciplines and learn their paradigms, their methods, and their jargon.

The danger of remaining solely within the academy—of not actively constructing an applied sociology of sport—is that we risk becoming the unwitting pawns of entrenched and powerful social interests. If we do not venture out to work actively among coaches, administrators, athletes, aspirants, and fans at all levels, our esoteric theories and abstruse jargon will remain accessible only to a technocratic elite who have the academic training to access and decode them. Indeed, elites have already begun to develop methods for putting social theories to practical managerial use (e.g., Pate, 1988).

There are sound reasons to conclude that the best applied sociologists of sport will be sociologists sui generis. In order to be applied, the sociology of sport must become self-reflexive. In order to build a self-reflexive sociology of sport, it is necessary to include those whom we study as active participants in the research process—from agenda setting through research interpretation. This is not to argue that our agendas or interpretations should be dictated by those whom we study. Rather, it is to point out that their agendas and interpretations help to locate the starting points for triangulation to increasingly adequate and useful comprehensions. If the sociology of sport is to be practical, it must become a sociology that empowers.

References

Anderson, C.A. (1982). Inoculation and counter-explanation: Debiasing techniques in the perseverance of social theories. *Social Cognition,* 1, 126-139.

Anderson, C.A., New, B.L. & Speer, J.R. (1985). Argument availability as a mediator of social theory perseverance. *Social Cognition,* 3, 235-249.

Anderson, C.A., & Sechler, E.S. (1986). Effects of explanation and counter-explanation on the development and use of social theories. *Journal of Personality and Social Psychology,* 50, 24-34.

Andreski, S. (1972). *Social sciences as sorcery.* London: Andre Deutsch.

Bredemeier, H.C. (1973). On the complementarity of "partisan" and "objective" research. *American Behavioral Scientist,* 1, 125-143.

Deutsch, K.W., Platt, J., & Senghaas, D. (1971). Conditions favoring major advances in social science. *Science,* 171, 450-459.

Ferber, R., & Hirsch, W.Z. (1978). Social experiments and economic policy: A survey. *Journal of Economic Literature,* 16, 1379-1414.

Foster, G.M. (1969). *Applied anthropology.* Boston: Little, Brown.

Fuhrman, E.R. (1980). *The sociology of knowledge in America, 1883-1915.* Charlottesville: University Press of Virginia.

Goodwin. L. (1975). *Can social science help resolve national problems?* New York: Free Press.

Gregg, G., Preston, T., Geist, A., & Caplan, N. (1979). The caravan rolls on: Forty years of social problem solving. *Knowledge: Creation, Diffusion, Utilization,* 1, 31-61.

Hansen, S.B. (1983). Public policy analysis: Some recent developments and current problems. *Policy Studies Journal,* 12, 14-42.

Harkins, S.G., & Petty, R.E. (1981). The effects of source magnification of cognitive effort on attitudes: An information processing view. *Journal of Personality and Social Psychology,* 40, 401-413.

Hinkle, R.C., & Hinkle, G.J. (1959). *The development of American sociology.* New York: Random House.

Ingham, A.G., & Donnelly, P. (1990). Whose knowledge counts? The production of knowledge and issues of application in the sociology of sport. *Sociology of Sport Journal,* 7, 58-65.

Janowitz, M. (1970). *Political conflict: Essays in political sociology.* Chicago: Quadrangle Books.

Johnson, J.M. (1975). *Doing field research.* New York: Free Press.

Knorr-Cetina, K.D. (1981). Time and context in practical action: Underdetermination and knowledge use. *Knowledge: Creation, Diffusion, Utilization,* 3, 143-166.

Lord, C.G., Ross, L., & Lepper, M.R. (1979). Biased assimilation and attitude polarization: The effects of prior theories on subsequently considered evidence. *Journal of Personality and Social Psychology,* 37, 2098-2109.

Luschen, G. (1986). The practical uses of sociology of sport: Some methodological issues. In C.R. Rees & A.W. Miracle (Eds.), *Sport and social theory* (pp. 245-254). Champaign, IL: Human Kinetics.

Mazur, A. (1968). The littlest science. *American Sociologist, 3,* 195-200.

Mead, G.H. (1899). The working hypothesis in social reform. *American Journal of Sociology, 5,* 367-371.

Miller, N.E. (1983). Behavioral medicine: Symbiosis between laboratory and clinic. *Annual Review of Psychology, 34,* 1-31.

Murphy, G.L., & Medin, D.L. (1985). The role of theories in conceptual coherence. *Psychological Review, 92,* 289-316.

Page, C.H. (1969). *Class and American sociology: From Ward to Ross.* New York: Schocken Books.

Pate, L.E. (1988). Using theories as "overlays" for improved managerial decision making. *Management Decision, 16*(1), 36-40.

Petty, R.E., & Cacioppo, J.T. (1979). Issue-involvement can increase or decrease persuasion by enhancing message relevant cognitive responses. *Journal of Personality and Social Psychology, 37,* 1915-1926.

Rees, C.R. (1986). Action knowledge and policy research: A response to "Luschen and McPherson. In C.R. Rees & A.W. Miracle (Eds.), *Sport and social theory* (pp. 289-291). Champaign, IL: Human Kinetics.

Rogers, E.M., & Leonard-Barton, D. (1978). Testing social theories in market settings. *American Behavioral Scientist, 21,* 479-500.

Rossi, P.H. (1981). Postwar applied social research: Growth and opportunities. *American Behavioral Scientist, 24,* 445-461.

Scott, R.A., & Shore, A.R. (1979). *Why sociology does not apply: A study of the use of sociology in public policy.* New York: Elsevier.

Sunesson, S., & Nilsson, K. (1988). Explaining research utilization: Beyond functions. *Knowledge: Creation, Diffusion, Utilization, 10,* 140-155.

Webber, D.J. (1986). Explaining policymakers' use of policy information: The relative importance of the two-community theory versus decision-maker orientation. *Knowledge: Creation, Diffusion, Utilization, 7,* 249-290.

Weiss, C.H. (1980). Knowledge creep and decision accretion. *Knowledge: Creation, Diffusion, Utilization, 1,* 82-105.

Yiannakis, A. (1989). Toward an applied sociology of sport: The next generation. *Sociology of Sport Journal, 6,* 1-16.

Yiannakis, A. (1990). Some additional thoughts on developing an applied sociology of sport: A rejoinder to Ingham and Donnelly. *Sociology of Sport Journal, 7,* 66-71.

Chapter 21

Issues and Practical Suggestions for the Applied Sport Sociologist

Andrew Yiannakis
The University of Connecticut

Given his reading and reactions to Ingham and Donnelly's critique as well as Chalip's challenge for future growth, Yiannakis sheds some additional insight into the future development of applied sociology of sport. His article is divided into two sections, the first of which addresses three issues raised by Ingham and Donnelly: (a) whose definition of knowledge is important; (b) the commercialization of knowledge and the sport sociologist as knowledge broker; and (c) whether or not Yiannakis's model is contextualized within the broader social structural framework of society. Yiannakis clearly disagrees with Ingham and Donnelly on all three issues, a bone of contention that suggests more discussion in the years to come. He then makes specific recommendations that extend the theoretical model depicted in chapter 1. In addition to outlining a typology of roles, Yiannakis describes essential skills and knowledge associated with those roles, and in doing so he suggests the variety of forms that applied sociology of sport may take in the future.

This book attempts to contextualize applied sport sociology in a framework that helps to organize our thinking and gives a clearer direction to this complex enterprise. The issue of application has been extensively debated, and coeditor Susan Greendorfer and I feel that it is now time to move sport sociology out of what I (1990) have called Stage I (the exploratory phase) and into Stage II, to address questions of structure and content of application. Consistent with this perspective, we have illustrated, based on my model (1989) featured at the outset of the book, the issues that paved the way to the model's development and have provided a detailed typology of the applied enterprise. In addition, we have advanced the notion that in order to link effectively the different types of applied sociology of sport with the various contexts of application, sport sociologists must be trained in the work roles of applied researcher, knowledge broker, and change agent. And we have endeavored to acknowledge the emerging debate by including two recent works by Ingham and Donnelly and Laurence Chalip.

The Emerging Debate

The model I have advanced is not without its critics. In particular, Ingham and Donnelly have expressed concerns relevant to this discussion. It seems appropriate, therefore, to address their concerns before proceeding with more practical recommendations for developing applied sociology of sport.

Although Ingham and Donnelly's article (published in this section) does not contribute substantively to the development of an applied sociology of sport, it does address significant issues regarding the definition of applied work and the political and philosophical implications of such work. Three issues in particular could influence future developments in applied sociology of sport.

The first issue is the question of who should define applied knowledge. Although there is broad consensus that sport sociology has produced knowledge with potential value to society (which we call explanatory knowledge), we argue that this body of knowledge is presently inaccessible, unusable, and often unreadable. It is published in academic journals and is couched in linguistic and epistemological jargon. Hence, there is need for a Knowledge Transfer Phase in which the knowledge broker prepares, packages, and disseminates valuable information in ways that do not alienate the public and that serve the needs of professionals in various contexts of application.

Ingham and Donnelly (1990) argue that "sociological knowledge is [already] practical knowledge" (p. 63). But according to whose definition? Clearly, those for whom such knowledge is intended either fail to understand it or find it mostly irrelevant to their needs. Who then should define what knowledge is applicable or practical—the producer or the user? By accepting the producer's definition that sociological knowledge is practical knowledge, Ingham and Donnelly appear to have imposed the scholars' definition of application on consumers.

If Ingham and Donnelly (1990) truly believe that the imposition of knowledge should not be left "to the sociologists and makers of social policy" (p. 265), then it is time to foray out of the ivory tower, mingle with the people, and discover what consumers actually want. They will then be able to develop a truly grounded, or reality-based, applied sociology of sport. Instead, Ingham and Donnelly fall prey to the same self-serving perspective that attempts to legitimate the producer's definition of knowledge, and they appear to accept unquestioningly Mills's (1959) assumption that sociology is a source of practical knowledge. As knowledge producers, we can lay claim to whatever definitions we want about our work. But if our work is not perceived by society as relevant, its usefulness is significantly diminished and our credibility is undermined.

The commercialization of applied sport sociology knowledge is a second potentially problematic issue, and on this Ingham and Donnelly (1990) and I (1989) agree. Many pitfalls exist for sport sociologists who hire out their services as consultants. However, I do not share Ingham and Donnelly's disdain for connecting "cultural capital to market capital" (p. 266). If, as sport sociologists, we claim to possess knowledge that has value, then the commercial sectors of society that need it and can pay for it should do so. My coeditor and I are not opposed, in principle, to applied sport sociologists acting as consultants in assisting the public and private sectors in the conduct of responsible and ethical management and marketing activity. For it is still possible to do good if one chooses carefully and retains one's independence. When academics, on the other hand, become full-time employees of the commercial sector, market demands and the profit motive may well contaminate their research activity, and they may eventually join the mercenary army that follows the directives of the ruling class (Dahrendorf, 1959). However, individual entrepreneurs who retain their independence have the freedom to act in accordance with the dictates of their consciences. Thus, we reject Ingham and Donnelly's position as an oversimplification.

Finally, Ingham and Donnelly argue that the model of applied sociology of sport presented in this anthology fails to address the influence of broader social structures and institutions. Although we agree on the importance of contextualizing microphenomena in larger social structures (when such links are possible), problematic issues arise when immediate intervention is needed. But the real question is, Should applied work be relevant and responsive to the more immediate needs of the microenvironment, or should applied researchers concern themselves solely with a problem's larger structural and institutional causes? Or are both responses necessary? Mills's distinction of "troubles" from "issues" is useful if we extend their meaning and embrace more fully micro- and macroenvironments and influences. Thus, the ability to locate the "personal troubles of milieu" in the broader "public issues of social structure . . . is an essential tool of the sociological imagination" (Mills, 1959, p. 8).

It should be made clear, however, that micro troubles at the level of the community or the group may require a set of intervention strategies completely different from those for the broader social structures underlying their continuation and sustenance. To save the "patient," a community or group often requires immediate intervention and solutions. But to solve problems in broader social structures may require major policy shifts and institutional change. An example from medicine illustrates this point. We believe that most of the major causes of lung cancer are clearly tied to the politicoeconomic structures that produce, support, and maintain various forms of environmental pollution. Although applied science must address these broader structural causes, in the meantime there are persons suffering from lung cancer who need immediate medical attention. Yet Ingham and Donnelly's argument would have us continue to focus on the broader societal influences and causes. Although such an approach helps perpetuate the philosophical discourse regarding the politics of involvement in the capitalist system, the patient either goes untreated or seeks help elsewhere.

Yet, despite the fact that the works of critical theorists often fail to go beyond critical analysis, the insights that such theorists generate can provide an invaluable foundation for grounding applied work at the macro level. By developing their analyses beyond the Explanatory Phase to include the Operational, Knowledge Transfer, and Implementation Phases (in the Marxian sense of praxis), critical theorists could greatly enhance their contributions to the amelioration of the human condition.

I have suggested in "Toward an Applied Sociology of Sport: The Next Generation" (see chapter 1) that applied work should be informed by broader theoretical perspectives. And I pointed out that applied work at the implementation level can generate inductive insights and understandings that may subsequently inform theory at the macro level. Therefore, in developing the model further, we envision an applied sociology of sport, consistent with Mills's distinction of "troubles" and "issues," that reflects work at both the micro and macro levels. That is, applied work may focus either on problems requiring immediate intervention and solutions (the micro level) or on issues needing long-term strategies (the macro level). And these two concepts should not be viewed as dichotomies but as polar ends of a continuum.

The model I presented at the outset of this book is clearly an attempt to address the micro level, where most "troubles" requiring immediate attention are located. But a complete model of applied sociology of sport must also embrace the macro level if we are to deal effectively with broader causes. For example, to help prevent lung cancer at the micro level, we must eventually eradicate the politicoeconomic structures and industrial systems responsible for polluting our environment and ultimately causing cancer at the individual level. Critical theory is especially suited to contributing to our explanatory knowledge of such phenomena.

Therefore, we envision an interlinking of micro- and macro-level theory, each reflecting at its level of abstraction the Explanatory, Knowledge Transfer, and Implementation Phases. At the micro level, pressing problems of management, marketing, teaching, coaching, and drug counseling, among others, may be fruitfully addressed. At the macro level, more long-term solutions may be sought by addressing broader structural issues, including inequality, poverty, and exploitation.

Further Refinements and Recommendations for Developing an Applied Sociology of Sport

Our involvement in applied work, coupled with considerable reflection, has, we feel, provided us with some additional insights regarding the development of applied sociology of sport. Ingham and Donnelly have challenged our thinking, and Chalip's thoughtful analysis has added a new dimension to the debate. We believe that if applied sociology of sport is to grow and mature, systematic efforts and long-range planning are called for.

Applied sport sociology (and sport sociology) must first gain greater academic legitimacy and acceptance, and structures need to be installed to foster such legitimation. Leaders in NASSS and related organizations must embrace the need for a concerted effort to develop a comprehensive strategic plan. Such a plan must speak to goals and objectives, funding sources, graduate training, rewards and incentives, marketing, and relations with the public and private sectors.

Second, applied sport sociology needs to develop visibility and recognition, especially within the media. Sport sociologists must be seen to be addressing social issues and problems, and their work must reach the organizations and practitioners who need it most. The knowledge transfer phase is clearly an important link in this process. Furthermore, applied work must be published and disseminated in ways that will convince agencies and organizations that sport sociology has something of practical value to offer. And most important, key media spokespersons must be targeted for cultivation, for most hardly know that sport sociology exists. Sport sociologists are invariably overlooked as consultants, discussants, and panelists in both print and broadcast features on sport-related issues. Instead, coaches, star athletes, sports journalists, and physicians offer "expert" testimony on such issues as children, racism, sexism, politics, and the like, in sport. But for a handful of exceptions, sport sociologists are conspicuous mostly by their absence!

Third, it should be clear by now that applied work can take many forms. To contribute effectively, the sport sociologist must assume roles appropriate to the task. But these roles, including the applied researcher and the knowledge broker, are not taught in universities, and in academia little emphasis is placed on applied research skills. Neither do graduate schools teach students to define problems in applied terms, that is, in terms whose findings may contribute to the life tasks of solving, changing, and ameliorating. What does such work entail, and how is it related to the Explanatory, Operational, Knowledge Transfer, and Implementation Phases?

The Applied Researcher

Work in the Explanatory Phase requires a commitment to addressing questions of practical importance or significance and tends to be of a higher theoretical abstraction than activity in the Operational Phase. Answers to such questions create the intellectual conditions for subsequent problem solving and decision making. Work in the Operational Phase emphasizes activities of a lower level of abstraction that seek to provide more narrow technical solutions, to test findings, and to verify their applicability in various contexts of application. In either case, the sport sociologist must assume the role of "applied researcher." Yet such preparation is often inadequate, if available at all.

The Knowledge Broker

An area that receives even less training or emphasis in graduate schools is the Knowledge Transfer Phase, which stresses the transfer and delivery of knowledge generated by explanatory and operational research to practicing professionals in different contexts of application. This phase requires a variety of diverse skills, including the ability to translate epistemological jargon and complex research findings into language that nonacademics can understand and use. It also requires an ability and a willingness to disseminate the findings of sport sociology through presentations and workshops and by publishing material in periodicals read by professionals and the public. Additionally, or alternatively, a knowledge broker must be willing to popularize applied research knowledge by writing books with the practitioner specifically in mind, making media appearances, and addressing parent and other community groups.

The Change Agent

Sport sociologists who choose to work in the Implementation Phase become change agents. This role is most difficult to enact because it is often fraught with conflicting demands and expectations. In this phase, the change agent is responsible for converting findings and policy recommendations into programs of action, installing them in specific contexts, and actually carrying them out.

The Consultant

A fourth work role is the consultant: someone who, by virtue of her or his knowledge and expertise, is hired by public or private organizations as a researcher, a knowledge broker, or a change agent (though these titles are not employed as such). Although the essence of a consultant's activities may not differ substantially from those of an academic applied researcher, knowledge broker, or change agent, consulting and academic applied work differ in several major ways. In consulting work, the goals and objectives of the task are defined primarily by the hiring organization, the consultant is invariably paid for such work, and consulting work is primarily for the purpose of helping an organization achieve its corporate objectives. Noncommercial applied work, however, may be funded or unfunded. Funded research is primarily supported by research foundations and other nonprofit organizations, which often place few constraints on the investigator. Generally, such foundations support research that benefits various segments of society or contributes to the body of knowledge in different fields of endeavor. And, most important, with funded research the goals and objectives are defined by the investigator and often reflect his or her particular research interests.

We propose in summary that it is possible to engage in applied work as a researcher, a knowledge broker, or a change agent as either an academic or a consultant. Figure 21.1 clarifies this relationship: When an academic (A) engages in role tasks (B_1, B_2, or B_3) defined and remunerated by an organization to achieve corporate objectives (D_1, D_2, and D_3), the individual is said to be a consultant. When such role tasks satisfy other criteria (C_1, C_2, and C_3), the individual is considered an applied academic. What do these roles actually entail, and how might we prepare sport sociologists to engage effectively in either?

Skills and Knowledge for Applied Researchers

Because applied sport sociologists concern themselves with answering questions of practical importance and significance, problems for possible investigation must

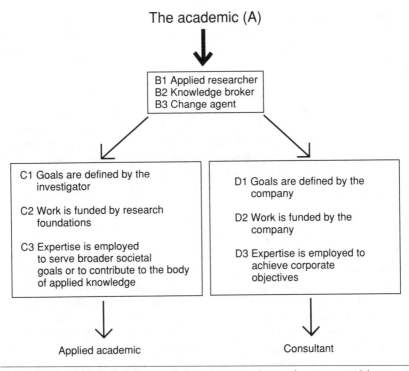

The academic (A)

B1 Applied researcher
B2 Knowledge broker
B3 Change agent

C1 Goals are defined by the
investigator

C2 Work is funded by research
foundations

C3 Expertise is employed
to serve broader societal
goals or to contribute to the body
of applied knowledge

D1 Goals are defined by the
company

D2 Work is funded by the
company

D3 Expertise is employed to
achieve corporate
objectives

Applied academic   Consultant

Figure 21.1   Criteria defining applied academics and consultants engaged in research, knowledge transfer, and change activities.

lend themselves to solutions of practical consequence. Such solutions enable the researcher and practitioner to clarify issues, select options or courses of action, and develop both policy statements and strategies for solving, changing, and ameliorating.

The first step in problem solving is reducing the scope of the problem to a manageable level so that key concepts may be operationalized. Defining and delimiting problems is not an activity unique to applied research, of course; it is essential to all forms of research. But because in applied research the goal is to clarify and solve problems of practical importance, definition and delimitation must be tied to concerns about utility and application. This has significant implications for the way research questions are framed and findings and recommendations are discussed.

In framing questions for applied research, investigators should define and delimit problems by reformulating them at lower levels of abstraction. Although this tends to decrease the theoretical import of findings, greater specificity is possible. And with greater specificity one is more likely to remain ''connected'' to the practical issues or questions being investigated. So whether one is attempting to provide narrow technical solutions or more general explanations that help ''enlighten'' decision making, applied work often requires sacrificing a great deal of scope and theoretical import for the sake of specificity and precision. This is clearly the case with problems requiring immediate attention and solutions.

Second, applied research is defined by its purpose and research questions—and most often the purpose is to provide solutions to problems demanding immediate attention. A researcher, then, must be able to define and delimit research problems in ways that will provide *timely* solutions that inform the processes of solving, changing, and ameliorating. Therefore, research questions must be anchored in problems and issues of the here and now.

Applied research of both the explanatory and operational types differs to the greatest degree from basic research in the way its questions and hypotheses are framed. A major distinction is whether research questions of either theoretical or practical consequence are addressed. At times, however, such distinctions are unclear, and research originally intended to address particular practical issues may assume significance because of theoretical insights that happen to shed light on problems of theoretical importance at a later date. Several earlier works by Coleman, Stouffer, Lazarsfeld, Duncan, and Park, among others, fall in this category (Rossi, 1980).

Third, applied research requires the ability to determine the best methodology and design for a given situation and problem. That is, a researcher must have the skills to define and analyze a problem and then select, from an array of conceptual and methodological alternatives, the research strategy that best fits the demands of the situation. Applied research, therefore, should be *problem centered*.

Finally, the applied researcher must be equipped to discuss findings and make specific recommendations that focus on solutions, change, and amelioration (the *applied consequences* of research). This differs greatly from basic research, in which the investigator is primarily concerned with the theoretical import of findings and with testing or developing theory.

In summary, then, applied research requires these skills and competencies:

1. The ability to reformulate a problem at a lower level of abstraction and tie it to concerns about utility and application
2. The ability to define the purpose of the project and to frame research questions and hypotheses in ways that provide timely solutions that inform the processes of solving, changing, and ameliorating in the here and now
3. The ability to apply appropriate (problem-centered) research methodology
4. The ability to develop discussion and recommendations that focus on the applied consequences of the findings

Skills for Knowledge Brokers

Knowledge brokers tend to be central, and therefore highly visible, figures in applied work. The role thus assumes great significance because it links academia with the public and with professionals in the field. To be effective knowledge brokers, sport sociologists need many and diverse skills. They must be well versed in the knowledge of the explanatory and operational domains and able to translate and communicate it to various publics. Knowledge brokers also must understand the needs of their clients and be able to advise professionals how knowledge from sport sociology can help them in their work. Because their activities can assume many forms (books and articles, speeches, workshops, media interviews, and the like), knowledge brokers need superior skills in written and verbal communication and in dealing with people. These are essential because they facilitate interaction, help establish rapport, and may promote more effectively the utility and worth of applied sport sociology.

Sport sociologists who wish to specialize as knowledge brokers, then, should include coursework in communications and marketing in their training. They must possess superior writing skills and be effective speakers. Familiarity with communications outlets, especially the media, is also beneficial in efficiently and effectively reaching appropriate publics and professional groups.

Skills and Knowledge for Change Agents

Change agents are persons who choose to actively involve themselves in the process of implementation. This phase incorporates diverse activities including the following:

- Using sport in a correctional facility to bring about changes in racial attitudes among inmates
- Offering organizational assistance to a sport group pursuing a grievance or fighting for reform
- Building and directing a sport program to meet particular community needs
- Teaching students or athletes desirable values, attitudes, and behaviors by employing insights and knowledge generated by applied sociology of sport research
- Implementing a program of sport activities to improve an organization's employee morale

Although the specific skills and knowledge required may differ with the activity, a variety of academic, technical, and social skills are invariably called for. Certain types of work may necessitate even additional skills. Programs with political agendas or that stress educational reform, for example, may depend for their survival on effective public relations, marketing, fund-raising, proposal writing, and political savvy.

Not all forms of change activity require such a complex arsenal of skills. However, to be effective change agents, sport sociologists need more than a desire to do good. Interfacing with other sectors of society requires specialized skills that often differ greatly from those required in academia. Coupled with the lower status accorded by universities to applied work, it is understandable that academics are often discouraged from engaging in such activity.

Skills and Knowledge for Consultants

Consultants are people who are hired to apply their expertise as researchers, knowledge brokers, and change agents in helping organizations achieve corporate objectives. Consultants explain, advise, clarify, design and conduct research projects, evaluate programs, and recommend courses of action. The consultant's role differs from those of the academic applied researcher, knowledge broker, and change agent in that it is often "reactive" in nature, meaning that the consultant is paid to apply his or her expertise, and the goals and objectives are defined by the hiring agency.

The pitfalls inherent in consulting work have been persuasively argued by Ingham and Donnelly (1990), by me (1989), and by many sociologists in the 1960s and 1970s (for a complete bibliography, see Yiannakis, 1989).

But caution notwithstanding, interfacing as consultants with the public and private sectors is a necessary element of applied work and is necessary for promoting sport sociology as a useful and relevant social science. Rather than shying away from such work, adequate training should be provided to those who aspire to applied activity. Because graduate schools are not likely in the near future to view such endeavors with enthusiasm, we propose that professional societies such as NASSS undertake the responsibility and provide training workshops and seminars on this topic. Such initiatives should focus on a number of areas including the pitfalls of such activity as well as the technical and social skills required in dealing with business and industry. And while every sport sociologist should have studied the sociology of organizations, additional exposure to the realities of such environments may be necessary. Skills such as proposal writing, billing, personal marketing, and presentation styles should also be discussed and debated. (Santomier elaborates further on this topic in chapter 18, "Marketing and Promoting the Sport Sociologist," and his paper should be of value to anyone interested in consulting work.)

A Plea for Action

We believe the development of an applied sociology of sport to be the most effective course for benefiting society, our discipline, and our profession. We urge all of you who care about the sociology of sport to employ your skills and knowledge to make a difference by solving, changing, and ameliorating. How so? By demonstrating the relevance of your work (regardless of ideological persuasion) by, for example, helping an organization improve employee morale, by showing how inequitable practices can be bad for business, by helping professional athletes deal more effectively with team owners, and by helping organizations more accurately (and ethically) reach their target markets. Engage in research as an applied researcher, in knowledge transfer as a knowledge broker, and in implementation as a change agent. Promote your knowledge, skills, and findings through print and broadcast media, by writing books for the public, and through speaking to community and social organizations. Let the private and public sectors, including government at all levels, know that our work counts and our contributions have value. Do not be satisfied with simply exposing social ills. Rather, ask yourself how you might work to solve, change, and ameliorate. Let your work make a real difference!

References

Dahrendorf, R. (1959). *Class and class conflict in industrial society.* Stanford, CA: Stanford University Press.

Ingham, A., & Donnelly, P. (1990). Whose knowledge counts? The production of knowledge and issues of application in the sociology of sport. *Sociology of Sport Journal,* **7,** 58-65.

Mills, C.W. (1959). *The sociological imagination.* New York: Oxford University Press.

Rossi, P. (1980). The presidential address: The challenge and opportunities of applied research. *American Sociological Review,* **45,** 889-904.

Yiannakis, A. (1989). Toward an applied sociology of sport: The next generation. *Sociology of Sport Journal,* **6,** 1-16.

Yiannakis, A. (1990). Some additional thoughts on developing an applied sociology of sport: A rejoinder to Ingham and Donnelly. *Sociology of Sport Journal,* **7,** 66-71.

Index

Note: References to tables and figures appear in boldface type.

UNITED STATES SPORTS ACADEMY
One Academy Drive
Daphne, AL 36526